Entering the Child's Mind

Entering the Child's Mind

THE CLINICAL INTERVIEW IN PSYCHOLOGICAL RESEARCH AND PRACTICE

Herbert P. Ginsburg

*Teachers College,
Columbia University*

CAMBRIDGE
UNIVERSITY PRESS

PUBLISHED BY THE PRESS SYNDICATE OF THE UNIVERSITY OF CAMBRIDGE
The Pitt Building, Trumpington Street, Cambridge CB2 1RP, United Kingdom

CAMBRIDGE UNIVERSITY PRESS
The Edinburgh Building, Cambridge CB2 2RU, United Kingdom
40 West 20th Street, New York, NY 10011-4211, USA
10 Stamford Road, Oakleigh, Melbourne 3166, Australia

First published 1997

Printed in the United States of America

Typeset in Palatino

Library of Congress Cataloging-in-Publication Data
Ginsburg, Herbert.
Entering the child's mind : the clinical interview in
psychological research and practice / Herbert P. Ginsburg.
p.   cm.
ISBN 0-521-49685-3 (hardcover). – ISBN 0-521-49803-1 (pbk.)
1. Cognition in children – Testing. 2. Interviewing. 3. Child
psychology. I. Title.
BF723.C5G557   1997
155.4 – dc21   97-5635

*A catalog record for this book is available from
the British Library*

ISBN 0 521 49685 3 hardback
ISBN 0 521 49803 1 paperback

With joy, for Jane

*And with sadness, for the memories of my father,
and of Mollye and Ed*

The search for method becomes one of the most important problems of the entire enterprise of understanding the uniquely human forms of psychological activity. In this case, the method is simultaneously prerequisite and product, the tool and the result of the study.

Vygotsky, *Mind in Society*

Contents

Preface

My goal as a psychologist has been to "enter the child's mind" – to discover as best I could how the child thinks, sees the world, constructs personal reality. Mostly I have operated as a researcher, trying to gain insight into such issues as the usually unrecognized learning potential of poor children. But I have also worked as a clinician, attempting to discover, for example, why a particular child is having difficulty with schoolwork. In both research and clinical work, I have found that the "clinical interview" is a powerful vehicle for entering the child's mind.

The clinical interview can provide a kind of "thick description" of the mind (to borrow from Geertz, 1973). The clinical interview – more than many standard procedures – gives me a chance of getting beyond the child's initial fear or defensiveness, of being sensitive to the cultural differences that separate us, of ensuring that the child understands the task I am presenting and that I understand the task the child decides to deal with, and of gaining some insight into the child's often hidden abilities. The clinical interview, I believe, provides me with more accurate information about children's minds than do standard procedures.

The phrase *clinical interview* refers to a class of flexible interview methods the nature of which is very hard to capture in a single phrase. These methods typically involve intensive interaction with the individual child, an extended dialog between adult and child, careful observation of the child's work with "concrete" intellectual objects, and flexible questioning tailored to the individual child's distinctive characteristics. Clinical interview methods require a kind of

ix

informal experimentation and testing which is deliberately nonstandardized, at least in part. The methods under consideration involve a
"clinical" sensitivity to the child's motivation and defenses, an interpretive orientation, and, as we shall see, a distinct ethic of "caring."
The clinical interview derives from a different world view, a different
scientific paradigm, from that undergirding traditional methods.

I am not entirely satisfied with the phrase *clinical interview*. To
some, Piaget's "clinical interview," the main inspiration for current
clinical interview methods, implies the clinic and hence pathology.
This is not what I mean (and was of course not Piaget's meaning)
because the method can be used to study the child's intellectual
strengths as well as any difficulties, even pathologies, that might
exist.

To others, *clinical interview* implies that the method must be used as
Piaget used it to deal with a particular class of problems –
conservation, logic, rational thinking. I do not mean this either. As we
shall see, clinical interview methods have undergone development
since Piaget's time and may be applied to problems in which Piaget
had no interest whatsoever.

If I could find a better phrase than *clinical interview* I would use it,
but so far I have not been successful.[1] I have decided to stick with
clinical interview because it has noble origins in the best of clinical
practice and in Piaget's monumental research. I hope that the name
will not be misleading or will not distract from the two basic points
alluded to above. First, clinical interview methods can help us gain
insight into many aspects of the child's thought – rational and irra-
tional, cold and hot – in the everyday world and in the classroom, as
well as in the clinic. Second, as one of Piaget's great legacies, the
clinical interview method can be adapted for our contemporary
needs.

When I first began my work, the clinical interview was considered
"unscientific" – a sloppy, unacceptable method. Now it has gained
more currency, in both psychology and education, but it is still not
sufficiently appreciated and understood. Indeed, many researchers
and practitioners still think that it is not a "rigorous" and scientifically
respectable method.

I am writing this book because I believe otherwise. I believe that the clinical interview is a powerful but not yet sufficiently appreciated method for both researchers and practitioners concerned with entering the minds of children. Of course, it is not perfect, it is difficult, and it can lead to wrong conclusions. It is poorly understood and can be used badly. But remember that our traditional procedures can be used badly too, and some of them – especially standardized tests – have a documented history of harmful effects and of negative contributions to the social welfare, including mislabeling of children, incorrect diagnoses, insensitivity to those who are in some way different, and distortion of the curriculum.

My goals in the book are to celebrate, examine, and teach the clinical interview method as a technique for gaining insight into the child's mind. First, I want to convince you that the method can make a useful contribution to research on children's thinking, to clinical practice, and to educational and other applications. Second, I want to advance analysis and understanding of clinical interview methods. Their effectiveness and reliability have seldom been investigated or evaluated in a productive way. Third, I want to help psychologists and others to conduct effective interviews. The book therefore presents guidelines intended to help novices learn to conduct clinical interviews and more experienced interviewers to perfect their technique. I also discuss how clinical interviewing can be taught and why it should be taught more widely than it is now.

The plan of the book then is as follows. Chapter 1 ("The Need to Move Beyond Standardized Methods") aims at helping you appreciate the need for the clinical interview. The chapter attempts to show that our cognitive orientation is often ill-served by traditional standardized methods, which, although developed to achieve noble purposes, suffer from several basic weaknesses. For one thing, standardized methods are often ineffective at measuring complex, dynamic aspects of cognitive functioning. New developments in theory demand corresponding developments in method.

Chapter 2 ("What Is the Clinical Interview? Where Did It Come From? Why Do It?") is designed to present the rationale for clinical interview methods. After presenting several examples of clinical interviews, illustrating the range of their application, I begin with a history, discussing how important origins of the clinical interview can be found in the work of Freud, who should be considered the first major theorist of cognition. Drawing on clinical practice and psychoanalytic theory, Piaget then developed the "clinical interview method," which is the first and most important example of the clinical interview. Suitably generalized, Piaget's rationale for the method can form the conceptual basis for an appreciation of the merits of clinical interview methods in general. I show next that Vygotsky's theory of the Zone of Proximal Development also has a good deal to contribute to the clinical interview. Then I attempt to make a strong case for the clinical interview by presenting in detail key justifications for use of the method. There are some very good theoretical and ethical reasons for believing that the clinical interview is a powerful method for entering the child's mind and that it can present a useful supplement and alternative to methods we have been accustomed to using. I describe, among other things, its constructivist rationale and its distinctive approach to "fairness." I also raise some issues of concern.

Then we need to examine the use of the clinical interview. Chapter 3 ("What Happens in the Clinical Interview?") begins this analysis by showing how the clinical interview takes different forms to achieve distinctive purposes. The clinical interview is used to explore, to discover, to specify cognitive processes, to test hypotheses. Depending on the purpose, it may vary along a continuum of "structure." Next, the chapter outlines what might be called the social psychology of the clinical interview as it is actually used in an attempt to accomplish these purposes. I describe key features of the interviewer–subject dyad interaction: the goals and motives of each participant and their expectations, maneuvers, feelings, and mutual adjustments. Also considered is the interesting issue of how the process of the clinical interview affects both the interviewer and the subject. This material is presented mainly through the analysis of one extended interview of a 6-year-old girl.

Chapter 4 ("Not a Cookbook: Guidelines for Conducting a Clinical Interview") presents the essential "dos and don'ts" of the interview. It is a practical guide, a training manual in the conduct of the clinical interview. Using many examples, I describe the nuts and bolts of the interviewer's strategies and give practical advice on how to conduct the clinical interview (and on what to avoid in the clinical interview). I hope that the chapter will help interviewers begin their work and guide their efforts at learning this difficult method.

But the clinical interview also needs to be evaluated. Not all clinical interviews are well done; some are clearly better than others. The question then arises as to how we can determine the scientific adequacy of clinical interview methods. How do we know when they work well or poorly? Information like this is essential to evaluating research and improving practice using the clinical interview. Unfortunately, we now possess little evidence relevant to judging the scientific adequacy of the clinical interview method. Indeed, it is not even clear what kind of evidence would be required. We do not even possess clear guidelines for evaluating the clinical interview. Consequently, chapter 5 ("Evaluating Clinical Interviews: How Good Are They?") speculates on what a useful evaluation of the various forms of the clinical interview should involve. It is not at all clear that conventional psychometric criteria of reliability and validity are fully appropriate for evaluating the clinical interview. Because the clinical interview derives from a paradigm shift in psychological theory, the old standards of evidence may no longer apply (at least not all of them) and new ones may need to be developed. But if that is true, what should the new standards entail? Discussing this is the heart of Chapter 5, which is more of a challenge and program for future work, more of a framework and set of hypotheses, than it is a finished evaluation. The detailed research on the nature of the method and on its evaluation remains to be done.

Chapter 6 ("Towards the Future: The Clinical Interview and the Curriculum") considers several senses in which the clinical interview should be an integral part of the curriculum. Students in psychology and other social sciences need to learn the clinical interview as a tool for research, and practitioners need to learn the clinical interview as an essential tool in assessment. The chapter describes various techniques, including reports, an interactive video method, and test-based procedures, for helping students to learn the method. The chapter concludes with a proposal concerning the use of the clinical interview as a central aspect of education at all levels: Its use can help foster thinking about thinking, which should be one of the primary goals of education.

My hope is that this book will be useful and accessible to all those who wish to enter the child's mind: undergraduate and graduate students and professionals concerned with children, in various fields of psychology (developmental, educational, clinical, school, counseling, and other branches as well). I think that *all* of our students who are concerned with children should learn the method (later I describe what this does for their understanding of children, even if they never use it again when they are no longer students). At the very least, clinical interview methods can help researchers do effective pilot work and can serve as an adjunct to traditional procedures. At the very least, clinical interview methods can help practitioners supplement the knowledge gained from standard tests.

Members of other disciplines dealing with children can benefit from learning about clinical interview methods as well: social workers, pediatricians, psychiatrists, and educators.

I think the book will be useful for another audience too: those who attempt to enter adults' minds. Certainly adults are different from children, but many of the techniques useful for interviewing the latter apply to the former as well. If you can interview children well, you should be able to interview anyone. Therefore, psychologists and others studying adults' thinking – ethnographers, political scientists, survey researchers, even journalists and lawyers – might benefit from this volume too.

Please read on!

Acknowledgments

Many people and institutions contribute to the happy completion of a book. I wish to acknowledge first the support and intellectual stimulation provided by the Center for Advanced Study in Behavioral Sciences in Palo Alto. The book was begun there during the academic year 1993–94, when I was a Fellow supported by The Spencer Foundation (Grant B-1074). Several colleagues at the Center – Barbara Hauser, Bob Linn, George Madaus, and Laura Stoker – were kind enough to discuss issues surrounding interviewing, to read chapters, and to suggest references. I also had the good fortune of being able to finish the book at the Center, in the summer of 1996, when I was involved in an Institute on Research in Urban Education supported by the Mellon Foundation. In the intervening years, I have had the benefit of valuable comments from Howard Gruber, Deanna Kuhn, Lynn Liben, Bob Schwartz, and Rhona Weinstein. Julia Hough, my editor at Cambridge University Press, provided some very useful suggestions. My students, particularly those who participated in my seminar on clinical interviewing, have always been a source of great stimulation, and I have learned at least as much from them as they from me. Many thanks to my daughter, Lizbeth Ginsburg, who prepared the appendix. Apologies to Eileen Tang for the entirely fictitious quote at the beginning of the last chapter (although she could have said it).

But most of all, I want to acknowledge the contribution of my wife, Jane Knitzer, who has been my most insightful and valuable critic (on this and many other matters) and who has always served as a perfect model of intellectual integrity.

CHAPTER 1

The Need to Move Beyond Standardized Methods

> [A]ny fundamentally new approach to a scientific problem inevitably leads to new methods of investigation and analysis.
>
> Vygotsky, *Mind in Society*

How can we discover what a child knows? Consider two different methods. The traditional approach is to investigate the child's thinking by employing tests or standard tasks. The practitioner administers IQ tests, language tests, achievement tests, and the like in a standardized fashion. All children receive the same set of questions or test items in essentially the same way. Responses are not difficult to score, and test results can easily be computed and compared. Similarly, the researcher gives all subjects the same series of tasks, each presented in a uniform fashion. The resulting behaviors can be coded with adequate reliability, and results can be quantified and analyzed with apparent precision.

The method of standardized testing is extremely influential, dominating the assessment and study of children's thinking. Indeed, this method has virtually come to define what we consider to be "scientific." Use of the standardized method is the dominant procedure in research, as can be confirmed by even a cursory examination of journals like *Child Development* or *Developmental Psychology*, and it is the typical procedure employed in the assessments conducted by practitioners, for whom various psychological tests are indispensable tools.

Consider, however, a radically different approach to understanding what a child knows – an approach that I will argue makes more sense than the traditional method. In a clinical interview, the examiner begins with some common questions but, in reaction to what the child says, modifies the original queries, asks follow-up questions, challenges the child's response, and asks how the child solved various problems and what was meant by a particular statement or response. The interviewer makes "clinical" judgments concerning the child's motivation and personality and uses these judgments to modify the questioning in appropriate ways, perhaps pressuring one child but treating another with kid gloves. The examiner is constantly engaged in interpreting the child's response so as to follow up on it in an incisive manner.

In employing the clinical interview, the examiner – practitioner or researcher – literally treats each child differently. Indeed, the clinical interview is *deliberately nonstandardized,* thus violating the central tenet of traditional testing. If the traditional method depends on uniformity, the clinical interview thrives on individual variation. In a collection of clinical interviews done for the purposes of either practice or research, it is possible that no two children are treated in an identical fashion and that no two children receive an identical collection of questions. The clinical interview is often considered to be preliminary, sloppy, imprecise, lacking in rigor, "unscientific" – in short, unsuitable for objective practice or rigorous research.

This book is an attempt to show that for certain key purposes the traditional methods of standardized testing are inadequate. Based on outmoded theory, standardized methods often fail to provide adequate insight into cognitive function; they are not effective techniques for understanding the processes of thought. By contrast, the clinical interview method offers a useful and seldom understood alternative to standardized testing. Although deliberately nonstandardized and difficult to employ, the clinical interview method can provide both researcher and practitioner with deep insights into children's thinking. Indeed, this nonstandardized, nontraditional, and, in some circles, controversial method is the "scientific" method of choice for the purpose of entering the child's mind.

Because the method of standardized administration has been so influential, it deserves a serious critique. This chapter therefore describes the method of standardized administration, explicates the assumptions underlying it, and finally points out flaws which weaken the method's usefulness for examining conceptual frameworks and strategies. Although useful for some purposes, the method of standardized administration is not effective for others. It should not be allowed to provide the exclusive definition of what is "scientific" in research and practice.

THE METHOD OF STANDARDIZED ADMINISTRATION

Consider first the basic procedures involved in the method of standardized administration, and second its underlying rationale.

The Basics of the Method

Suppose that I want to gain insight into such aspects of the child's mind as changes in moral judgment from childhood to adolescence, a student's conceptual abilities in mathematics, the differences between boys and girls in logical reasoning, or the comprehension abilities of a child diagnosed as suffering from "learning disability." To answer questions like these, the traditional method is to employ a *task*,[1] or a series of tasks, which I will call a *test*, with or without norms. For example, if as a practitioner I am interested in examining processes of logical reasoning in an individual child, or if as a researcher I want to study age differences in logical reasoning in groups of 4- and 6-year-olds, the traditional procedure would be to

- develop a test involving a series of logical-reasoning problems or tasks ("Jane rides a bicycle. Bicycle riders are athletic. Is Jane athletic?");
- develop instructions which make clear what needs to be done ("I want you to tell me whether the answer to the question is yes or no");
- use procedures for establishing rapport and motivating the children ("We're going to have a lot of fun playing some games today. Listen carefully to the stories I tell you.");
- present the problems in as attractive a way as possible (perhaps use a colorful picture of Jane on a bicycle as part of the procedure);

3

- make sure that the physical surroundings are comfortable and conducive to diligent work;
- use a checking procedure to determine whether the subject pays attention and seems to understand the basic information in the problems ("What does Jane do?");
- administer the entire procedure in a standardized fashion, perhaps with several such problems or tasks given in the same order to all subjects;
- limit the children to responses that can easily be scored in an objective fashion, such as simple "yes" or "no" responses (so that independent judges would easily agree on the scoring);
- if the responses must be longer (as in the response to a moral-judgment dilemma), develop clear criteria for coding the responses; and
- carefully record the child's behavior, responses, and overall performance.

This example of logical thinking illustrates several basic features of traditional methods. First, it involves a *task* – a situation contrived by the psychologist to elicit behavior (activities, verbalizations, etc.) that will provide information concerning the "dependent variable" of interest, in this case, the child's logical thinking. In general, the task is of limited scope, focused on a particular topic, like the problem concerning Jane and the bicycle. The task elicits a fairly limited response, like the yes or no answer to the specific question concerning Jane's athletic prowess. The task is not modified regardless of what happens in the study; once decided upon, the task does not change.

Second, the task or series of tasks (the test) is administered in a uniform fashion to all subjects. This kind of *control* and *standardization*[2] is the essence of the traditional methodology. Both researcher and practitioner attempt to hold constant the test "stimuli," to make sure that all subjects receive the same problems in the same way. The controlled conditions must involve precise and uniform directions for administering the test, including use of the same questions, materials, tasks, instructions, and even the same tone of voice and pace in talking to different subjects. The testing environment should be the same for all subjects, including "lighting, ventilation, seating facilities, and working space" (Anastasi, 1988, p. 34), although this is difficult to achieve in practice (as all of us who have had to test children in the school nurse's office know full well).

Third, standardized administration often contains devices for promoting rapport, attention, and motivation. Obviously, both researcher and practitioner want children to take the test seriously, cooperate with the examiner, work hard, concentrate, and in general do as well as possible. As a result, we normally stress having the children attend to the test, we minimize distractions, and we encourage the children to work hard. Sometimes we build into the test techniques for checking our assumptions about rapport, attention, and motivation.

Fourth, tasks and tests may or may not be based on norms. I may develop the logical-thinking problems myself, perhaps relying only on informal pilot work. Or I may use already existing tasks about which various amounts of information may be available. If I borrow the problems from an existing research study, I will at least know how that researcher's subjects performed on the test (and other subjects in similar studies). If I use a test with extensive norms concerning age, ethnicity, social class, etc., then I know a good deal about how children "typically" respond to the test. In research, we tend to use tests which do not involve extensive norms; in assessment practice, we tend to use normed tests. But whether the tests are original or borrowed, normed or not normed, their essence is standardized administration as described above.

Two Rationales for Standardized Administration

Standardized administration can be justified on both scientific and ethical grounds.

SCIENCE

The basic scientific justification for standardized administration originated in the 19th century, when experimental psychologists, concerned mainly with sensation and psychophysics, required rigorous control over the conditions of testing. Suppose that you as an experimental psychologist want to investigate the ability to discriminate different colors. You want to know, for example, whether people can see the difference between red and green, or between one reddish color and another not so red. To find out, you need to make sure that all subjects are presented with the same two colors – in the first case, the same shades of red and green, or in the second, the same "reddish" color and the same "not so red" color. (It would help tremendously if you could define these colors in precise, physical terms, rather than just describing them as "reddish" and "not so red.") You would not obtain useful information were some subjects to see two very similar colors and other subjects two extremely different ones.

Similarly, you need to make sure that the lighting conditions are the same for all subjects. It would be a mistake for you to arrange conditions so that illumination was "bright" for some subjects and "dim" for others. (Here again, precise, physical measurement is helpful: What are "bright" and "dim"?) You also need to use the same instructions for all subjects. Thus it would be a mistake if some subjects were told to indicate when they "thought" one color was different from the other, whereas the other subjects were required to say when they were "sure" that the colors differed.

This then was the model of scientific procedure as developed by 19th-century experimental psychology. And it makes a good deal of sense: if anything is to be learned from investigations like these, the experimenter must have control over the stimuli and must be able to ensure that procedures are fully standardized.

In an effort to provide "scientific" measurement, this logic of control and standardization was then applied to the psychological testing developed in the late 19th and early 20th centuries. The argument was as follows: The goal of testing is to measure variation in some trait across individuals. We want to know whether A is more intelligent, aggressive, or depressed than B. We may want this information in order to compare groups of individuals (are boys more aggressive than girls?), to compare traits within individuals (is intelligence related to lower amounts of depression?), or to compare the effects of independent variables (does increasing stress heighten aggression?). In all of these cases – the comparative study of groups, the study of individual differences, or experimental research – the aim is to get reliable and accurate measures of psychological traits.

How to do this? The basic rationale is again control and standardization. According to Anastasi (1988), who has brought a good deal of sound judgment to bear on the subject of psychological testing: "If the scores obtained by different persons are to be comparable, testing conditions must obviously be the same for all" (p. 25). All subjects must receive the same test stimuli – whether this be a list of nonsense syllables or a paragraph to read or an IQ test – in the same manner. To do otherwise, the argument goes, would be to render the data uninterpretable. If subjects received different test stimuli, then the tester could not confidently attribute subsequent variations in performance to individual differences in a particular trait.[3] Consequently, strict uniformity of administration is required. "Such a requirement is only a special application of the need for controlled conditions in all scientific observations" (Anastasi, 1988, p. 25). This scientific argument then leads to the whole apparatus of standardized administration.

ETHICS

Standardized administration can also be justified on ethical grounds, particularly in terms of a specific kind of fairness. As far back as 1845, Horace Mann offered several reasons for introducing standardized testing to the schools (Wainer, 1992):

They are impartial.
They are just to the pupils.
They prevent the officious interference of the teacher.
They take away all possibility of favoritism.
They make the information obtained available to all.
They enable all to appraise the ease or difficulty of the questions.

(p. 15)

In one way or another, these reasons revolve around *fairness* or impartiality. One justification is that standard tests prevent the teacher from favoring some children over others (perhaps by giving some children easier questions than others) or from interfering with the process of testing. Another justification is that the tests make the process public, so that an outside observer can judge whether the questions are too hard or too easy. In this way, testing can be fair and "just."

The originators of psychological testing were also vitally concerned with fairness. In the France of the early 1900s, "alienists" (assessment specialists) used subjective methods to perform diagnoses of mental retardation in schoolchildren. Those children identified as retarded were pulled out of regular classes and assigned to special instruction. Although the alienists' goal was laudable – to identify children "unable to profit . . . from the instruction given in ordinary schools" (Binet & Simon, 1916, p. 9) – the accuracy of their diagnoses was by no means guaranteed, with the result that children were often mislabeled and then denied a mainstream education. Binet and Simon (1916) were particularly critical of the unstandardized nature of the alienists' testing, which seemed to involve

> haphazard decisions according to impressions which are subjective, and consequently uncontrolled. Such impressions . . . have at all times too much the nature of the arbitrary, of caprice, of indifference. Such a condition is quite unfortunate because the interests of the child demand a more careful method. To be a member of a special class can never be a mark of distinction, and such as do not merit it should be spared the record. . . . [T]he precision and exactness of science should be introduced into our practice whenever possible. (pp. 9–10)[4]

Binet and Simon felt that fairness demanded standardized, uniform administration. Their goal in developing the standardized intelligence test was to be *fair* to the child, whose "best interests" demand a precise and exact diagnosis. Haphazard, subjective assessment can result in the child's being labeled as retarded, which is never a "mark of distinction" and which can cause the child to miss out on normal instruction and be consigned to the special classroom. It is a great irony that Binet and Simon's motivation underlying the creation of the intelligence test, which is today so severely criticized for its bias and lack of fairness, was to avoid inaccurate and unreliable diagnoses of schoolchildren.

Similarly, modern testers are also concerned with the issue of fairness, particularly in the case of minority students. Anastasi (1988) argues that when "prejudice may distort interpersonal evaluations, tests provide a safeguard against favoritism and arbitrary or capricious decisions" (p. 67). She maintains that tests provide an opportunity for bright students of minority background to reveal their abilities in a forum not subject to the bias of teachers. The tests are a level playing ground on which all may compete equally. She argues that if standardized tests were eliminated, we would have to fall back on subjective judgment, which is subject to "unreliability, subjectivity, and potential bias" (p. 68), much as Binet and Simon had earlier maintained. In her typically wise summation, Anastasi claims that "tests can indeed be misused in testing cultural minorities – as in testing anyone else. When properly used, however, they serve an important function in preventing irrelevant and unfair discrimination" (p. 68).

I have tried to show that standardized testing springs from the noble motive of ensuring fairness. As articulated by Mann, by Binet and Simon, and by Anastasi, fairness has the goal of eliminating bias, discrimination against minorities, stereotyping, haphazard judgments, "officious" (or other) interference, and distortions of judgment.

The method for achieving this kind of fairness is to treat all people alike, to give everyone the same conditions for running the race. From this point of view, no one should be given easier questions than anyone else; no person should be judged on a different basis from another. A wrong answer should be a wrong answer for all. The same solution should not be judged incorrect if the child is African-American and correct if she is White. This kind of fairness is *color-blind:* It treats all children in the same way and ignores irrelevant attributes.[5]

The arguments in favor of the method of standardized administration are both scientific and ethical. The method aims at accurate measurement, unconfounded by variation in test administration, and it aims at fairness in the sense of impartiality.

Some Flaws in the Method

I claim that for certain purposes, the method of standardized administration (which I will sometimes designate as "traditional") often falls short on both ethical and scientific grounds. There is a sense in which the method is often distinctly unfair and can provide us with only limited information concerning children's thinking. The method of standardized administration suffers from several basic flaws, each of which will be described in some detail below:

- Despite standardized administration, subjects nevertheless interpret tests in idiosyncratic ways, in ways not intended by the examiner.
- It is often not clear what cognitive activities are actually measured by standardized tests.
- Standardized achievement tests are usually based on outmoded assumptions about cognition.
- Standardized methods are not suitable instruments for studying complex thinking.
- Standardized methods are not suitable instruments for studying dynamic change.
- Standardized procedures cannot effectively motivate all children.
- Traditional methods are often not suitable for tapping the competence of those who are in some way "different" by virtue of culture, ethnicity, health status (e.g., the hearing impaired), or other reasons.
- Traditional methods are inadequate for the kind of exploration often required in research and practice.

CHILDREN MAY NOT INTERPRET THE SAME TESTS IN THE SAME WAYS

As we have seen, traditional psychological research uses the method of standardized administration for a critical reason: to hold test stimuli constant; to ensure that all subjects receive the "same" problems. Although this method may work for the psychophysical experiments in which it originated, it often fails when other situations, including cognitive problems, are involved.

It fails because different people interpret the same *objective* stimuli in different *personal* ways. Given the "same" stimulus, we see different things in it. In Piagetian terms, we always *assimilate* objective reality into our own schemas. We interpret the world, and we respond more to the subjective interpretation than we do to the objective reality. As Shweder (1991) puts it: "'stimuli' are not external to or independent of our understanding of them" (p. 79). So a stimulus is not a stimulus is not a stimulus. It is what we make of it.

The effect is most apparent in cross-cultural research. Suppose we give Americans and unschooled Africans the same logical-thinking test of the type described earlier (Jane's bicycle). Let's even suppose that both groups are equally familiar with bicycles. It turns out that Americans and Africans answer such questions quite differently. The Americans give answers of the type we expect, but the Africans do not (Cole & Scribner, 1974). Africans say essentially that they cannot answer because they do not know Jane. Does this mean that the Africans cannot reason logically? Not necessarily; we simply can't tell from the results. The problem is that the Africans may have interpreted the question in an unexpected way. For whatever reasons, they convert the question into one about a particular person, whom they don't know, so that the problem cannot be solved. But when the same people deal with questions involving people they do know, they are able to reason logically in the way demanded by the test.

The view that individuals "construct" their realities has important implications for testing as well. It means that different children may interpret in idiosyncratic ways the very same task, the very same instructions. For example, once I asked a child to count some toys. I said, "Count the toys out loud." She proceeded to say, "Ball, block . . ." and to name all of the objects in front of her. But when I said instead, "How many toys are there altogether?" she had no difficulty in counting.[6] If I had limited myself to standardized instructions ("Count the toys out loud"), I would have learned only that she did not understand those particular words; it would have been wrong for me to claim that she could not in fact count.

We do not know how often this sort of misinterpretation of standardized instructions (from the examiner's point of view, not the child's) occurs. Obviously, the less clear the instructions, the more likely is misinterpretation to take place. (It would be interesting to conduct some research on the extent to which children develop idiosyncratic interpretations of problems and instructions on popular tests in the areas of "intelligence," cognitive abilities, and achievement.) But we do know that misinterpretation does occur with some frequency and that researchers and practitioners cannot ignore it.

11

Indeed, a useful approach to interpreting a "wrong" answer is to discover the question to which the child's answer is correct. In other words, the child's wrong answer to *your* question may be a correct answer to a different question – the one that the *child* was posing.

The danger that children may not interpret tests as we would like is particularly acute when we are attempting to compare children of different cultures, age-groups, social classes, and the like.[7] *Instructions and questions* may be misunderstood or understood differently by children varying in age. The "typical" 8-year-old may understand the request "Tell me how these pictures are alike" differently from the typical 5-year-old. *Procedures* may also vary in familiarity for members of various groups. Suppose, for example, the investigator asks middle- and lower-class children to write down their dreams from the preceding night. The middle-class children, who typically attend better schools and are more skilled at writing, are likely to produce more numerous and vivid (written) dreams than their lower-class peers. But do the poor children really dream less often or less vividly? Probably the groups differ mainly in their facility with the procedure employed in the research. As Cole and Means (1981) maintain:

> Simply following the same procedure or using the same instructions and materials with two groups does not automatically constitute equivalent treatment. . . . In general, there is reason to expect that most standard experimental procedures are neither equally motivating for, nor equally well understood by [all groups of subjects]. . . . Every aspect of an experimenter's method – the materials, instructions, and procedure – can be a source of treatment inequivalence for different comparison groups. (pp. 43–44)

In brief, standardized administration does not automatically result in presenting children with the "same" tasks and tests. Objective equivalence may differ from subjective equivalence, which should be our main concern. We must always be alert to the possibility that different children interpret the same task in different ways.

At the same time, we should recognize that for most practical purposes, standardized administration sometimes comes close enough to establishing subjective equivalence among some children. Thus, if we are testing two children or groups of children from similar, mainstream backgrounds, we need not be overly concerned about possible widespread idiosyncratic interpretations of test materials. Most middle-class American children probably would interpret the logical-thinking problem of Jane's bicycle in similar ways.

But without further checks, we cannot be sure. And we should be even less sanguine concerning our efforts to "hold the stimuli constant" if the children are from different age-groups, and especially if they are from different cultures, social classes, and the like – that is, if they are *different* from the mainstream.

What can we do to make sure that tests are interpreted in the same way by all who take them? As we shall see, the only solution is to create *objectively different* tests that have *equivalent subjective* meaning for the people in question. Standardized administration won't work. We have to find alternatives.

TESTS MAY NOT MEASURE WHAT THEY ARE INTENDED TO MEASURE

We use tests to tell us something about underlying thinking. We are not interested in subjects' responses to the test items themselves but in what subjects' behavior indicates about their psychological processes, like logical thinking. But how do we know whether the test measures what we think it does? The usual procedure in developing a test of this type is straightforward. It begins with a task analysis. We invent or borrow items that seem clearly to require a certain cognitive process for their solution. If we want to measure logical thinking, we may create problems that seem to involve syllogisms. We are careful to construct the items in such a way that other methods of solution will not be effective; only use of the syllogism will work. If we want to measure multiplication ability, we create multiplication tasks. We assume that if subjects get the right answer they must have used the process that the task was designed to measure. Then we administer the tasks to the subjects under investigation and make inferences from performance on the test (and related tests) to underlying cognitive process.

But matters are not as simple as they may initially seem: We should not be so quick to assume that tests measure what we think they measure. "Perhaps the greatest pitfall in all experimental work about thinking processes arises from a confusion between what we think the task entails and what subjects who enter these tasks actually deal with in their efforts to comply with the demands placed on them" (Cole & Means, 1981, pp. 136–137).

Suppose that you want to measure children's knowledge of number facts. You simply want to know whether children can remember the elementary addition combinations, like 3 + 4 = 7. What could be simpler? You just pick a few problems of this type, administer them with an instruction such as "I'm going to give you a number fact problem like 2 + 2. What is 2 + 2? That's right, it's 4. Now I'll give you some more problems, and I'd like you to tell me the answers as quickly as you can." We then observe a certain level of performance on items such as these and conclude that the child has a "good memory for number facts" or a poor one.

Often such inferences may be correct. But unfortunately they can be dead wrong too. Here is an example. When asked, "How much is 7 − 4?" a first-grade student, Becky, said that the answer is 2. We might assume from the nature of the test that she had simply misremembered the number fact that her teacher tried to convey. If she were given a series of such items on a test, we would add up her correct answers and, if there were few of them (Becky actually got only one of three correct), conclude that she has poor memory for number facts. But suppose we go beyond the standard test procedure. When asked, "How did you get that answer?" Becky replied: "I knew that 7 take away 4 is 2 because I know that 4 plus 2 is 7. And if 4 plus 2 is 7, then 7 take away 2 must be 4."

This example shows how things were more complicated than the test seemed to indicate. First, Becky began with a mistaken idea, namely that "4 plus 2 is 7." This was her basic premise; probably it was a faulty memorization of a number fact, and this was indeed what the test was intended to measure. But there was more to her cognitive process than rote memory. Indeed this second ingredient in the cognitive stew was much more interesting and significant than the first, the faulty memory. She introduced the correct idea that if 4 + 2 = 7, then *it must be true* that 7 − 4 = 2. Her underlying and unspoken assumption was that subtraction nullifies addition: What addition produces, subtraction can undo. She then combined these two ideas by means of a classic syllogism: If it is true that $4 + 2 = 7$, then *it must be true* that $7 - 4 = 2$.

So the tester's initial inference that the incorrect answer was a result of faulty memory was correct only in an accidental and trivial way. It is true that Becky misremembered a number fact. But the faulty memory involved $4 + 2$, not $7 - 4$. And the faulty memory was trivial when compared with her creative use of the syllogism.

We see then that it is dangerous to make inferences from test performance to underlying cognitive process, especially when all we usually observe is a right or wrong answer to a test item. In general, test items are deliberately designed to elicit very little behavior from subjects. In particular, they usually do not elicit subjects' verbalizations concerning strategies and methods of solution – verbalizations which might provide considerable insight into children's thinking. No doubt the standard impoverishment of subjects' behavior simplifies scoring and thereby helps ensure that raters can agree on how to score the items (high "inter-rater reliability"). But there may be a serious price to pay for this apparent "objectivity": incorrect inferences concerning what most interests us, children's thinking. Tests allow us to be objective and wrong – that is, to come up with incorrect conclusions – at the same time!

STANDARDIZED ACHIEVEMENT TESTS ARE BASED ON OUTMODED ASSUMPTIONS ABOUT COGNITION

Test theorists themselves are beginning to advance similar criticisms of standardized tests, particularly achievement tests. For example, some argue that standardized tests are based on outmoded psychological theory (Mislevy, Yamamoto, & Anacker, 1992). In a sense, tests use a rather elaborate and sophisticated form of 20th-century technology (think of how many books have been written about the details of testing and testing statistics!) to implement archaic 19th-century psychological theory. In this view, most standardized achievement tests are based on an incorrect psychological theory which views learning as the passive accumulation of facts provided by instruction. The job of the test then is to count up the number of such facts or skills, which can be done by scoring the subject's answers as "right" or "wrong." No doubt some learning is rote and

15

mechanical. But this is not the only phenomenon achievement tests should focus on, even though it is often encouraged by our educational system. Traditional achievement tests ignore students' construction of psychological knowledge, their thinking, and their underlying conceptions. As anyone who has navigated the educational system knows, it is quite possible for students to perform well on standard achievement tests, even through the college level, and yet understand very little and indeed continue to hold basic misconceptions concerning the subject matter (see, e.g., Clement, 1982, who cites the example of physics).

Others argue that standardized achievement tests do not provide information useful for teaching. The tests are "more likely to confirm what the teachers already know about the student than provide them with new insights or clear indications of how best to help the student. The global score simply does not reveal anything about the causes of the [student's] problem or provide any direct indications of what instructional strategies would be most effective" (Linn, 1986, p. 72).

Dissatisfaction with standardized testing is even more rampant among those who use tests than it is among those who create them. There is widespread consensus in education, particularly in mathematics education, that standardized testing provides little useful information concerning students' knowledge and learning and in fact has created more problems than it has solved. For example, it distorts the curriculum because teachers often teach to the rather trivial demands of the tests (Madaus, West, Harmon, Lomax, & Viator, 1992).[8]

STANDARDIZED METHODS ARE NOT SUITABLE
FOR STUDYING COMPLEX THINKING

There has been a "cognitive revolution" in psychology and other fields (Gardner, 1985), and as the 21st century approaches, psychologists are more vigorously and variously than ever engaged in cognitive research and practice. Researchers study topics as diverse as children's understanding of distinctions between body and mind (Inagaki & Hatano, 1993), their memories of abuse (Ceci & Bruck, 1993), their understanding of self (Damon & Hart, 1992), their "internal working models" of others (Greenberg & Mitchell, 1983), their racial stereotypes (Bigler & Liben, 1993), and their academic knowledge (Ginsburg, 1989a).

Practitioners are also vitally concerned with understanding children's minds. The diagnostician evaluates the child's cognitive abilities. The clinical psychologist attempts to learn how the child conceptualizes the self and conceives of others, particularly parents, siblings, and peers. The school psychologist investigates the cognitive processes underlying the child's difficulties with school learning. The pediatrician inquires into the child's understanding of his or her illness and of the steps proposed to ameliorate it.

Of course, our common concern with entering the child's mind does not guarantee that we will agree on what we find there. The cognitive revolution has hardly resulted in unanimity! As researchers and practitioners, psychologists are as contentious a lot as they have always been, employing theories almost as diverse as the phenomena they investigate. Psychologists have produced a proliferation of theories and points of view. They may be information processors or Piagetians or Self theorists or followers of Vygotsky or cognitive scientists. Psychologists may even hold to one of several brands of constructivism: simple, social, or radical. Nevertheless, regardless of orientation, researcher and practitioner alike agree that a major aim of psychology is the understanding of children's minds.

Methods are based on theories and need to keep up with them (T. Kuhn, 1962). The question then is whether the traditional method of standardized testing is adequate to the new theoretical task of understanding the complexity of children's thinking and its development. I think the answer is no, for several reasons.

First, the tests simply do not allow for the child to employ much rich thought. Interesting, complex thinking generally does not take place in a short period of time in response to a narrowly focused test item. Thinking is more like a stream – shifting its course and ever changing – than it is like a static pebble in the stream. Tests are more appropriate for picking up pebbles than for capturing the flow of the stream.

Indeed, children learn *not* to think – or not to think deeply – in response to test items. Too much thought might lead you to believe that none of the four multiple-choice answers is really correct, that the question was not very good in the first place, and that another issue is really involved. And if you try to work all this out, you will not have enough time to get the (wrong) right answer that will get you credit on the test. I have heard that in training sessions designed to promote successful test taking, children are taught not to spend too much time on individual items because doing so will hurt their overall test score. In other words, they learn not to think too much about something that might be challenging.

Second, standard methods are not suitable for depicting complex cognitive *systems*. Researchers and practitioners are interested in gaining insight into such matters as children's "conceptual frameworks" – their relatively complex theories or belief systems concerning the physical, social, and psychological worlds. For example, researchers have examined how children's conceptualizations of teachers and schooling affect academic motivation, and ultimately achievement (Weinstein, 1993). This research arises from a perspective which sees children's motivation as stemming not simply from teachers' instructions, behavior, constraints, and rewards and punishments but from children's *interpretations* of the social context of schooling. More important than the "objective reality" of teachers and schools is the child's "construction" of that reality, the ways in which the child interprets and comprehends the educational experience.

Weinstein finds that children are well aware of the different ways in which teachers treat children seen as high or low achievers. For example, "It's a way that [teachers] talk to you . . . about your grades. . . . A very soft voice lets you know you are doing well and a hard tone of voice – they shout and scream to let you know that you are not doing well" (1993, p. 206). Children are also sensitive to the relations among children considered "smart" and "not so smart." "Not so smart girls can't play with the smart, smart girls because smart girls just act like they ignore them." Children also have ideas about what it means to be not so smart. "When the kids [who] don't pay attention, when they see they have a sad face [a mark of failure given by the teacher] on their paper, they say 'I'm not smart.' . . . They be mad, then they start kicking the college kids" (p. 207).

Understanding children's conceptual systems concerning teachers and schooling is vital for both researchers and practitioners. As a researcher, I cannot explain children's achievement without understanding what schooling means to them, and as a practitioner, I may not be able to help the individual child who is failing unless I understand how he or she interprets the teacher's behavior and what happens in school. Yet simple standardized tests are inadequate to capture the complexity of cognitive systems like these.

Third, we know that cognitive competence is often "situated" in various environmental contexts. In the natural environment, problems are complex and people deal with them over time, with various tools, with the help of other people, and with many different kinds of motivation. Thus, children may engage in effective mathematical thinking in connection with selling candy on the streets but may not achieve similar levels of success in their school mathematics (Carraher, Carraher, & Schliemann, 1985). Standardized procedures, however, do not tap rich environmental contexts. Tests are designed to be narrow, asocial, and myopic. The usual testing situation is so devised that subjects must deal with a narrow problem over a short period of time and are allowed to respond only in limited ways. Tests demand impoverished responses because to permit richness would be to make scoring difficult.[9] It is harder to see complex phenomena than simpler ones, so test constructors choose to look at what is easier to see. These constraints of standardized tests limit what subjects can do and what can be learned from what they do.

Because of this decontextualization, tests are often not effective in tapping children's intellectual competence. McDermott describes the everyday problem-solving activities of Adam, a boy considered learning disabled. His behavior was quite variable. In everyday situations, he acted quite competently. In the cooking club, when allowed to work with his friend, he was able to bake cakes. But in testing situations, "Adam stood out from his peers not just by his dismal performance but by the wild guesswork he tried to do" (McDermott, 1993, p. 279). Adam's guessing on tests may be important to know about. For one thing, he may engage in similar behavior in school. But it would be a mistake to think that the tests tell us the whole story about Adam's mind.

19

STANDARDIZED METHODS ARE NOT SUITABLE INSTRUMENTS FOR STUDYING DYNAMIC CHANGE

Tests do not allow for the study of the *development* of thinking in the individual. Often, a child's conceptual frameworks and strategies seem to shift even within a short period of time. In the course of an interaction with the psychologist, the child's concept may seem to change, several different strategies may be used, or different aspects of the child's world view may be emphasized, elaborated, or obfuscated. The child believes that the teacher treats "smart" kids differently from others, but in the next breath points out how the teacher behaves in the same way toward all. Or on the first subtraction problem the child incorrectly uses the "subtract the smaller number from the larger" strategy, or "bug," and concludes that $12 - 4 = 12$ because the 2 must be subtracted from the 4 (J. S. Brown & VanLehn, 1982; Ginsburg, 1989a), but on the next problem a different bug is used, or perhaps the strategy used is correct.

Some of the changes may reflect instability in the child's emerging mind: Conceptual frameworks and strategies are not yet firmly established; the structures are not solid. Other changes may reflect learning: The experience of thinking about a topic or using strategies may in itself lead to learning and development. But whether we posit instability or learning or something else, one thing is clear: Conceptual frameworks and strategies are not conveniently static. It is rare that we can say with confidence that at a given point in time the child "has" exactly Concept X or Strategy Y and no other. "[I]t may be more accurate to view change, rather than static states, as the norm" (Siegler & Crowley, 1991, p. 614).

Perhaps tests and tasks can sample relatively static forms of knowledge at discrete times. But they are poor tools to employ in examining the processes of change. Indeed, tests tend to depict change as an undesirable lack of reliability which must be eliminated. Partly because of such limitations of method, developmental psychology has unfortunately devoted insufficient attention to the study of what should be central to the discipline: the study of development itself.

STANDARDIZED PROCEDURES CANNOT
EFFECTIVELY MOTIVATE ALL CHILDREN

Traditional test theory stresses the necessity for establishing rapport and motivation in order to ensure adequate conditions for testing. Some tests suggest specific statements the examiner can make in an effort to establish rapport. More often, before administering a test, psychologists engage in informal conversation with the child, asking about brothers and sisters or favorite games and activities and the like, all in an effort to put the child at ease, to relax the child so that full attention can be given to the test and serious work on it can begin.

In many cases this works. If the child is a good student, a mainstream middle-class child who is confident in school, comfortable with professional adults, even familiar with testing, then he or she is likely not to be too upset and to work reasonably hard at taking the test. Some children even *like* to take tests, seeing them as an opportunity for demonstrating their prowess. Given a standard test, one child, 4 years and 9 months, repeatedly exclaimed with great enthusiasm, "I like these puzzles!"[10] Other children will cooperate with the tester because they like to get out of class. How bad could the "games" be compared with what is happening in class?

Many children, however, do not enter the testing situation with this constellation of motives and attitudes. Some children are frightened of adults; some children see the researcher's games as evaluations or do not know what to make of them; some children think that taking the test will make them look stupid; some children think that their parents send them to a psychologist to punish them or that the psychologist will tell parents their secrets. These children are likely to have negative attitudes toward testing and are not likely to work hard at taking them. In response to a tester's statement that he would enjoy the "game," one child, 3 years 6 months, responded, "This is no game. I know so many games that's better."[11] And as the years go on, children who do poorly in school gradually seem to lose their motivation for taking tests (Paris, Lawton, Turner, & Roth, 1991).

All this is obvious to anyone who has ever worked with children. But the key point is that standardized administration – treating all children the same way – cannot succeed in establishing rapport with and motivating *all* children. Chitchat about brothers and sisters may work with some children, but it is not enough to reduce the fears of a child who is consistently ridiculed for being "dumb." Describing the tasks as games may convince some children not to worry, but it cannot motivate the child who feels that whatever happens in school is not to be taken seriously. To establish rapport with many children and motivate them, you need to treat them as individuals, which is exactly the opposite of what standardized administration involves. Treating all children the same cannot lead to knowing many children as individuals; and if you do not know them as individuals, you cannot establish "rapport" and create motivation.

STANDARDIZED METHODS ARE OFTEN NOT SUITABLE FOR TAPPING THE COMPETENCE OF THOSE WHO ARE "DIFFERENT"

Difficulties in standardized administration are particularly evident when it comes to the fair and accurate testing of minority groups. Suppose we wish to understand minority children's intellectual abilities. If we use standardized tests to get information of this type, we need to ensure that minority children are properly motivated to take the tests. As we have seen, many middle-class children seem to have little difficulty with test-taking attitudes or motivation. But the same may not be true of many lower-class and minority children. For example, lower-class African-American children may consider doing well in school, which presumably includes taking tests seriously, to be a sign of being "White" and hence to be undesirable (Fordham & Ogbu, 1986). In some cultures, it is not considered polite for children to offer opinions or even talk with adults. This must certainly interfere with test taking.

If children do not work hard at taking the test, the results are uninterpretable.[12] A low score on an ability test, for example, might indicate low ability, as it is intended to and is usually interpreted to mean, or it might merely indicate low motivation to perform well on the test and therefore permit no inferences about ability. Of course, the test score will accurately predict that the child is not doing well in school. But we already knew that. The issue is not school performance but underlying ability.

Given all this, we must try to identify and reduce factors that might interfere with minority children's display of their competencies on standardized tests. Or conversely, it is incumbent on us to make sure that minority children are well motivated to do their best on tests. What can be done? According to Anastasi (1988), some special precautions can be taken: "A desirable procedure is to provide adequate test-taking orientation and preliminary practice" (p. 64). But can this really be accomplished in a brief period of time with methods of standardized administration? Can our little games overcome deep-seated cultural differences and suspicions?

Anastasi (1988) also recommends avoiding use of materials that are "unfamiliar in a particular cultural milieu" (p. 307) or that may alienate minority children by referring repeatedly to suburban, middle-class family scenes, by picturing only affluent White children, or by stressing artifacts and customs of middle-class culture. (Similar arguments have of course been made about gender bias.)

This logic sometimes leads to the elimination of test items that reflect differences among cultures. The strategy is to keep only those items common to all, yielding a "culture-fair" test.[13] But I believe the strategy is likely to be counterproductive: These "culture-fair" tests are bound to fail because they are really "culturally deprived" tests. Culture-fair tests try to *remove* what is important to individual cultures. They eliminate culturally specific knowledge and practice – precisely the material that might stimulate motivation and allow members of the culture to demonstrate their competence.

The well-intentioned attempt to eliminate bias in testing may result only in empty, lifeless tests that cannot succeed at promoting motivation and otherwise providing insightful information about children's thinking. The solution, as we shall see, is just the reverse of what has been proposed: Play to the culture's strengths; do not try to eliminate them.[14] In brief, if we wish to motivate those who are different, standardized administration is not an effective method. And eliminating culture from tests may only reduce their power to interest and motivate.

TRADITIONAL METHODS ARE INADEQUATE FOR EXPLORATION

One of the most important activities for a researcher or practitioner is to explore, to become familiar with the lives of those who will be studied. Before doing more "rigorous" investigation or assessment, the psychologist needs to get a feeling for the child, to develop an informal understanding of the topic under investigation, to develop some "common sense" about the issues.

How do you explore? You observe children, you talk with them, you work with them as teacher or friend, you spend time with your younger relatives, you engage in informal conversations. Basing your knowledge of children solely on what you read in textbooks or on what you learn from test scores leads to a severe case of intellectual deprivation. Both researchers and practitioners need to draw upon and be constrained by informal knowledge – common sense – about the children they are studying.

Suppose we want to understand the language competence of African-American adolescents. Suppose we know nothing about the topic except for the fact that research shows that these youths perform extremely poorly on standardized tests of language administered in the schools. This limited set of data almost inevitably leads to the conclusion that African-Americans' language is impoverished.

Suppose, however, that we have informal contact with these youths, observing them and talking with them in nonschool situations. This shows immediately that their language, although different in some respects from the mainstream, is far from impoverished (Labov, 1970). Given this informal knowledge, this "common sense" resulting from informal observation and exploration, we would not be likely to fall into the trap of misinterpreting the data (and perhaps we would not even bother to collect standard test data in the first place). The tests may tell us something about performance in the school setting, but they do not provide insight into African-American adolescents' basic linguistic competence. To gain deeper insight into this competence, we must employ techniques other than standardized tests and we must conduct research outside the school setting, as indeed Labov then proceeded to do, producing important results.

So if we lack common sense and familiarity with the local culture, we may be led to faulty conclusions. If we do not interpret the data provided by standard research through the lens of rich informal experience, we may reach conclusions which are in serious error, as was true of many researchers investigating poor children's intellect (as cited in Ginsburg, 1986b).

You cannot do good research or clinical practice unless you use your head. First, you have to explore, and indeed, sometimes you learn more from exploration than from formal, "rigorous" procedures used later.[15] But standardized tests cannot be used effectively for exploration. This should come as no surprise: They are not *designed* for purposes of exploration. Restricted and focused as they are *intended* to be, they cannot give you the lay of the land; they cannot provide you with intuitive knowledge of your subject matter. The point is not to criticize standardized tests for not being able to do something they were not intended to do but to emphasize that if you want to explore, as you *must*, you need other methods. Don't get locked into the narrow, myopic world of standardized tests.

Conclusions

There are some things that standardized tests can do reasonably well. Often, instructions are reasonably clear to many children, who arrive at more or less common interpretations and are adequately motivated to work hard at the test. If so, a test may tell us something about a child's cognitive ability: for example, a child is skilled in comprehension but weak in productive vocabulary. A cleverly designed test, interpreted with sophistication, may even provide information about children's cognitive processes. From such a test, we may learn that a child seems to have some competence in logical thinking or seems to be in Stage 3 of moral judgment. Unless tests gave us *some* useful information, they probably would have been replaced long ago.

At the same time, we should not ignore serious shortcomings in the method of standardized administration. Different groups of children may interpret the "same" stimuli in different ways, so that the logic of "holding stimuli constant" is inevitably compromised. The tests may not measure what we think they measure, and achievement tests often attempt to measure the wrong sorts of things. Tests are not useful for studying complex thinking or development. Standard administration is ineffective in motivating many children, particularly those who are in some way different. Indeed, it is a contradiction in terms to believe that standardized administration can motivate all children. And tests are particularly inappropriate for understanding children who are "different" in terms of culture or in other ways.

For all these reasons, the method of standardized administration reveals only the tip of the iceberg with respect to children's thinking. Testing modeled on psychophysics is a poor vehicle for entering the child's mind; standardized methods are not well suited for obtaining a rich and sensitive view of cognitive processes.

NEW DEVELOPMENTS IN METHOD

I have argued that psychologists have been slow to abandon or at least deemphasize methods rendered obsolete by the new theoretical developments associated with the cognitive revolution. Yet progress can be noted in several important attempts to develop techniques appropriate for the study of mind.

Some of these are modifications of existing methods. In the bastions of psychometrics, attempts are being made to make tests sensitive to the needs of individuals. In "tailored testing," the difficulty of test items is adjusted to the needs or previous responses of the individual (Green, 1983). Thus, in the case of computerized testing of attitudes or personality traits, a statistical algorithm determines a subject's basic tendencies and then uses this information as a decision rule for omitting items which are likely to be irrelevant or redundant. If a subject believes "Abortion is a terrible sin," there is likely to be no point in asking him or her whether "Abortion could be legalized if there is an acceptable definition of when life begins" (Kamakura & Balasubramanian, 1989).

Tailoring has also been applied to educational achievement testing. Here tests are "tailored" to local conditions when they employ only items which are relevant to a particular local curriculum (Rudman, 1987). If Johnny or his class has not studied long division, then items on that topic are eliminated from the test. In both cases, the goal is to produce an alternative to a standardized administration, in which subjects all receive the same content, regardless of predisposition or local conditions.

Moreover, researchers are currently attempting to develop new testing procedures that can measure underlying understanding, strategies, and the like (Glaser, 1981; Nichols, 1994; Royer, Cisero, & Carlo, 1993). Indeed, I have participated in this effort myself, helping to develop a test intended to measure mathematics concepts and strategies (Ginsburg & Baroody, 1990). No doubt new approaches to testing will help us gain greater insight into cognitive processes, although we do not yet know how substantial these improvements will be. I suspect that the very nature of standardized testing sets limits on what it can accomplish with respect to entering minds.

Other methodological innovations are more far-reaching. Thus, researchers have gone outside the laboratory to investigate memories of everyday life (Pillemer & White, 1989). Investigators have employed "think-aloud methods" to examine complex problem solving (Ericsson & Simon, 1993; Schoenfeld, 1985). The microgenetic method – repeated observations and interviews of individual children working on a set of problems over a relatively long period of time – has been used to examine development (D. Kuhn & Phelps, 1982; Siegler & Crowley, 1991). Others have called for methods that will allow for consideration of meaningful activities in their social context (D. Kuhn, 1992). Ethnography – the detailed observation of persons in their natural environment and culture – is traditional in anthropology and has much to offer research in some areas of psychology (Fetterman, 1989).

Innovations like these have "opened up" our methods, freeing them from traditional constraints. Consider next a powerful method that is relatively "old."

THE CLINICAL INTERVIEW

This book is about one class of nontraditional methods, the *clinical interview,* originally developed by Jean Piaget. In recent years the clinical interview has achieved some popularity in research and practice related to developmental psychology. (I often refer to "the clinical interview" in the singular. But remember that the reference is to a *class* of methods, of which there are many, not just one.) Contemporary investigators have developed forms of the method, to be used alone or in conjunction with other procedures, to investigate topics as diverse as moral judgment (Smetana, 1982), mathematical thinking (Gelman, 1980), reading (Garcia, 1991; Wixson, Bosky, Yochum, & Alvermann, 1984), understanding of maps (Liben & Downs, 1991), and understanding of physics (Johansson, Marton, & Svensson, 1985). It is also used in clinical practice (Garbarino, Stott, & Faculty of The Erikson Institute, 1992; Greenspan & Thorndike-Greenspan, 1991; Hughes & Baker, 1990) and in vocational counseling and medicine (Millar, Crute, & Hargie, 1992). Use of clinical interview methods is increasing in mathematics education (Ginsburg, Jacobs, & Lopez, 1993), where the National Council of Teachers of Mathematics encourages its members to conduct flexible interviews in the classroom (National Council of Teachers of Mathematics, 1989, 1995), and in educational research generally. I have even found an example of the clinical interview used by police investigators to enhance the accuracy of eyewitness testimony (Kohnken & Brackmann, 1988). Clearly, use of clinical interview methods is not limited to the topics originally investigated by Piaget.

Despite its emerging popularity, the clinical interview method is not sufficiently understood. This is partly because the method violates the standard paradigm. It directly challenges the traditional point of view concerning scientific method in research and practice. It forces us to think very differently about how we should enter children's minds.

The purpose of this book is to introduce you to the clinical interview and to convince you that it offers a viable alternative, or at least a supplement, to traditional methods. The clinical interview can help you understand how children construct their personal worlds, how they think, how their cognitive processes (at least some of them) operate, how their minds function. I believe that the clinical interview can make important contributions both to basic research and to applications in the clinic, the school, and elsewhere too, like the courts and the physician's office. It can help us understand such phenomena as problem solving in school, world views and concepts of reality, understanding of one's illness, memories of abuse, stereotypes of others, and basic concepts of the self. It can be useful both for investigators in search of general knowledge concerning children and for clinicians seeking to capture the individual child's uniqueness.

Although the method has attracted increased interest in recent years, particularly in cognitive developmental research and in education, some psychologists continue to hold misconceptions concerning its scientific status or do not fully understand its strengths. Many researchers seem to believe that unstandardized clinical interview methods of the type I will describe are merely "informal" or even sloppy and suitable at best for "pilot work," preparatory to more rigorous research. Clinicians, school psychologists, and others often tend to assume that the more "standardized" the assessment, the more "valid" it is, and that "clinical judgment" may perhaps supplement such standardized procedures but is inferior to them in accuracy and reliability (not to speak of scientific respectability). Indeed, perhaps because of their devaluation of it, some practitioners are not as skilled in "clinical interviewing" as they should be.

If you think this, I hope to broaden your view. No doubt, both basic researchers and those doing applied work can derive some benefits from traditional procedures like standardized tests. These have an important (although more limited than usually assumed) place in our array of research and assessment methods. But I hope to convince you to be more catholic in your approach. Because people's minds are so extraordinarily complex, we must expand our methodology to include the *deliberately nonstandardized* approach of the clinical interview.

CHAPTER 2

What Is the Clinical Interview? Where Did It Come From? Why Do It?

> Now from the very first questionings I noticed that though [the standardized] tests certainly had their diagnostic merits, based on the numbers of successes and failures, it was much more interesting to try to find the reasons for the failures. Thus I engaged my subjects in conversations patterned after psychiatric questioning, with the aim of discovering something about the reasoning process underlying their right, but especially their wrong answers. I noticed with amazement that the simplest reasoning task . . . presented for normal children . . . difficulties unsuspected by the adult.
>
> Piaget, "Autobiography"

The previous chapter argued that traditional research and assessment methods involving standardized administration are often inadequate for understanding the complexities and dynamics of the child's mind. The theme of this chapter is that the cognitive tradition provides the theoretical rationale for an alternative method which can help us achieve the goal of gaining insight into the child's mental constructions. The clinical interview, a class of powerful techniques, can help us enter the child's mind.

In this chapter I begin by presenting examples of clinical interviews, so as to highlight key features, including their flexibility and ethic of respect. Next I describe the ideas of three seminal cognitive theorists – Freud, Piaget, and Vygotsky – who provide the theoretical rationale for use of clinical interview methods. I then attempt to expand upon this rationale by offering what I hope are basic and convincing arguments supporting use of the clinical interview.

SOME CLINICAL INTERVIEWS

Interviews are not the invention of psychologists. People have always engaged in dialogs with others to find out what they think. Over time, specialized forms of interviews have evolved in various professions: the law, journalism, medicine. Clinical interviews are to some extent distinct from the others in nature and purpose. In this section, I present several clinical interviews, the first revolving around a classic Piagetian topic, the conservation of number. After that, I give examples of how clinical interviewing has been used in connection with a variety of research efforts and in applications like IQ testing. Each example highlights distinctive features of clinical interview methods.

Jimmy's Concept of Number

I began by putting five dolls in a straight row in front of 4-year-old Jimmy.

> Interviewer (I): Watch what I'm going to do. I'm going to put out these little dolls. Now what I'd like you to do is put out just as many hats as there are dolls – the same number of hats as dolls.
> [Jimmy (J) placed one hat immediately below each doll.]
> I: Are there the same number now?
> J: Yes.

The problem presented to Jimmy has two major characteristics. One is that the basic test was decided upon beforehand. The initial presentation of the task is essentially standardized – given in the same way to all children. Unless the goal is unstructured exploration, both researcher and practitioner prepare several tests, in a fair amount of detail, before beginning the interaction with the child. In this case, my goal was to present a "conservation" task, and I knew

31

Before

After

The conservation of number

that I would ask several key questions, such as "Are there the same number now?"

A second characteristic is that the task involved objects for the child to work with. These objects happened to be "concrete" – dolls and hats. In other cases, the "objects" could be words on a page or spatial puzzles in a mental test.

At this point in the interview, it appeared that Jimmy understood *same:* He was successful in constructing equal sets. But as Jimmy watched, I then made the line of hats longer than the line of dolls.

That is, I rearranged one of the sets so that it looked different from the other, although its number was unchanged. The question was whether the child would recognize that the equivalence between the two sets remains the same (or is *conserved*) despite the irrelevant change in appearance. This is a classic, and again standardized, feature of conservation experiments.

> I: Are there more dolls now or more hats or just the same number?
> J: More hats.
> I: How do you know there are more hats?
> J: Because they are spreaded out.

Another major feature of the interview is a question designed to elicit the subject's account of how he solved the problem. "How do you know?" Or "How did you do it?" Or "*Why* are there more hats?" and so forth. Next, the interviewer must *interpret* the response, on the spot. In this case, Jimmy's statement that "they are spreaded out" is typical of children his age, who base their judgment on the lengths of the lines of objects and not on their number, and so was easy to interpret. In other cases, the child's response may be distinctive. Nevertheless it must be interpreted without reference to a previously decided upon scoring system, such as is available for tests like the WISC-R or Binet. To interpret what the child says and does, the interviewer must rely on specific knowledge of the domain under investigation, general knowledge of children, context, and the rules and norms of conversational interaction.

At this point, Jimmy's answer seemed to indicate, in the classic manner described by Piaget, that he believed that there were more hats because the line of hats was longer. But I wondered whether his error could have been the result of a mere misunderstanding of the instructions. My hypothesis was that perhaps he misunderstood the word *more* to refer to length rather than number. To find out, I introduced counting and number directly. I showed Jimmy two identical rows of candies, one designated as his and the other as mine. After Jimmy agreed that the rows were the same, I added one to my own row but spread Jimmy's apart so that although I had more candies than he did, his row was longer.

I: Can you count them for me?

J: One, two, three, four.

I: So you have four. And how many do I have?

J: One, two, three, four, five.

I: So who has more?

J: Me.

I: You? But you have four and I have five.

J: You put yours like that [meaning the interviewer's line was shorter] and put mine right there [i.e., spread it out].

So counting does not yet help Jimmy, because his judgment is still based on appearances. Things that *look* bigger *are* bigger.

Note that in the last part of the interview there was a good deal of improvisation: The interviewer has the freedom to vary questions as seems necessary. There is room in the interview for unplanned, unstandardized questioning. Indeed, my very last remark was a challenge ("But you have four and I have five"), which had been unplanned but seemed to be useful in eliciting the child's thinking. This kind of on-the-spot hypothesis making and testing is basic to the interview process. Obviously, the whole process is very different from the standardized administration of a test. Note too that the process evolves and that the interview may take some time to complete.

To summarize, a few major features (we will see more later) of the clinical interview are

- initial standardization of the task,
- use of objects around which the task revolves,
- a "How did you do it?" or "Why?" question,
- an immediate interpretation of the subject's response,
- on-the-spot hypothesis making and testing,
- the freedom to improvise, and
- evolution of the interview process over a period of time.

Of course, the clinical interview need not be limited to classic Piaget problems. Next follows a more contemporary example.

Fantasy and Reality on Television

Children's ability to distinguish between reality and fantasy has been an important topic for therapists and researchers alike. One way of approaching this issue is to examine children's judgments concerning whether characters on television are real or imaginary. Is the video image itself alive, or can it be separated from what it is supposed to indicate?[1] Is the Mister Rogers on the TV screen a living person, or is it an image depicting a live person? And if the child believes that the image is itself not real but merely depicts Mister Rogers, is Mister Rogers a real person or a character depicted by an actor? These are very complicated questions indeed. The concept of fantasy and reality on television is multilayered, involving video displays which present images of actors (who presumably are real) pretending to be characters (who in a sense are not real).

One way to provide answers to questions like these is to interview children. Here is an excerpt from an interview conducted by my student Anne Kaplan. The subject is "M," age 6. The questions revolve around a children's show called *Charles in Charge*, which is not a cartoon.

Interviewer (I): Is this boy on the show a real boy?

M: Yes.

I: He is? How do you know?

M: Because if it's not a cartoon, then it's a real person.

I: If you could reach inside your TV set, could you touch him and the furniture that's in his living room?

M: No.

I: How come?

M: Because if you could reach inside your TV set, you'd just break your TV.

I: I see. How do you think that Douglas got inside the TV?

M: Well, he didn't get inside. He got taped. Like they took a video camera and put him on video and then like you take that video and just put it in here [the VCR] and it shows what they taped.

I: After the show is over and you're not watching TV anymore, is Douglas and his family . . . are they still a family?

M: Well, only if they were like a family and the family got taped *as* a family. But if they were separate people, just friends doing it, then they wouldn't be a family.

Note that the clinical interview presents a sophisticated method for examining complexities like these. At first, M agrees that the character on the show is "real." This could mean either that the character depicts a real person or that the image on the screen is itself real – that is, alive. The interviewer follows up with "How do you know?" which elicits an answer indicating that M takes *real* to mean a "real person" rather than an imaginary character: "Because if it's not a cartoon, then it's a real person." But is that "real person" alive inside the TV set or is it merely a video image? The interviewer asks a clever question (probably prepared beforehand), "If you could reach inside your TV set . . . ," which elicits M's clear knowledge that what is seen on the screen is a video image, not a "real person." But then the question arises as to whether M sees "Douglas" as a real person or as a character portrayed by an actor. A question about the family – "After the show is over . . . are they still a family?" – reveals that M makes a very clear distinction between actors and the characters they portray. He is perhaps naive only in thinking that the actors are "friends" (although perhaps he really means only "acquaintances"). It is hard to see how standardized interview questions could reveal the same level of complexity in children's thinking.

The Meaning of IQ Test Responses

An IQ test like the WISC-R yields various scores and patterns of scores that are considered to provide information concerning children's "intelligence." They may tell us something useful concerning children's general level of intellectual functioning and even about relative levels of verbal and performance abilities. But IQ data – total scores, performance and verbal scores, and scale scores too – are at best incomplete; they do not provide a detailed portrait of children's thinking. Indeed, these scores are hard to interpret with confidence because, although correct and incorrect answers to any single IQ item may result from any number of strategies, the test provides no direct information about which strategies might have been employed to solve that and other items. The tester has no way of knowing from the response alone what strategy, what thought process, was actually used.

What can be done? To learn about thought in any depth, the psychologist must examine the processes of solution that underlie the individual child's performance on IQ problems. Clinicians interested in the "diagnostic" interpretation of IQ tests often do this when they "test the limits," which in effect involves conducting informal interviews concerning IQ responses.[2]

Here are some examples of how clinical interview methods can be used for this purpose. Sometimes, informal questioning reveals competence where none was shown by standard testing. Thus, when Jo, age 12, was given a standard question[3] from an information subtest, "What is a thermometer?" she did not get the right answer. Of course, the examiner employing standardized administration is prohibited from following up on the child's mistake. But the clinical interviewer need not be constrained in this way. When the question was only slightly rephrased as "What does a thermometer do?" Jo answered immediately, "Measures heat in the body."

In response to another IQ item, Jo had been unable to provide any information about hieroglyphics. Ignoring standardized procedure, the interviewer returned later to the question.

I: You had trouble with the question about the hieroglyphics. Do you know anything about the Egyptians?
J: Oh, now I know what it is. It's that Egyptian writing.
I: Where do they write it?
J: They write it on the walls.
I: What does it look like?
J: It looks like pictures, like funny little pictures.

We see then that a small amount of structuring – placing the question in context without giving away the answer – was sufficient to allow Jo to produce a correct response. The interviewer did not "give away" the answer; he merely provided the means for Jo to access preexisting knowledge.

Here is another example: Jo had been given a problem in which she had to determine how much change would be left over from a dollar if she had bought two dozen eggs at 45¢ a dozen. Her answer was 20¢.

I: Say out loud how you did it.

J: Since it was 45¢ for one dozen and 45¢ for the other, and 45 and 45 is 80, so 80 from 100 or a dollar is 20¢.

I: So you said 45 and 45 is . . . ?

J: 80 . . . [She hesitates, drawing out the word *eighty*, and looks very unsure.]

I: Are you sure?

J: No, 90.

I: So the answer is?

J: 10.

In this case, the questioning revealed that her strategy was sensible. She knew that she had to add up the two amounts and subtract the sum from the total to get the answer. The only faulty part of her procedure was the number fact. She believed that $45 + 45 = 80$ (which she did in fact subtract correctly from 100). But the incorrect number fact was mere sloppiness. When given the chance to reconsider the number fact answer, she spontaneously corrected it and then completed the problem correctly. Clearly, her analysis of the problem was correct, her procedures were mostly correct, and the minor flaw in her recall was easily corrected.

In all of these examples, the standard IQ testing failed to reveal the true extent of Jo's competence. Only a small amount of additional support or questioning – which did not teach her anything – was sufficient to reveal that she possessed the relevant knowledge or skill to solve the various problems.[4]

Conclusions

The clinical interview can be used to examine different aspects of the child's (or adult's) thinking, including the understanding of basic concepts of number, complex ideas about reality, moral judgment, and solutions to IQ test items. The clinical interview can be used by the researcher interested in the prototypical child or by the practitioner attempting to understand the individual child. At the heart of the clinical interview method is a particular kind of flexibility involving the interviewer as measuring instrument. Although usually beginning with some standard problems, often involving concrete objects, the interviewer, observing carefully and interpreting what is observed, has the freedom to alter tasks to promote the child's understanding and probe his or her reactions; the interviewer is permitted to devise new problems, on the spot, in order to test hypotheses; the interviewer attempts to uncover the thought and concepts underlying the child's verbalizations. The clinical interview seems to provide rich data that could not be obtained by other means.

In the most general sense, we can say that the interviewer partly controls what the child does and partly is controlled by the child. On the one hand, the interviewer sets the child an initial task and devises further tasks to test hypotheses. In this sense, the interviewer (or more precisely, the interviewer's theory) determines what happens. On the other hand, the interviewer attempts to respond to the child, to follow where the child leads. In this sense, the child's talk and behavior control what the interviewer does and how the interviewer thinks and theorizes about what the child does. In the clinical interview, control passes back and forth between interviewer and child. What could be more different from the method of standardized administration, in which the test instructions rigidly control the tester's behavior, the test items direct and limit the child's response, and the whole affair has been devised beforehand by the test constructor, the only actor in the process with any freedom, who is not even there?

A Note on Respect

Finally, I note an ethical dimension. The interviewer, whether researcher or practitioner, usually displays an attitude of respect toward the child. The interviewer conveys the impression, in word and deed, that he or she is deeply interested in the child's thinking and acknowledges that it is the product of a genuine attempt to make sense of the world, to create meaning. The interviewer makes clear that mistakes are not taken as evidence of flaws in intelligence or character. In the ethic of interviewing, it is quite acceptable to make mistakes, and what is more important than the wrong answer is the thinking that underlies it. The interviewer helps the child to understand that the primary goal is not to evaluate in the same way that a test evaluates – that is, to produce a scorecard of successes and failures. Rather, the goal is to understand the underlying thinking, to enter the child's mind.

Given such respect, the child usually responds with trust and is gradually willing to reveal his or her thinking, including doubts and ignorance. As we shall see, children even find the clinical interview interesting and enjoyable. For one thing, the clinical interview is one of the few occasions in which an adult is genuinely interested in the child's thought.

By contrast, in the method of standard administration, the ethic revolves around control and evaluation. Whatever the tester says about "having a good time" or "playing games," the child believes (for the most part quite accurately) that he or she is being evaluated, that right answers are better than wrong ones, that it is both possible and undesirable to fail the test, that the tester is firmly in control, and that, in this situation, guardedness is more adaptive than openness.

THE INTELLECTUAL ORIGINS OF THE CLINICAL INTERVIEW

The clinical interview has a distinguished theoretical lineage in the ideas of Freud, Piaget, and Vygotsky. Freud taught us that cognitive phenomena are complex and sometimes deceptive and need to be deciphered by devious methods. Piaget showed that to uncover children's thought – their constructions of reality – we must use the flexible techniques of the "clinical interview method." And Vygotsky argued that we must broaden our concept of children's thinking to include the child's budding cognition and that we must measure it in the social context.

Freud: Decoding the Deception

Why begin with Freud?[5] Partly because Freud influenced the young Piaget. At the beginning of his career, Piaget was a member of the Psychoanalytic Society, he attended the International Congress on Psychoanalysis in Berlin (a congress at which Freud himself appeared) in 1922, and he underwent psychoanalysis under the supervision of one of Freud's disciples (Bringuier, 1980). One of Piaget's first psychological papers, written in 1920, bore the title "Psychoanalysis in Its Relations With Child Psychology" (Piaget, 1977). Strongly influenced by psychoanalytic theory, Piaget felt – at least in the 1920s – that Freud was a significant cognitive theorist. "It will . . . be apparent how much I owe to psychoanalysis, which in my opinion has revolutionized the psychology of primitive thought" (Piaget, 1955, p. 21).

Freud's cognitive approach seems to emerge most clearly in his treatment of dreams (S. Freud, 1961) and slips of the tongue (S. Freud, 1953). The work is "cognitive" in two senses. First, the empirical phenomena – dreams and slips of the tongue – are clearly the sorts of psychological events we could term "cognitive": Dreams can be seen as reports of mental images and slips are a special case of speech, both classic problems of cognitive psychology.

More important, Freud's theoretical treatment of the empirical phenomena is cognitive in postulating underlying mental processes that generate the observed data. In this view, the objective observer (analyst, psychological researcher) encounters *manifest* phenomena, or what some would call "behavior," such as reports of dreams or slips of the tongue. The explanation of these observables (the surface phenomena of verbal reports and speech acts) involves an account of the mental mechanisms generating them; they are "constructed by a highly complicated activity of the mind" (S. Freud, 1961, p. 122).

Complicated, indeed. To account for dreams, a kind of construction of unreality, Freud postulates an elaborate mental apparatus which begins with a latent dream (or "dream-thoughts"), which is not acceptable to consciousness. For example, a child's latent dream might involve decapitation of a new sibling. But then a censor – the superego – intervenes to determine which aspects of the latent dream may emerge to consciousness and which may not. Thus, the censor

41

may decide that decapitation is unacceptable but that the sibling's departure is tolerable. Next, the child employs a system of mental operations, the "dreamwork," to transform the latent dream into something acceptable to the censor. The dreamwork includes cognitive processes like condensation (combining two thoughts into one), whose goal is to disguise unacceptable elements of the latent dream so as to transform them into something innocuous, confusing, or obscure. Thus, the child may dream that the sibling loses a cap and goes off to find it. The result of the dreamwork's transformation of the latent dream is the manifest dream – what the dreamer experiences and what the observer hears about.

Key to the theory, and to cognitive psychology generally, is the distinction between the manifest and the latent, between what is observed on the surface and what underlies it. For Freud, as for Piaget, psychology is not the science of behavior but the science of the (sometimes hidden) workings of the mind. The aim of psychology is to understand how the mind works; the observation of "behavior" (e.g., verbal reports of dreams) is undertaken not for its own sake but only to achieve the goal of portraying the mind. In his focus on underlying process, Freud's work is clearly consonant with the theories of those in psychology and artificial intelligence who postulate underlying mechanisms (e.g., concrete operations, information-processing models, computer simulations) that generate (and hence provide sufficient explanations for) overt behavior.

Freud's ideas led him to an "interpretive" methodological stance which is instructive for cognitive psychology. The clinical aim of psychoanalysis was to discover and make conscious the thoughts that the patient finds unacceptable and disturbing. Yet these are disguised or hidden by various cognitive operations (the dreamwork, the defense mechanisms), so that the process of discovery must be subtle, even devious.[6] The work of the analyst is therefore like that of the code breaker, the detective, or the archeologist. The analyst can rely only on limited, sometimes misleading information and must infer from these clues hidden meanings and underlying patterns. The surface data cannot be taken literally; they must be penetrated to see what lies beneath. One must listen with "the third ear."

Cracking the cognitive code requires flexible and sophisticated procedures. For Freud this meant several things. First, even if the aim is to discover general laws of human nature, it is necessary to undertake the intensive study of the individual, of the particular case. This is required because the cognitive disguises are highly individual. Although the processes of the dreamwork are general across individuals, one person's dream symbol for a particular thought is not the same as another's. Second, because it is necessary to deal in depth with individuals, the short-term study of large numbers of "subjects" (the standard statistical method of conventional psychology) is likely to prove insensitive for research into psychoanalytic issues. Third, it is necessary to obtain a rich corpus of data from which to make inferences concerning underlying processes. A detective cannot get very far with only one clue. A given datum can be generated by any one of a number of underlying operations; hence, further evidence is needed to decide among them.[7]

Thus, for Freud, the goal was to interpret behavior to illuminate the underlying process. The method must be subtle, involving the intensive study of the individual and the gathering of a rich corpus of data over a period of time. Consider next how Piaget, sharing many of these goals and principles, developed an interpretive method suitable for studying children's thinking.

Piaget: The Clinical Interview Method

HISTORY

Picture the young Piaget around 1919, when he was 23 years old, with a doctorate in the sciences and a thesis on mollusks and already the author of several published zoological papers, some dating from his childhood.[8] Freud had written his *Interpretation of Dreams* some 20 years earlier, Gestalt psychology was barely under way in Germany, and about 15 years earlier, Binet had developed the first successful intelligence test. Piaget's overall goal was "to consecrate my life to the biological explanation of knowledge" (Piaget, 1952a, p. 240). But he was at odds and ends; after receiving his doctorate, he searched for a systematic and empirical method for studying the "embryology of intelligence" (p. 245) – that is, the evolution of the various forms of knowledge. Deciding to explore psychology, he wandered from one research laboratory to another, studied with the psychiatrist Bleuler, learned to interview mental patients, read psychoanalysis, and attended Jung's lectures.

Then an event occurred which gave direction to Piaget's career. He had the good fortune to receive an invitation to join the Binet laboratory in Paris around 1921. Working under the loose supervision of Simon, who ran the laboratory after Binet's early death, Piaget's job was to standardize a French version of an English reasoning test. He began the work "without much enthusiasm, just to try anything" (Piaget, 1952a, p. 244). It is easy to see why Piaget felt this way. Standardizing a test involves administering it, in the same way each time, to large numbers of children in order to establish detailed norms, in this case for French children. Imagine the boredom that this mindless task would have created in the immensely talented and creative Piaget!

But fortunately Simon was living in Rouen, far away from the laboratory in Paris, "and couldn't oversee what I did – luckily!" (Piaget, quoted by Bringuier, 1980, p. 9), so that Piaget was his own master, in control of an entire school for purposes of research. Piaget writes that the experience allowed him to discover his field of research. "I became interested immediately in the way the child reasoned and the difficulties he encountered, the mistakes he made, his reasons for making them, and the methods he came up with in order to get to the right answers" (p. 9). For Piaget, the test scores – the right and wrong answers – were of little interest. What fascinated him instead was the child's mind, the child's thought, and it was to this topic that Piaget devoted approximately 60 years of the most influential and, I think, insightful research on children's thinking ever conducted.

One of the first issues Piaget confronted was that of method. He felt that the method of standardized administration was too constraining for purposes of investigating thought. For one thing, this method precludes follow-up questions; it inhibits exploration. If the child gives an interesting response, the standard test format does not allow the examiner to probe it, to attempt to go beneath the surface, in order to discover something about the underlying pattern of thought that produced the response. It is as if a psychoanalyst were forced to take at face value the patient's manifest dream and were prohibited from using additional evidence in an attempt to uncover the latent content. From Piaget's point of view, the method of standardized administration limits attention to the superficial – literally, to what is on the surface. Of course, a defender might argue that standard tests do this for a good reason: Their goal is to rank children objectively by common criteria, not to investigate their thought. But from the perspective of cognitive psychology, that is the whole point: The very goal of standardized tests precludes insight into underlying thinking.

In any event, Piaget decided to pursue the investigation of thinking in the following way: "I engaged my subjects in conversations patterned after psychiatric questioning, with the aim of discovering something about the reasoning process underlying their right, but especially their wrong answers" (Piaget, 1952a, p. 244). Like Freud, Piaget's goal was to interpret surface phenomena, to uncover the latent, to listen with a cognitive "third ear."[9]

Piaget chose the "clinical interview method" in a very deliberate and principled fashion. It was not an afterthought; it was not the result of ignorance about scientific methods. Indeed, Piaget accepted the standard scientific criteria, believing that methods must be systematic, objective, and replicable (Cowan, 1978, p. 60). Piaget did not enter lightly into a method that he knew was unorthodox, not to speak of difficult to implement. In one of his first books, *The Child's Conception of the World* (Piaget, 1976a), originally published in 1926, Piaget gave several arguments for use of the method (although after that he wrote virtually nothing about methodology), and it is worth presenting them in some detail.

THE METHOD OF TESTS

Piaget realized almost immediately that the method of standardized administration (what Piaget called the "method of tests") was inadequate for implementing the kind of research he wished to undertake into children's thinking. The method of tests can of course be useful for several purposes. It can provide accurate individual diagnosis, as Binet originally claimed. If a child scores below a certain level determined by statistical norms on the intelligence test, administered in a standardized fashion, the tester can reasonably infer that the child is likely to be retarded. (Basically, this amounts to saying that if the child behaves like a retarded child, consider him or her retarded.) Such a test may or may not provide useful insight into the child's thinking; but under certain conditions, which need to be carefully specified, it is a reasonably "fair" method (as we saw in chapter 1) for ranking children's performance.[10] The method of tests may also provide some general information that might be used to make general inferences about children's thinking. Thus, if 8-year-olds but not 2-year-olds can solve logical syllogisms on a standard test, the researcher might reasonably conclude that the latter group of children generally experience difficulty in logical reasoning.

All this is fine, but if the goal is to study thinking in depth, the method of tests falls short. Piaget's first criticism is that the method of tests "does not allow a sufficient analysis of the results . . . [which] are too often useless as theory, owing to the lack of context" (Piaget, 1976a, p. 3). The child's brief responses to the questions (which are required by the "stereotyped conditions which the test method demands") are each considered in isolation. But all responses are not equal. One may not be as informative as another. An answer cannot be fully understood if it is considered apart from the child's comprehension of the question, from what the child has done in response to previous questions, from the child's motivation, and from the way in which the child has used certain words in other parts of the test. Context is all; single bits of behavior extracted from the larger stream lose their meaning.[11] Lack of context stifles interpretation.

Piaget's second criticism is that the method of tests "falsifies the natural mental inclination of the subject or at least risks so doing" (1976a, p. 3). The very phrasing of a question may impose the adult framework of interpretation, restrict the child's freedom to employ his or her own point of view, and thus fail to elicit the child's spontaneous (and uninfluenced) way of thinking about the topic. Thus, if the examiner poses a rather specific question, like "What makes the sun move?" the child may quickly accept the premise of the question (that something does indeed make it move) and invent an answer based on that premise, for example, that God pushes it – an answer which fails to reflect his or her "natural mental inclination." Or if the test involves multiple choice, the available answers may not reflect the child's methods of solution.

The method of tests, Piaget felt, was clearly inadequate for the kind of cognitive research he wished to conduct. "The only way to avoid such difficulties is to vary the questions, to make counter-suggestions, in short, to give up all idea of a fixed questionnaire" (1976a, p. 4). Piaget's solution was radical indeed: *Abandon standardized administration*. For many psychologists, this meant that Piaget had stepped over the line into nonscientific territory and that his methods were inherently weak, sloppy, and suitable only for pilot work – in short, unscientific.

PURE OBSERVATION

If the method of tests based on standardized administration is inadequate, what are the alternatives? One possibility that appealed to Piaget, who after all began his career as a naturalist in biology, was "pure observation," that is, observing the child's behavior in everyday life, particularly those questions the child poses in a spontaneous fashion. Such observation may yield very important data. Spontaneous questions can reveal the topics with which the child is struggling and even the way in which the child is framing answers. If the child spontaneously asks, "Who pushes the sun along in the sky?" the adult knows that the child is concerned with explaining the sun's movements and also that the child seems to believe that an external agent must cause them. Without such spontaneous questions, the researcher may not have realized that the topic was of concern to the child or that the child even had begun to formulate a way of thinking about it.

Having made such naturalistic observations, the psychologist can then devise more focused studies to investigate the qualities of thought which the spontaneous questions suggested. And after these more formal studies are completed, the psychologist can return to naturalistic observation in order to check on their results. Spontaneous questions can thus provide confirmation of claims made by "laboratory" studies.

Despite these substantial advantages, observation also suffers from basic limitations. The most important of them is that the child's spontaneous behavior and speech may reveal very little about thought. Children seldom express their thoughts spontaneously, articulately, or coherently, at least in the absence of direct questioning. As Piaget (1976a) put it, ". . . alongside of those thoughts which can be expressed . . . how many inexpressible thoughts must remain unknown so long as we restrict ourselves to observing the child without talking to him?" (pp. 6–7). The observer may watch for a long time and may gather tons of data without seeing anything very interesting insofar as thinking is concerned. Observation is tedious, and all the labor that goes into it may pay off with only meager results. Observation is useless if what the investigator is interested in does not happen with any frequency.

CLINICAL INTERVIEW

Piaget therefore found it necessary to develop a third method, "the method of clinical examination," modeled after psychiatrists' methods of diagnosis (but of course *not* focused on their subject matter, psychopathology). Attempting to combine the best of testing and observation and at the same time to avoid their defects, Piaget designed the method to accomplish three goals: to depict the child's "natural mental inclination," to identify underlying thought processes, and to take into account the larger "mental context." All of the goals require the abandonment of rigidly standardized administration; each of the goals requires distinctive forms of flexibility. As we shall see, to depict spontaneous thought, the clinical interviewer depends on an "observation" guided by the child's responses. To identify thought processes, the interviewer introduces special questions and problems and in effect conducts on-the-spot experiments to test hypotheses. And to establish context, the interviewer introduces and varies conditions designed to examine such matters as the child's attention and motivation.

1. *"Natural mental inclination."* One of Piaget's primary goals was to access the child's spontaneous thought. Piaget was interested in depicting the "natural mental inclination" of the child, in describing how the child sees the world, how the child thinks, and how the

child solves problems – even, and especially, when these are qualitatively distinct from the adult's world view and methods. (As we shall see, Piaget's later notion of "constructivism" expanded upon these ideas and is now almost an axiom of cognitive psychology.) This is fundamentally at odds with an adult-centered approach in which the goal is to determine whether the child comprehends the concepts adults think are important, whether the child has learned what adults have taught, whether the child can respond accurately to questions which stem from adult assumptions, and whether the child can solve a problem using the methods that adults teach or consider proper.

From the Piaget perspective, the interviewer asks the child, "What does fairness mean to you?" or "What is your way of adding the numbers?" From the adult-centered point of view, the tester asks the child, "How do we define fairness?" (which really means "Can you define fairness the way we do?") or "Can you use column addition to add these numbers?" (which really means "Solve this the conventional way, not the way you usually do.").

If identifying the child's natural mental inclination is the goal, then attempts to enter the child's mind must entail a substantial element of exploration. If the child's thought may be distinctive, the interviewer would be foolish to limit herself to the standard questions stemming from adult categories. Instead, the interviewer must have the freedom to abandon adult preconceptions and to follow where the child's thought leads. A research method sensitive to natural inclination must entail sufficient flexibility to allow exploration. As Piaget put it, "How can we, with our adult minds, know what will be interesting [to the child]? If you follow the child wherever his answers lead spontaneously, instead of guiding him with preplanned questions, you can find out something new. . . . we can explore the whole area" (Bringuier, 1980, p. 24).

Taking this approach, Piaget often began his clinical interviews with open-ended questions[12] that were intended to discover the child's world view, not to impose the adult's, and he would then follow up on the child's initial response as appropriate. Thus, in *The Moral Judgment of the Child* (Piaget, 1962, p. 140) he begins by asking CLAI, a 6-year-old: "Do you know what a lie is?" The child responds, "It's when you say what isn't true."

Piaget (P): Is 2 + 2 = 5 a lie?

CLAI (C): Yes, it's a lie.

P: Why?

C: Because it isn't right.

P: Did the boy . . . know it wasn't right or did he make a mistake?

C: He made a mistake.

In this case, open-ended questioning revealed a distinctively childlike definition of *lie* (that a lie is any kind of error and need not involve the intention to deceive) and then followed up this "natural observation" with a little intervention (the question about deception) designed to check the hypothesis that the child's view differs from the adult's.

2. *Thought processes.* The clinical interviewer, unlike the naturalist, does not simply observe and explore. Instead, in the course of interacting with the child, the interviewer develops hypotheses about the child's thought processes and tests them with miniature experiments. Thus, in the case of moral judgment, Piaget conjectured that the "naughtiness" of a lie, as defined by the child described above, is determined by the magnitude of the mistake. The greater the mistake, the naughtier the lie: Moral culpability is directly correlated with factual error. To test this hypothesis, a little experiment is required in which the child is presented with several "conditions" (e.g., a small mistake and a larger mistake) and then must produce a judgment of naughtiness in each case. Piaget clearly recognized the power of the experimental method.[13]

Here is how Piaget (1962, p. 140) examined the relations between factual error and naughtiness with the same child.

P: You see this gentleman [a student]?

C: Yes.

P: How old do you think he is?

C: Thirty.

P: I would say 28.

The student then reported that he was 36.

P: Have we both told a lie?

C: Yes, both lies.

P: Which is the naughtiest, yours or mine, or are they both the same?[14]

This interchange may be considered an experiment. In Condition A, the child's "lie" is incorrect by 6 years, whereas in Condition B, Piaget's lie is incorrect by 8 years. The question is whether Condition B produces a judgment of greater naughtiness than Condition A, as predicted by the hypothesis. The child replied, "Yours is the naughtiest, because the difference is biggest." Note that the child's answer came in two parts. First, his judgment concerning which lie is naughtier ("Yours is the naughtiest") was in the direction predicted by the hypothesis. Second, he spontaneously provided a justification that revealed the basis for his decision ("because the difference is biggest"). Clearly, the child believed that Piaget's was the greater mistake, hence the bigger lie and the naughtier.

What is remarkable, demanding, and distinctive is that the clinical interviewer must create such an experiment on the spot, in the course of interacting with the child, without having planned for it in advance. As Piaget's great collaborator Inhelder (1989) put it: "Throughout the interview, the experimenter has to formulate hypotheses about the cognitive bases of the child's reactions . . . and then devise ways of immediately checking these hypotheses in the experimental situation" (p. 215).[15] The interviewer must continually engage in a process of experimental design in response to what is observed in the course of interacting with an individual child.[16] This is freedom and flexibility indeed![17] And this is one of the reasons why the interview is so hard to do, why according to Piaget a year's daily training in the method is required to achieve expertise.

One fascinating aspect of Piaget's investigations of cognitive process is that his interviews seldom employed questions asking children how they solved problems. Piaget rarely asked the child, "How did you get the answer?" or some equivalent. Instead, Piaget devised little experiments like the one described above in which the child was presented with two conditions (a larger and a smaller factual discrepancy) and was simply asked, "Which is the naughtiest, yours or mine, or are they both the same?" In such experiments, an inference about cognitive process (the equating of naughtiness with factual error) could be made from the child's simple judgment that one person is naughtier than the other and did not depend on the child's introspection (although in the example given above, the child *spontaneously* came up with a verbal description of his method). Piaget avoided the "How did you get the answer?" type question for a basic theoretical reason: He believed, on the basis of some good evidence (Piaget, 1976b), that young children are incapable of extensive introspection.[18]

3. Mental context. The last basic aspect of the clinical interview we shall consider is the interviewer's attempt "to keep every answer in its mental context" (Piaget, 1976a, p. 9). By this Piaget meant that responses to individual test items cannot always be taken at face value; they must be interpreted in the context of the child's other answers, motivation, and beliefs – in the context of the child's whole *psychology*. (Recall that Piaget felt that the method of tests is impoverished because it fails to do this.)

Suppose that the child is asked, as on the IQ test, "How are a sparrow and a cow alike?" At first Sally says simply, "I don't know." If we take the child's answer at face value, we might infer that she fails to see the abstract relation of "animal-ness" or has difficulty with similarities, and hence abstract thought in general. But if we attempt to establish the context in which to interpret this answer we might come to a very different conclusion.

One basic aspect of context is whether the child is motivated to deal with the task: whether Sally is trying hard and taking the task seriously. If we observe that she looks bored or tired or does not seem to be paying attention, we might be skeptical of the idea that she has difficulty with abstract thought. And we might test our hunch by observing her behavior under several very different conditions, including one in which we make special (nonstandardized) efforts to get her to attend, to perk up, and in general to try harder.

Another aspect of context is the child's understanding of the question. How does the child interpret *alike?* Although most children readily understand this term, perhaps Sally does not. And although she does not understand the word *alike*, perhaps she nevertheless understands the concept, at least with respect to the class of animals.

How to find out? Abandon the standard question; rephrase it as seems necessary. Ask new (unstandardized) questions like "Can you think of some ways a sparrow and a cow are the same?" or, at least as a start, "Tell me about sparrows and cows. Do they do any of the same kinds of things?"

The third type of context refers to strength of conviction. Piaget pointed out that sometimes children say what they believe the adult wants to hear and in fact do not believe what they are saying. On other occasions, children have thought through their answer with great care and are unshakable in their conviction. If all responses are not produced with equal conviction, they cannot be interpreted as equally revealing of the child's underlying thought.

The interviewer's job then is to distinguish among these various types of answers. Piaget's favorite methods for this purpose were repetition and "countersuggestion." Piaget would ask a question several times and from several angles to see if the child maintained a belief or repeated a judgment. If consistency was evident, then Piaget might present a countersuggestion. If the child said that A is true, Piaget would contradict him by asserting that B is true. Would the child then maintain his original judgment or, having little conviction, take up the cause of B as presented by the interviewer, perhaps in an effort to please?

For example, Piaget (1964, p. 85) asked an 8-year-old, Labert, whether he had a brother, and he replied in the affirmative that he had a brother, Arthur. Did his brother, Arthur, have a brother? Labert said no.

Piaget (P): How many brothers are there in the family?
Labert (L): Two.
P: Have you got any?
L: One.
P: Has he got any?
L: None at all.
P: You are his brother?
L: Yes.
P: Then he has got a brother?
L: No.

Note that in this case, Piaget asked the original question in several forms and then concluded with a countersuggestion asked in the form of a question ("Then he has got a brother?"). The result is more convincing than if a single response had been elicited by a single test item or even by a collection of similar items.

In brief, from a Piagetian perspective, the interviewer cannot understand what a response means without knowing the interviewer's previous question and the child's previous response, whether the child took the question seriously or was just guessing, how the child interpreted the question, whether the child was tired, whether the child was trying, whether the child was anxious, and the like. Getting answers to questions like these requires flexibility of method.

CONCLUSION

Early in his career, Piaget did a great service by teaching us that to examine the child's spontaneous thought, to identify the underlying thought process, and to place the child's responses in a larger psychological context, we require more flexibility of method than is allowed by the method of standardized administration. Piaget himself, along with his colleagues and students, used the clinical interview method to produce what is arguably the single most brilliant and influential body of research ever produced in developmental psychology. Surely, given Piaget's arguments and his accomplishments, we must consider the clinical interview a serious contribution to scientific method.

Vygotsky: The Zone of Proximal Development

Vygotsky considered the clinical interview method to be "a truly invaluable tool"[19] for studying intellectual development. At the same time, he felt that Piaget used the tool in too narrow a fashion precisely because Piaget's notion of intelligence was overly restricted (Vygotsky, 1978). In Vygotsky's view, Piaget and other psychologists normally consider only one aspect of intellectual functioning, namely the child's "actual developmental level" (p. 85). This refers to the concepts, strategies, processes, and the like that children can perform "on their own," independently of adult assistance. The actual developmental level refers to "functions which have already matured, that is, the end products of development" (p. 86). This view of intelligence demands testing procedures which ensure that the child operates independently, receiving no adult assistance, in coping with test problems.

But Vygotsky maintains that this approach neglects another aspect of intellectual functioning, namely those functions that are in the process of development, "functions that will mature tomorrow but are currently in an embryonic state. These functions could be termed the 'buds' . . . of development rather than the 'fruits' of development" (1978, p. 86). Changing the wording slightly, I would refer not to the "buds" but to the "budding" of intellectual functioning, as opposed to its ripe fruits.

To illustrate the difference between buds and fruits, Vygotsky presents the hypothetical example of two 10-year-old children who have a mental age of 8. Of course, we can say that they are the "same" in their actual developmental level because both can independently solve tasks the average 8-year-old can solve. But that is not the end of the story. Suppose that the adult tester or clinical interviewer then helps the two children to deal with the test problems they failed to solve the first time around. The help might consist of indirect hints, suggestions, leading questions, demonstration of the solution, and so forth. The hypothetical result is that under these conditions of adult assistance, one of the children performs at the 12-year level, whereas the other achieves only the 9-year level.

What would be the meaning of such a result, which is by no means far-fetched and can easily be observed? Clearly, although the children's "actual developmental levels" (as defined by their initial independent performance) were identical, their mental abilities differ in important ways. One child cannot "get it," or gets very little of it, even when offered considerable assistance; the actual developmental level is relatively static. By contrast, the other child shows dramatic progress; given adult assistance, the intellectual functions undergo a budding process, and the child reaches a significantly higher level of intellectual development.

In Vygotsky's (1978) famous definition, the "Zone of Proximal Development" refers to the "distance between the actual developmental level as determined by independent problem solving and the level of potential development as determined through problem solving under adult guidance or in collaboration with more capable peers" (p. 86). For the first child, the distance between the two was small. For the second child, the distance was large, indicating what might be called a flexible set of intellectual functions, a healthy amount of learning potential, and a high level of potential development, given adequate social support.

Although many aspects of Vygotsky's theory require clarification[20] (e.g., how does one measure this "distance," what are the different forms of "adult assistance," and do they differ from one another?), his contribution is to direct our attention to the "dynamics" of the child's intellect, to its flexibility, its learning potential, its ability to profit from experience and assistance. Clearly the intellects of Vygotsky's two hypothetical (but entirely plausible) children differ in important ways that we need to understand. And methods of assessment which investigate only the child's independent problem solving cannot help us to do this (Minick, 1987). From the perspective of Vygotsky's theory, the clinical interview must be reshaped to include an investigation of various forms of adult assistance.

Piaget's position was drastically different. His goal was to identify the child's natural mental inclination, the way in which the child spontaneously approaches problems and constructs the world *without adult assistance*. In Piaget's view, adult assistance is to be avoided, as it may involve suggestion and thus distort the child's natural knowledge. Indeed, Piaget often tested the child's degree of conviction in her beliefs by presenting what is in a way the *opposite* of adult help – a countersuggestion. If the child said the world is round, Piaget might say it is flat to determine whether the child could *resist* this misleading bit of adult "help" and thus demonstrate the depth and spontaneity of her belief. So Piaget's strategy was not to determine how the child's intelligence buds with adult assistance but to see whether the child's mind is strong and structured enough to resist adult influence.

How can the apparently discordant voices of Piaget and Vygotsky be reconciled in a useful way? Perhaps we might say that Piaget's clinical method aims at establishing the child's "competence" in what

Vygotsky called the "actual developmental level" – that is, the level of development which has already been completed. It is crucial to determine this lower boundary of the Zone of Proximal Development, and that is the goal of Piaget's clinical method, using various techniques, including the reverse of adult help (countersuggestion). But Vygotsky goes further and uses various forms of adult assistance, hints, and the like, deployed in flexible ways, to investigate the child's potential intelligence. This is a valuable extension of the goal and method of Piaget's clinical interview. One might even say that Vygotsky's theory can broaden the Zone of Proximal Development of the Piagetian clinical interview.

REASONS FOR USING THE CLINICAL INTERVIEW

We have seen then that several basic ideas underlie the development of clinical interview methods. Freud stressed the necessity of deciphering manifest content in order to identify underlying cognitive (and other) processes. Piaget developed the clinical interview method in an attempt to depict the child's spontaneous thought, to test hypotheses about underlying process, and to interpret the child's behavior in its psychological context. Vygotsky argued for the examination of the child's potential for development; his ideas can broaden the zone of the clinical interview.

Since these giants of the field introduced their ideas, the cognitive revolution has triumphed and cognitive theories have proliferated. Yet, as I argued earlier, research and assessment methods have generally not kept pace with theory, and until they catch up, the promise of the cognitive revolution cannot be realized. Some researchers have been searching for and experimenting with new methods of investigation, including modifications of Piaget's clinical interview method. As part of this effort, there is a great need to clarify the rationale for employing clinical interview methods and other innovative procedures (and conversely for abandoning, at least for some purposes, standardized administration).

I now make an effort to present a contemporary rationale for the clinical interview. It is important to employ, elaborate upon, and examine clinical interview methods for the following reasons, each to be discussed in some detail:

- Acceptance of constructivist theory *requires* that clinical interview methods be used.
- They offer the possibility of dealing with the problem of subjective equivalence.
- They help us to examine the fluid nature of thinking.
- They aid in the investigation of learning potential.
- They are useful for understanding thinking in its personal context.
- They allow us to deal with the individual as well as the general.
- They embody a special kind of methodological fairness, especially appropriate in a multicultural society.

Constructivism

If you accept the constructivist position, you have no choice. You *must* use the clinical interview or some other method that attempts to capture the distinctive nature of the child's thought. Constructivism requires us to take a methodological leap in order to achieve a new level of psychological understanding.

As we saw, Piaget's early intention was to investigate, without distortion, the child's natural mental inclination. Piaget's basic idea was that children develop spontaneous modes of thought, often different from the adult's, and that the psychologist's task is to describe the child's mind with as much fidelity to its "natural" form and functioning as possible. Over the years, Piaget expanded on this notion, eventually arriving at the overarching concept of *constructivism*, which now is at the heart of theorizing in almost all domains of psychology, from developmental to social to clinical.

The main point of constructivism is that humans actively construct their knowledge rather than receive it, fully formed, from external sources, which include the physical world and the various forms of social wisdom and which range from other persons to language, schooling, or television. Humans use information from these various sources to create theories of the world, methods for overcoming physical and social obstacles of various sorts, concepts of other people and of society, and modes of problem solving. Thus, the child constructs a schema of the mother, a notion of physical cause and effect, a stereotype of another ethnic group, a method for computation, and heuristics for comprehension of texts.

Constructivist theorists stress different aspects of the process. Some, like Vygotsky, stress the extent to which constructions are influenced by language, adults, and, indirectly, by the social and economic systems. Others, like Piaget, emphasize the child's private construction of reality.[21] Yet, despite the many forms and styles of constructivism, and the theoretical disagreements, there is widespread consensus among psychologists that the child does not develop concepts and ways of thinking primarily because the world imposes them, parents or teachers inculcate them, culture provides ways of thinking about them, or the mind innately contains them. Instead, the child actively uses information from the world, the lessons provided by parents and schools, the cultural legacy, and the species' biological inheritance as bases for constructing knowledge.

Several things follow from the constructivist world view. First, we must keep in mind that constructions are always *personal. Persons* construct knowledge, and persons are always separate, private, and different from one another (Ginsburg, 1989b). What I take to be the meaning of the word *justice* (or any other word) may be at least somewhat different from how you construe it, even though we share enough meaning to be able to communicate, albeit imperfectly. A child may be even more different from you than I am. Perhaps this stems from the fact that, as Piaget claimed, the child's thought is qualitatively different from the adult's. Or perhaps the child's distinctiveness simply results from a learning history that differs from the adult's. In either event, the child's meaning of *justice* is likely to be more distinct from yours than mine is, and hence it is more difficult for you to communicate with the child than with me.

This insistence on the personal nature of constructions does not gainsay the fact that persons are also the same in many basic ways, sharing basic biology and modes of thought. But the claim is that despite shared social influences, despite widespread universals and commonalities in mind, everyone's constructed world is to some extent personal and therefore distinct. This is true of the intellectual

59

world of the child at various stages of development, the unconscious world of the neurotic, and the cultural world of an ethnic group.

The first demand of constructivism is that we truly believe this. It is easy to *say* it, to "buy" constructivism as the latest theoretical style. But incorporating constructivism deeply into our thinking requires that we always recognize that the child's ways (and those of other people) may not be ours. The child may see the world differently, approach it differently, understand it differently.

Then, if we truly believe this, entering the child's mind requires methods that do not impose on the child our world view, our methods of coping, or our meanings. For example, if we truly understand the constructivist position, we must not begin the research or assessment by saying, "I will give the child this problem, which I think is important and which must logically be solved in the following manner, and I will determine whether or not the child does it this way." This is tantamount to saying, "I will give the child this problem, which is important to me and which I think ought to be solved in this way, or which I prefer to solve in this way, and I will find out whether the child does it my way." In fact, this is the basic logic behind a good deal of research employing "task analysis" and behind most of educational assessment.

Instead, if constructions are personal and if children may be different from adults, we should say, "I will give the child this problem, which seems to be important in his or her life, and I will try to find out the child's way of doing or seeing it, even if I do not do it or see it in the same way." This means that I cannot rely only on my adult experience, modes of thinking, and values. I have to discover what is important to the child, regardless of whether I value it, and how the child constructs a way of dealing with it.

As I have argued, the method of standardized administration – usually seen as the scientifically rigorous approach – is often poorly suited to accomplish this goal. Our task as "scientists," as researchers and practitioners, is to employ methods more sensitive than standardized administration for entering the child's mind, for understanding the other's distinct world to the fullest extent possible. Noddings (1990) argues that we must create a "methodological constructivism," which "develops methods of study consonant with the assumption of cognitive constructivism" (p. 10).[22]

Our methods must be at least as intelligent as our thinking.

Subjective Equivalence

As we saw, one of the fundamental problems of traditional methods is that even standardized administration cannot guarantee that all subjects receive the "same" problems. Children are asked which of two toys is "bigger" than the other. The wording is the same, the stimuli are the same, the administration is perfectly constant, and yet one child *sees* the problem differently from the other child. One child indicates that the taller is bigger; another says the heavier is bigger. Each child is answering a different question (and perhaps neither is answering the question the tester intended to ask); both are right. In short, the objective equivalence of standardized administration cannot guarantee subjective equivalence – that is, that all subjects *interpret* the problems in the same way.

Clinical interview methods appear to be useful for establishing subjective equivalence. The flexibility inherent in these methods allows the interviewer first to vary the questions and tasks for each child in order to establish subjective equivalence and then to determine whether the child has in fact interpreted the task in the way intended. Thus, if I wish to present the child with a problem involving weight, I may begin by asking, "Which is heavier?" But if my questioning reveals that the child does not understand that word or thinks it refers to color, I may reword the question, asking, for example, "Which weighs more?" and in this way help the child to interpret the problem in the same way as other children who understand "Which is heavier?" in the same way I do.

Of course, the particular ways in which the interviewer varies the "objective" problems may not succeed in their goal of producing subjective equivalence. Clinical interview methods provide no guarantee. But clinical interview methods should not be ruled out; their flexibility – their deliberate nonstandardization – offers the possibility of a fresh approach when traditional methods fail.

The Fluid Nature of Thinking

In recent years, psychologists have begun to consider thinking in a broader sense than did some earlier theorists, particularly Piaget. In Piaget's view, thinking is based on a set of more or less stable logical structures like the child's concrete operations or the adolescent's propositional logic (Inhelder & Piaget, 1958). Similarly, other cognitive psychologists conceptualize thinking in terms of a collection of information-processing operations or strategies. At a given stage of development, the child uses one or another set of logical operations, information-processing routines, or strategies. It's like knowing that you can call up on your computer this piece of software or that. Although complex, and even capable of learning (as when we put a new word in the spell checker), the software is stable, relatively fixed, and operates with a particular degree of effectiveness at a given stage of development (as when Version 2.1 eventually is replaced by Version 2.2). In this static world, the psychologist's job is to discover what kind of logical structure or information-processing routine or strategy underlies the child's performance (or what software is available for your computer). Clinical interview methods, I have argued, are useful for doing this.

Other writers have stressed the fluidity of thinking. For example, Flavell, Miller, and Miller (1993) point out that in studying children's thinking we usually find "all sorts of in-between patterns of performance: children who succeed on some versions of the task but not on others, and who thus seem sometimes to 'have' the concept and at other times to 'not have' it" (p. 321). Why this fluidity? Some familiar performance factors might be involved, such as failing to understand the instructions, failing to attend to relevant features of the problem, forgetting relevant aspects of the problem, lack of interest, and fear of the examiner. But other, more subtle cognitive factors may contribute to the child's inconsistency as well.

The "in-between patterns" take several forms. The child may reveal her knowledge only in those cases where she has real expertise (e.g., she can apply a memory strategy to dinosaurs, with which she is familiar, but not to other animals). The child may possess knowledge but can exhibit it only in situations that are not too demanding on her cognitive resources (e.g., she has strategies for remembering up to four things at a time but cannot cope with five or more things). The child may know a rule only imperfectly so that she fails to realize the conditions under which it generalizes to new problems (e.g., she knows how to add with two columns but does not know whether the same procedure is used for three columns). The child may know what ought to be done in a given situation but may not know how to do it (e.g., she knows she ought to protect her queen, but she doesn't have the strategy for accomplishing this sensible goal). The child may solve a problem but be unable to explain in words how it was done or why.[23] Other writers have stressed the fluidity of thinking as it evolves (e.g., over a period of several weeks or even months) in response to the demands of a problem and to other circumstances (D. Kuhn & Phelps, 1982; Siegler & Crowley, 1991).

These are only a few of the complexities we may observe. The general conclusion, according to Flavell et al. (1993), is that the child's thinking is "more like a developmental succession of different things than like a unitary, present or absent cognitive entity" (p. 322).[24]

I would expand on this notion by offering the following metaphor, an enlargement, one might say, of James's "stream of consciousness." Thinking is like a flowing, ever changing river. It looks very different in different places and seems to change continuously. It ebbs and flows, swirls around obstacles, fills in empty places, changes the environment it flows through (even eventually cutting through granite). It can be angry, menacing, or serene (no one would ever say that about Microsoft Word 5.1). It does have some permanence and constancy. It is after all a river, and rivers generally do some things but not others and can be distinguished from lakes or oceans. But it would be foolish to say that the essence of the river is here, swirling around this boulder in Minnesota, and not here, in the broad expanse of the waters slowly flowing by New Orleans.

So too the child's thinking. Like the river, it does have some general features. It is different, for example, than conditioned response or reflex. But it is always changing in response to its environment, fluid, swirling, shifting, meandering. If you dip into it in different places, you seem to place yourself in different rivers, as in a sense you do.

If thinking is not a thing, not an entity, not a trait, not even a stable collection of logical or other mental operations, but a shifting, ever changing process, then the job of assessment is by no means easy. The method of standardized administration seems unsuitable for the measurement of such complexity; it is like dipping into the stream in one place all the time with the same little ladle. We require flexible methods like the clinical interview to assess the "river of thought."

Learning Potential and Development

Clinical interview methods are also useful, indeed crucial, for examining several dynamic aspects of thinking. We have already reviewed Vygotsky's concept of the Zone of Proximal Development and his argument that we must examine the ways in which thinking changes and develops in response to help from those more knowledgeable than the child. Feuerstein, drawing both on Vygotsky's theory and on Piaget's method (he trained with Piaget and Inhelder), has developed "dynamic assessment" procedures to examine "learning potential" in the context of adult interaction. Feuerstein's Learning Potential Assessment Device (LPAD) involves a "radical reshaping of the test situation from a rigidly standardized procedure to a flexible, individualized, and intensely interactive process among the three partners involved: the task (may be changed according to need), the examinee . . . and the examiner (changes his or her orientation according to the detected transformations in the examinee's functioning . . .)" (Feuerstein, Rand, Jensen, Kaniel, & Tzuriel, 1987, p. 45). Within the LPAD, the flexibility of clinical interview methods is essential: The tasks and questioning procedures are modified, on the spot, in response to the child's shifts in performance.[25]

The Personal Context

Finally, the method is especially suited for examining the complexities of thinking in relation to its general psychological context. Recall that Piaget developed the clinical interview method partly in an effort to interpret the child's behavior within its "mental context." He wanted to know whether a response reflected a fundamental aspect of thought or whether it was the result of transitory factors such as lack of interest or fatigue.

Piaget himself was interested in the enduring and basic structures of the mind (at least within a period of intellectual development) and not with its vicissitudes in the course of everyday life. "I'm not really interested in individuals, in the individual. I'm interested in what is general in the development of intelligence and knowledge" (Piaget, in Bringuier, 1980, p. 86). Thus, in placing the child's answer in its mental context (i.e., in the context of emotion, interest, motivation, and the like), Piaget had no interest in context itself. In a sense, for Piaget, context was a nuisance, an irrelevance, merely something to transcend on the way to investigating what he considered more fundamental, namely the basic and universal structures of mind. For Piaget, the psychological analysis of the subject – that is, an analysis of thinking in relation to its psychological context – was secondary to the analysis of basic forms of knowledge. When asked by Bringuier, "You don't deal with the affective level at all?" Piaget replied: "Only because I'm not interested in it. I'm not a psychologist. I'm an epistemologist" (p. 49).[26]

Many of us, however, do not follow Piaget's lead in this matter. We agree instead with theorists like Dewey (1933) who claim that "no separation can be made between impersonal, abstract principles of logic and moral qualities of character" (p. 34), with those like Scheffler (1991) who assert that "cognition without emotion is vacuous" (p. 4), and with A. L. Brown, Bransford, Ferrara, and Campione (1983), who stress the importance of "hot cognition." Because we have more of an interest in understanding children than in knowledge in general, we believe that the mental context is not something to be shunted aside in order to study thinking; rather, the two, being inseparable, must be examined together. We want to know as much about the child's fear of reading and the conditions that elicit it as about the reading strategies the child employs. We want to know what the child likes to remember, as well as how the child remembers it. And for these purposes, clinical interview methods may be extremely useful. Placing the child's thought in the psychological context of emotion, value, and character is essential both for practitioners concerned with the functioning of the whole child in the everyday world and for researchers interested in broadening their theoretical perspective.

The Individual and the Group

Psychologists enter minds for different purposes. Most researchers aim at creating general knowledge, laws or theories designed to explain the minds of children-in-general – for example, all children learning to talk, all preoperational children, or all Latino children. Almost all researchers want to help children, in a general and rather abstract sort of way; but they are not concerned with helping the individual, particular children they investigate. Most practitioners, on the other hand, are primarily concerned with understanding and helping the individual child. Practitioners want to develop a theory of this particular child who is learning to talk, this particular preoperational child, this particular Latino child, and they want to improve this child's speech.

Clinical interview methods are useful for both purposes. As mentioned above, Piaget developed the clinical interview method to conduct research on what he considered to be cognitive universals, not to understand individuals. It is ironic that although Piaget's focus is thus quite consistent with that of most academic researchers, they have tended to denigrate his method, feeling that it needs to be sanitized (i.e., standardized) to achieve scientific respectability.

It is doubly ironic that Piaget's method is also suitable, indeed especially powerful, for practitioners devoted to understanding the individual case. As I pointed out above, when Piaget attempted to understand the mental context – the child's motivation, attention, indeed individuality – it was only to identify obstacles on the route to entering the world of the general "epistemic subject," the knower. Thus, one of the few psychologists (cognitive or other) whose method is genuinely *psychological*, sensitive to individual variation in motivation, affect, and the like (after all, the clinical interview was drawn from psychiatric practice) was fundamentally uninterested in these issues, preferring instead to highlight general aspects of cognition.

It is perhaps triply ironic that Piaget as an interviewer exhibited a deep concern for individuals. Indeed, according to Gruber (in

Bringuier, 1980), Piaget was so successful as a researcher because he showed great respect for children as individuals: "if you think of what he did with children, it was thanks to the great respect he has for what they say. . . . Piaget respects the child. He genuinely wants to understand the child for what he is" (p. 69). So the same Piaget who claimed he was not interested in children and who did not see himself as a psychologist nevertheless behaved toward them with a great deal more respect than those psychologists who "run experiments" with children or give them IQ tests.

What are we to make of this? My advice is to enjoy the ironies and use the method. Use it to create theories of both the general mind and individual children.

A Different Kind of Fairness

Both the method of standardized administration and the clinical interview methods emerge from a laudable concern for "fairness." Both achieve it, albeit in different ways. As we saw in chapter 1, the method of standardized administration is concerned with fairness as impartiality. Clinical interview methods aim at a very different kind of fairness.

The second type of fairness, *fairness as sensitivity to the individual*, conflicts with the first because it *treats people differently* in order to identify their competencies. The logic is that treating people in the same way often prevents us from identifying their strengths. Children from nonmainstream cultures may fail to exhibit their true competence because they do not easily interpret standard problems or are not interested in them or are uncomfortable in the standard testing situation, and the like. For example, Garcia (1991) maintains that under standardized testing conditions,

> Hispanic students' reading test scores seriously underestimate their reading comprehension potential. . . . [They exhibited] poor performance on the scriptally implicit questions (which required use of background knowledge) . . . [and a] tendency to interpret the test literally when determining their answers. . . . The Hispanic children's [open-ended] interview responses tended to elicit more information

about their . . . comprehension than did their test performance. (p. 371)

For reasons like these, "getting through" to many children, not only minority children (every child is in some way a minority of one, a distinctive "culture"), requires that we treat them in a special, non-standard way. The second type of fairness treats people differently – as individuals – in an effort to identify their abilities and problems, strengths and weaknesses. Having done this, the examiner can then make more insightful statements about the competencies of individuals or groups.[27]

The two methods are clearly very different. Using standard administration, the tester acts like an evaluator, a judge. Using flexible procedures, the interviewer is like a clinician, an artist.

So we are faced with what seems to be a real dilemma. If we assess all children in the same manner, we are in danger of ignoring their special, individual characteristics. Thus, using uniform procedures, the magistrate is in danger of imposing blind justice.[28] Yet, if we assess each child differently, we are in danger of making biased and unreliable judgments. Using methods tailored to the individual, the artist is liable to construct a fantasy.

Is there a way out of this dilemma? At least we should be aware of our purposes in testing; we should consider which standard of fairness we wish to employ. On some occasions, fairness as color blindness may be appropriate; in other circumstances, fairness as sensitivity to the individual may be required. Suppose that I have to take a civil service test to get a job as a policeman. I don't want considerations of race or other kinds of stereotypes to distort the assessors' judgment. That is why I might want the test to be in a standard form and my performance on it to be scored without the assessor knowing anything about me. The results may show that I do not do very well under the particular testing conditions employed; that is the reality – or at least one reality.

But if I want people to understand why I performed as I did, I want the examiner to treat me as an individual. Doing so, the examiner might discover that I am afraid of tests or don't speak the language well. The flexible method of testing may help the examiner to discover aspects of my psychology that explain my performance and may indeed qualify me for the job. The flexible method might reveal that what seems like a wrong answer on the test really was based on a good deal of thought which indeed indicates that I am well qualified for the job.

In general, if we want to obtain unbiased judgments of children's performance (e.g., how do they compare at the end of the school year in remembering their number facts or reading English words?), we need to test them in more or less standard ways, attempting like the judge to distribute color-blind justice. But if we want to understand what they are capable of and what lies beneath their performance, we must test them in flexible ways, acting like the artist attempting to capture their individuality.

CODA

I have tried to make as strong a case for the clinical interview as possible and hope to have so convinced you of its potential merits that you are willing to consider it seriously and read on. At the same time, I am not unaware that every method has limitations which must be acknowledged and then confronted. Perhaps both strengths and weaknesses of the clinical interview will become evident and even comprehensible as you read the next chapter, which offers a detailed account of what occurs in an extensive clinical interview.

What Happens in the Clinical Interview?

And since you know you cannot see yourself
So well as by reflection, I, your glass
Will modestly discover to yourself
That of yourself which you yet know not of.

Shakespeare, *Julius Caesar*

In the last chapter, we saw that the essence of the clinical interview is deliberate nonstandardization and flexibility. In an attempt to gain insight into the child's thinking and learning potential, the interviewer presents problems, modifies questions if the child seems to misunderstand them, devises new problems to test hypotheses arising in the course of the interview, and challenges answers to test the strength of the child's conviction. We also saw that the clinical interview can be used in a relatively brief, intensive, and focused manner or in a more lengthy and exploratory fashion.

But much more needs to be said about what happens in the clinical interview. My goal in this chapter is to examine the clinical interview in some depth to shed light on the activities of the interviewer and of the child and on the interaction between the two. At a time when so little is known about the clinical interview, my questions are of a general nature. What are the interviewer's thoughts and goals? What does the interviewer do to encourage the child to reveal and express thinking? (The next chapter has a more narrow focus and deals with specific tactics that the interviewer uses to put the child at ease, to explore thinking, and to test hypotheses about what is in the child's mind.)

We must also consider the interaction from the child's point of view. What does the child think is happening when an adult takes him or her from the classroom to discuss "how you think?" How does the child feel about it and cope with it? How does the child interpret this unusual situation? How does the child learn the rules of interaction in this distinctive form of discourse? What does the child learn from the clinical interview?

And then there is the interaction itself. How do interviewer and child affect each other? What goes on between interviewer and child during the intricate interaction that comprises the clinical interview? What kind of relationship do they form?

I raise these questions, and hope to provide preliminary answers to them, for two reasons. One is that understanding the clinical interview may help researchers and practitioners to appreciate its power – and its limitations too. Most researchers and practitioners do not have a very accurate idea about what the clinical interview *is*. They tend to think that it is a sloppy form of pilot work, a hit-or-miss procedure, based largely on "intuition." This is perhaps to be expected because the clinical interview is usually not considered to be an essential part of the methodological canon and is seldom taught. And unfortunately, little has been written about the method. As we have seen, even Piaget, whose output was vast, produced only a few (but extremely insightful) pages about the clinical interview (reviewed in chapter 2). By contrast, a voluminous literature, offering perhaps a bit more than anyone needs to know, has been devoted to standard testing, that overrated technique!

The other reason for examining the clinical interview in depth is that understanding it may help us to use it more skillfully. In my experience, it is true that some people seem to be "natural" interviewers, whereas others struggle with the method. But we all need to improve our technique, and explicit analysis of the method should provide useful guidelines about what to do and what to avoid.

THINKING ABOUT THE CLINICAL INTERVIEW

How should we think about the clinical interview? Several of its characteristics are immediately obvious. One is that it involves talk between two people. In some ways, the clinical interview resembles that naturally occurring form of interaction, the conversation, "the everyday situation in which two or more people address each other for a period of time, communicating something about themselves and their experience in the process" (Labov & Fanshel, 1977, p. 1). In both clinical interview and conversation, talk flows back and forth and is not "standardized" or routine, and often one person in the dyad tries to find out what the other thinks.

It is also clear, however, that the clinical interview is more than informal talk. Unlike ordinary conversation, the clinical interview is a focused, specialized, and indeed artificial form of discourse. The adult conducts the interview for a specific professional purpose, not to exchange experiences or pleasantries or to make friends. The clinical interview is dedicated to and designed for the task of "entering the child's mind." From the child's point of view too, the clinical interview, which may be identified as a "game," will appear to be out of the ordinary. When was the last time an adult spent a half hour asking questions about the child's thinking, ideas, and beliefs? What unprecedented interest!

Moreover, the clinical interview is an enormously complex form of social interaction. It often lasts a half hour or more, involves intense give-and-take between the participants, and is unlike much of what happens between adults and children. As we shall see, the interviewer deploys intricate strategies of probing and constructs sophisticated interpretations based on language, behavior, and context; the child engages in difficult attempts at introspection and expression.

How can we come to understand such a complex interaction, at least in a preliminary way? No doubt many approaches are possible. My own is to examine the minds and actions of interviewer and child and to attempt to decipher the relationship that develops between them. I use the interviewer's and the child's speech and behavior to make inferences about their thought and actions and to understand how their behavior is intertwined. I hope that this very preliminary theoretical framework, describing *ideas, goals, acts,* and *relationship* – you might think of it as a blend of individual psychology, social psychology, and discourse analysis – will prove useful for raising important questions, for directing attention at key issues, and for thinking about what occurs in the clinical interview.

Ideas

Social interactions are built around the actors' *ideas.* I *anticipate* that the police officer who stops my car will ask me in a polite but threatening way why I was going so fast; my *knowledge* of the social norms indicates that I am expected to respond in a serious manner and that some excuses are more socially acceptable than others; I *interpret* the police officer's speech, manner, and style as indicating excessive rigidity and an unforgiving attitude; I *believe* that speeding is generally not good, although in this case it was clearly justified. As all this is going on in my head, the police officer's mind is similarly active. Seeing an apparently speeding (let's not concede too much) car of a certain type with a driver of a certain age and appearance, the officer immediately *infers* that the vehicle is not stolen; *expects* that the interaction will be polite; and *believes* that no threat to safety is imminent. Of course, our cognitions can be more or less accurate. Particular difficulties of misunderstanding and miscommunication can arise when interviewer and child are members of different cultures.[1] But accurate or not, all these ideas, these "cognitive" phenomena – knowledge of social norms, expectancies, interpretations, beliefs, prejudices, and the like – shape our interactions with the socially constructed other.

Mental activity is as central to the clinical interview as to any other form of social interaction. Interviewer and child constantly expect, believe, interpret, and infer. The interviewer expects a 5-year-old to act differently from a 10-year-old, believes that a child's consistent refusal to respond indicates shyness, interprets a child's statement "They both have the mostest" to mean that both have the same number. The child expects the adult to ask questions that will be hard to answer, believes that giving correct answers is essential, and interprets the adult's request "Tell me more about how you got the answer" to mean that the answer must have been wrong.

To understand the process of interviewing we need to gain insight into these mental events. In particular, it is important to explore how expectations and norms concerning children's behavior and abilities influence the interviewer's questioning, and how the interviewer goes about interpreting behavior and talk in order to create hypotheses and theories concerning the child's mental abilities. It is also important to understand how the child develops ideas concerning what is happening, what the interviewer's questions mean, and what is expected in this strange activity which we think of as the clinical interview. Presumably the child understands something of the rules of ordinary conversation but at the outset does not know how to respond to the unique interaction of the clinical interview. The child does not know when to talk and when not to talk, what to talk about, what is proper to introduce spontaneously, and how much direction to take from the adult. How does the child learn the "rules of the game," the assumptions and social norms underlying the clinical interview?[2]

Goals

To understand social interaction, we also need to consider the participants' *goals*. What do they hope to get out of the situation?

The interviewer's behavior seems to be dominated by at least one broad goal, namely to understand the child's thinking. But as the interview evolves, the interviewer seems to develop various subgoals or purposes – for example, to put the child at ease or to explore or clarify. We need to understand the interviewer's major goals and subgoals. How do they evolve? How are they related to what the child does and to what has been learned about the child?

The child's goals are less clear (maybe because I have more recently been an interviewer than a child). Experience in many interviews leads me to conjecture, however, that the child's initial goal is in a broad sense to please the examiner and to look good. The child wants to do what is thought to be required by the interviewer. Further, I believe that in the course of a good interview the child may acquire a new goal, namely to introspect and to describe thinking so that another can understand it. In a less stimulating or competent interview, the child's goal remains saying whatever the child thinks the adult wants to hear.

Acts

Social interaction comprises not only ideas and goals but *acts*. Acts are large-scale (psychologists sometimes call them "molar") and meaningful behaviors like asking penetrating questions or refusing to answer. A penetrating question may be asked in many particular ways; refusing to answer may be accomplished with word or gesture. Acts are not discrete behaviors like saying "What are you thinking?" or shaking one's head from side to side. The acts are what lie beneath those particular behaviors; acts are what they signify.

In the case of the interviewer, we are concerned primarily with acts of questioning and of motivating. How does the adult act so as to achieve or fail to achieve the goals of exploring, uncovering the child's thinking, putting the child at ease, and motivating the child? Does the adult probe, encourage, mislead, dominate, reassure? In the case of the child, we need to learn about acts of cooperating and resisting, introspecting and expressing,[3] thinking carefully and guessing. What are the child's main actions, and how do they change in the course of the interview?

Relationship

The two[4] participants in the clinical interview become more than two individuals. They form a relationship which evolves over the course of the session. The conventional relationship between adult and child is one of "constraint" (Piaget, 1962). The adult has power, dominates the child, and controls (or attempts to control) the interaction. Thus, the teacher tells the child what is to be learned, controls the course of "instruction," and then tests the child to determine whether the process has worked as intended. As Waller (1932), in his remarkable book *The Sociology of Teaching*, put it, "Education, as has been truly said, is the art of imposing on the young" (p. 296).

What kind of relationship do we observe in the clinical interview?

In chapter 2, I pointed out that the clinical interview (or at least the successful clinical interview) is characterized by an "ethical dimension" of "respect." In part this refers to a particular kind of relationship that may be observed in the clinical interview. The interviewer generates trust in the child, and the child takes the risk of revealing the self to the interviewer. It will be interesting to examine the development of this unusual relationship and the conditions that foster it.

STUDYING THE CLINICAL INTERVIEW

To gain insight into goals and acts, ideas and interactions, we need to examine the clinical interview in detail. We begin with what we can observe.

The Observed Interaction

The behavior observed in the clinical interview is rich and plentiful. Seated in close proximity to one another at a table, upon which may be toys, other objects, or pencil and paper, interviewer and child talk to each other. The adult says, "Why are there more here than here?" and the child responds, "Because you spreaded them out." Obviously their "conversation" is crucial for understanding the clinical interview, and if we could record only one aspect of the interaction it would be the words.

But other aspects of the situation are important too. As we saw in chapter 2, Piaget felt that young children's ability to introspect is limited, with the result that their self-reports do not provide useful information about thinking. For this reason, Piaget felt, it is important to observe the child's behavior, particularly as it revolves around concrete tasks. Hence we pay careful attention as the child is writing on a piece of paper, or as the child moves the toys and objects, saying nothing. We also note gestures, facial expressions, expressions of affect, tone of voice, and other paralinguistic cues. There are shrugs and sighs and grimaces.

As we shall see, it is also vital to take into account the behaviors making up the social interaction. The adult is often serious and businesslike, although not harsh and punitive. Sometimes, the child appears uncomfortable or confused; sometimes, involved and excited. On some occasions adult and child look at each other, on others they do not. Most often the adult seems to initiate the interaction, but sometimes the child does.

To investigate the clinical interview, we must record these living events and then use our recording, or reductions of it, to make inferences about behavior. My practice has been to use videotape to record and preserve as much of the interaction as possible. But any interesting human interaction is enormously complex, and even videotape is inadequate to capture all the relevant detail.[5] Our video camera may miss the particular expression of affect that is crucial for understanding the child's intention or the sparkle in the eye that signals the interviewer's meaning. Usually, I also make use of a transcript which attempts to capture as much of the interaction as possible, recording all of the spoken words and describing in an informal way the major actions, expressions of affect, and intonations. But the transcript is clearly an inadequate account. Comparing the transcript with the videotape quickly reveals how impoverished are the mere written words.

Once the interview is recorded, my approach has been to study and restudy the videotape. (I seldom work with the transcript, unless it is to check on the exact wording of a remark.) For the purposes of the initial investigation to be presented below, I have not made use of any formal coding system or measurement devices. Instead, I have attempted an interpretive analysis, drawing on "ordinary-language" concepts describing ideas, goals, acts, and relationships, and drawing heavily on context and history. Of course, even with a videotape, different researchers or practitioners will choose to focus on different phenomena. What one sees in the interview is at least in part a function of one's interests and theoretical orientation.

Interpretation, Context, and History

My approach is to take an "interpretive" stance involving several elements. First, I am interested, not in the behaviors per se, but what they can reveal about the processes underlying the clinical interview. Suppose that after the adult says, "What did you do on that problem?" the child sits in silence. In itself, this behavioral sequence is ambiguous. It may mean that the child is thoroughly confused, that the child knows the answer but is defiant, or that the adult has asked an unanswerable question. The behavior of sitting in silence is of no interest in itself; it is valuable only insofar as it sheds light on the child's confusion, defiance, or the adult's lack of interviewing skill.

Second, simply examining the frequencies of behaviors like these can tell us very little about what is really going on – in the sense of underlying processes. If we observe that the adult does almost all of the talking, we might conclude that the interview process is askew. But we cannot tell why it is out of balance: Perhaps the child does not understand what is being said or is very shy, or perhaps the adult won't let the child talk. If we observe that the child cries during the session, we can surely conclude that she is unhappy. But why? Perhaps she is very insecure, or perhaps the adult has been badgering her. If we observe that the adult often says, "Why?" we may infer that he is asking the child to explain her thinking. But we cannot be sure. "Why?" can also be used to challenge the validity of a response. So it is not very useful merely to observe and then count up the number of "why's" or cries.

Third, to gain insight into the processes underlying speech and behavior it is essential to consider context and history. Consider again the case in which the adult says, "What did you do on that problem?" and the child then responds by sitting in silence. What does the "behavior" of silence mean? In human interaction, *"Nothing never happens"* (Pittenger, Hockett, & Danehy, 1960, p. 234). Even silence can have interesting meanings if we understand the context and history.

Imagine a scenario in which the child first solves several problems and in each case gives a reasonably articulate description of her solution process. Then when given a new type of problem, she does not seem to have a clue, appears to guess, gets the answer wrong, and looks miserable. In this case, her silence seems to indicate lack of knowledge, frustration, unhappiness. But imagine another scenario in which the child easily solves a series of problems and indicates by word and tone that dealing with such tasks is "childish" and indeed beneath her. As the session goes on, she gets more and more indignant and eventually tosses off answers haphazardly and refuses to say how she got them. In this case, the "behavior" of silence has a different meaning. It says nothing about cognitive skill and a good deal about hurt feelings and defiance.

In brief, the behavior exhibited in the clinical interview – the talk, the actions, the gestures, and the displays of emotion – is often quite rich and meaningful. But to understand it, we need to undertake a process of "rich interpretation" (Bloom, 1991) in which we assign meaning to words or actions on the basis of how they fit into the entire context of the session and what we know about the interviewer and child.[6]

In our ordinary conversations, we continually infer meaning and make interpretations in subtle ways. Why should we abandon these skills when we do psychology?

Focusing on an Individual Interview

If interpretation of behavior must involve consideration of context and history, then the researcher must pay careful attention to the individual case. Each child's context and history are unique. Each child's interview responses must be interpreted in the context of that child's personal history and that child's interactions with a particular interviewer.

Consequently, I have chosen to present in this chapter an intensive analysis of a single interview that I conducted with a 6-year-old girl, whom I will call Toby. Of course, study of the individual case raises issues of generalization. The main limitation of an individual case study is evident: It does not allow us to make precise statistical statements about the prevalence of the phenomena in question. In some respects Toby is not typical, and some of the interactions with her will never be repeated with another child (or for that matter with Toby) in exactly the same way. Studying Toby does not allow me to make claims concerning how children in general use introspection in the clinical interview. Similarly, studying an individual patient in psychotherapy does not permit the investigator to make statements concerning the frequency with which, say, White middle-class males use denial at the outset of the process.

Nevertheless, a strong argument can be made concerning the utility of studying the individual case. Examination of the individual allows us to base our theories in rich observations, to identify important issues "from the bottom up." When we do this, we are "ascending to the concrete" (Luria, 1979, p. 178). That is, close attention to and respect for the details of an individual's behavior, in context, over a period of time, can afford us a sound basis for developing abstract propositions concerning basic processes. Also, the rich data obtained from the intensive study of the individual provide opportunities for "replication" – that is, for establishing the consistency of the observations within the single case.[7] Thus, within the case study, a single observation may be treated as a fluke; but repetitions of the behavior lead one to take it more seriously.

Indeed, the intensive study of the individual is a great and powerful tradition in psychology. For example, consider Itard's account of *The Wild Boy of Aveyron* (Itard, 1962); almost all of Freud's work, which was largely based on case studies of individuals in psychoanalysis; Piaget's observations on the everyday behavior of his three infants (Piaget, 1952b); Luria's case study *The Mind of a Mnemonist* (Luria, 1968); Gruber's (1981) historical study of Darwin's creativity; or even almost all of Skinner's work, based on the study of individual pigeons.[8] Of course, in the long run, the proof is in the scholarly pudding. If we learn something interesting and enduring from the single case, we will value research of this type.[9]

Therefore, from this point of view, and in this tradition, Toby's interview can be used to raise many issues that are important for the clinical interview in general and, I think, to give a good sense of what interviewing is all about.

Focusing on a Prototypical Case

Toby's interview is distinctive in another sense too. It is lengthy and exploratory. It ranges over a good deal of material, and it involves me as the interviewer. I could have chosen for analysis a shorter, more focused interview, or I could have chosen to look at the work of a different interviewer.

Why the lengthy and exploratory interview? I wanted a prototypical case, not a watered-down, more or less standardized interview.

Some people might find the latter more palatable than the former, but it is the deliberately nonstandardized clinical interview, the intentionally nonconventional method, that needs to be understood and appreciated. The other is already familiar.

Why me as the interviewer? Two reasons. One is that people tell me I am a pretty good interviewer. To get insight into the possibilities of the clinical interview, would you want to study a poorly done interview? And the other is that I know (more or less) what I was thinking at the time, which helps in the analysis of the data.

TOBY AND ME

I present the account of Toby's interview in several sections, beginning with the context for the interview and then proceeding to a description and interpretation of the interview itself. I have omitted what I think are some nonessential events, but for the most part everything Toby and I said is given in detail.[10] (A transcript of the interview[11] is given as an appendix.) I do not use technical means, like phonetic transcription, to describe Toby's verbalizations. Instead, I indicate stretched-out words thuuuuuuus, stressed words *thus*, inflections thus! and thus?, and actions, rather than words, [thus].

Before the Interview

The interviewer typically engages in considerable preparation before the actual interaction with the child. In both research and clinical work, the interviewer usually begins by devising a set of problems or tasks for the child, developing preliminary questions to ask, gathering together some materials for the child to use, and in general attempting to acquire as much knowledge about the topic under investigation as possible. What is in the interviewer's head is as important as the toys on the table or the questions on the page. Successful interviewing demands judgment and knowledge as much as it requires particular questions or tasks. To interpret the meaning of the child's response, the interviewer, whether researcher or practitioner, must be a theorist – a theorist of the individual, but a theorist nonetheless. In clinical work, but usually not in research, the preparation may also involve learning as much as possible about the individual child in question: background, the nature of the child's performance and difficulties, and the like.[12]

My goal in interviewing Toby was unusual. In this case, I was acting, not as researcher or practitioner, but as a kind of video producer. I was involved in preparing a series of videotapes designed to illustrate for teachers the major phenomena of children's learning of mathematics. My interviews with children like Toby would provide teachers with vivid examples of children doing math and thinking about it. Asked to interpret what was going on in the interview, the teachers would then actively construct their own understandings, their own theories of children's learning. The insights gained in this way would help them to reorganize their teaching. (Things did not really work out as expected, but that was the idea.)[13]

The goal of my interview was therefore not to help Toby with some problem or to investigate some particular aspect of mathematical thinking. It was instead to make an interesting videotape – a tape that would illustrate through Toby's behavior some basic aspects of mathematical thinking. (Don't get scared off by this: Although the specific content was mathematics, the interaction around the clinical interview is of general interest.) Consequently, preparation for the interview involved reviewing the available research on this area of thinking, making up some questions, and assembling the materials (toys, blocks, cubes, chips, paper and pencil, and other common paraphernalia) necessary for posing problems in this area.

As a clinician, I might have obtained information from the school concerning the performance of the children I was scheduled to interview, but in this case I decided not to. I wanted to see the children with a fresh eye; in my experience, educators sometimes misjudge the children, underestimating their abilities. Consequently, I simply asked the school personnel to send me a certain number of children to be interviewed and did not know anything about them except their grade level.

In any event, I was now prepared to conduct the interview. Although one of my goals was exploration, in my head were some ideas about children's mathematical thinking and a list of topics that I thought important to cover. (The clinical interview is seldom –

indeed, it should not be – a nondirective and atheoretical fishing expedition.) And on the table in front of me were various materials with which the child could work.

From the child's point of view, there could have been no preparation. The teacher simply told her that she would leave the room to do something interesting, perhaps to "play some games," with a "doctor" somebody or other.

The Setting

The interview was conducted in a somewhat cluttered resource room, a place where children needing special attention were seen. Toby and I were seated next to each other at a large round table, on which there were some papers with my notes and some materials for Toby to use. Facing us was a video camera and its operator, Takashi Yamamoto. On the side, out of camera range, was my colleague Rochelle Kaplan, who observed the session and occasionally suggested new tasks for me to explore. Announcements occasionally intruded over the loudspeaker system, which everyone in the school was subjected to. A phone rang now and then.

You might think that these are inauspicious conditions for an interview. Actually, in some respects, the conditions were not bad. The room was reasonably quiet and larger and more comfortable than many in which children and I have had to work. Sometimes we get put in the nurse's office and sometimes in something resembling a broom closet. The most difficult part of the conditions were the presence of all the adults and the video camera. We try to make this palatable to the child by first demonstrating how the camera works (if this is not known already) and allowing the child to see himself or herself on the monitor. Children usually enjoy this and it puts them somewhat at ease.

Episode 1: Getting to Know You

Traditional testing often begins with an attempt to establish "rapport," often unsuccessful. I can't say I did much better at the outset of my interview with Toby.

The interview began in a rather bizarre way. Before Toby entered the room, I had written on the board "Children's Math," which was to be the name of our television show. I began with a theatrical introduction including fanfare.

> Herbert Ginsburg (H): Let's start here . . . this is a show and it's on now? Let's have a little music, Toby. Da da da da – Welcome to Children's Math. [I pointed at "Children's Math" written on the board.] And Toby wrote her name on the board. [I then asked the cameraman whether he had got a picture of Toby's name and then directed him to turn the camera back on us.] All right. Very good. Now we come over here and I say, "Hi Toby, how old are you?"
>
> Toby (T): 6.
>
> H: 6 years old. And what grade are you in?
>
> T: First.
>
> H: How do you like that? I already knew that already, didn't I?

Now I said this was bizarre. Why did I do it? This rather strange behavior was an attempt to put the child at ease, to set up a relaxed atmosphere. In effect, I was saying to her, or trying to say to her, "This is a special, unusual event, different from school. You don't have to act here the way you do in school. We can laugh and have some fun." In retrospect, I think that there was something else going on too: I was acting as if onstage, playing to the camera. I knew that I was making a video that might turn out well or poorly and that it might be seen by others; perhaps this induced some anxiety that I coped with by being a somewhat hyperactive performer.

What did Toby think of all this? Imagine the expectations with which she arrived at the interview. She must have thought that we would be doing something related to schoolwork and that as an adult I would act in a serious and task-oriented way. Perhaps then, the first seconds of introduction only served to violate her expectancies about what might and should happen in interaction with an adult in a school setting. Toby seemed bewildered, not knowing what to make of me.

I continued to put my foot in my mouth:

H: OK, and what we're going to do today is to do some fun math things. OK? And we'll start off real easy by asking you to count, as high as you can. Let's hear you count.

There were two problems with this particular interaction. First, my attempt at making the task seem enjoyable was heavy-handed. For many children the idea of "fun math things" is an oxymoron. And you can't *tell* children that something is going to be fun; you have to show them. Second, it was not a good idea to say that we would "start off real easy." Although I had intended to relax Toby, my statement might have had the opposite effect because it implied that things might get harder or otherwise more unpleasant later on. And what if she had experienced difficulty with the counting task? She would have felt very badly and would probably have been terrified of what was to come next.

Note too several other aspects of the interaction. One is an event that did *not* occur. I did not explain to Toby anything about the purpose of the interview. Usually I say something like "I am interested in finding out how kids think about math so that we can learn how to teach them better. So we will do some math together, and we will talk about how you do it." Probably this does not mean a great deal to many children at the outset of the interview. But the statement communicates to them a certain respect. It gives the message that I will not simply tell them what to do. I am at least trying to help them understand our purpose, even if it is initially unclear. But with Toby, I simply forgot to do this. Second, up to this point, Toby has said only 2 words, "Six" and "First" (both extremely important for an interview on mathematics), whereas I said approximately 111. This ratio of adult to child talk does not bode well for a situation in which the child is encouraged to reveal *her* thinking.

We see then that literally in less than a minute, the attempt at "rapport" reveals itself to have several features. The subtext of the interviewer's speech (rantings and ravings) seems to say: "We will do something here that is special and different from what you usually do in school. I am cool, a pretty good performer, so this television gig will turn out OK. We can have a good time and you should relax." The child's overt response is very limited (mostly because she hasn't had much of a chance to say anything) but her underlying reaction is probably "What in the world is this person doing?"

Episode 2: Norms

The previous episode ended with my asking Toby "to count, as high as you can. Let's hear you count." Why did I ask her to do this? Because I wanted her to begin with an easy task on which she could in fact do well. Instead of just telling her to relax, I now wanted to give her an opportunity to experience some success over a protracted period of time. I chose counting as a way to accomplish this because I expected that a first-grade child would enjoy the task and would be likely to demonstrate some competence at it. (Also, she could do something and not just sit there listening to me!) My expectancy was based on experience in working with many children and on knowledge of the literature on counting.

To accomplish motivational goals like having the child feel competent (and other goals too) the interviewer must operate with internal norms. The "qualitative" method of interviewing depends in part on intuitive "statistics" concerning children's performance and abilities. The interviewer knows or expects that a first grader is likely to find counting easy but probably wouldn't have a clue about how to do written division. Although not as explicit as the statistical norms of standard tests, the intuitive norms of the interviewer have an important role to play in guiding the choice of problems and in evaluating the child's response.

Episode 3: Monitoring Motivation and Flexibility

Asked to count, Toby shrugged her shoulders as if to indicate that she found the task a cinch.

> T: 1, 2, 3, 4, 5, 6, . . . , 44. [She counts correctly and deliberately, with little expression, until she reaches about 12, when she shows a slight smile. She continues without error until 44, whereupon I interrupt her.]
> H: OK, why don't you start now with 87. Just keep going from 87.

I interrupted Toby when she reached the 40s and introduced a new task, mostly because I did not want her to get bored (and I also didn't want her to bore me). I knew from my internal norms that if a first grader gets up to the 40s in counting, she is likely to continue with ease at least up into the 80s. But if she had to count for so long, the process might prove tedious. So by changing the task, I would stand to lose little information about her counting abilities and at the same time would decrease the chances of spoiling her motivation.

This episode illustrates two key aspects of the clinical interview. First, the interviewer enjoys the freedom to change the task, on the spot. This flexibility must be employed for good reasons, but it is there to be employed. In the example, my internal norms and knowledge of the normal development of counting provided these good reasons for interrupting Toby's counting and changing the task. Second, the interviewer constantly monitors the child's emotional state. The primary goal of the clinical interview is to understand the child's cognitive functioning, but the means must include "clinical" sensitivity to the child's affect. The interviewer must be a careful observer of affect as well as of other events.

Episode 4: Neutrality and the Rules of Discourse

I asked Toby to continue in the 80s because I knew from previous experience and research that she might experience some difficulty with those numbers. My suspicions were immediately confirmed.

T: 87, 88, eighty-niiiiiine – [Long pause.] a hundred?
H: OK, keep going.

On reaching 89, Toby clearly knew she was in trouble. She dragged out "89" – "eighty niiiiiine" – as if she were buying time to figure out what came next and needed help. In saying "A hundred?" she raised her voice as if asking a question. But I reacted in a neutral, nondirective way ("OK, keep going"). She continued:

T: A hundred and one, a hundred and two, a hundred and three, hundred and four, hundred and five, hundred and six, hundred and seven, hundred and eight, hundred and nine?

H: Yeah, keep going.

Again in saying "hundred and nine?" she raised her voice as if asking a question. She did not seem to know what came next. And again I reacted to her difficulty in a neutral way – the nondirective technique used frequently in the clinical interview. I did not confirm her suspicion that she was in trouble. I deflected the conversation away from an evaluation of specific answers. The implicit message was "Don't be so concerned with right and wrong answers. I am not going to correct you all the time. This is not school. Just do your best."

In a way, the interviewer's neutrality has the function of beginning to teach the child the rules to a new mode of discourse between adult and child, a new "game" that the two are playing. In the typical discourse of the traditional school, the teacher asks the child questions to find out whether the child has learned something the teacher thinks the child ought to know. The child can indicate successful learning by producing the answer that the teacher has defined as "correct" and would like to hear. Now, at the beginning of the clinical interview, the child is being introduced to a new framework for discourse. At this point, the new rules of the game are not yet clear. From the child's point of view, they must seem to have something to do with an absence of evaluation, or perhaps a different kind of evaluation. But what is expected? And why is the interviewer acting this way? These matters are probably not yet clear to the child.

Episode 5: "Failure" and Reassurance

At this point, Toby had reached her counting limit and knew it.

T: That's all. [With a shrug and a bit of a nervous laugh and smile.]
H: That's all. Oh, wow, you counted real high. OK? [She seemed to frown and does not look too happy.]

Not only did Toby know that she had reached the end of the line (her whole-number line), but she indicated by her shrug and nervous laugh that this made her uncomfortable. After all, in the world of the classroom, the child is usually asked to do things that should be done accurately. The teacher does not ask interesting questions to which there might be no good answer, which is to say, an answer of which the teacher is unaware. Rather, the teacher asks questions to which the answer is already known (and defined as correct by the teacher).[14] In this type of discourse, if you do not know the answer to something, or cannot complete a task, the problem cannot be that the task is so interesting or complex that the answer is difficult to know or produce. Rather, the fault must be in yourself: You should have known the answer or the teacher would not have asked you for it in the first place. The traditional rules of classroom discourse can lead a child to see failure where there is none.

If this is so, then Toby might have interpreted her inability to count beyond 109 as failure. She did not yet know the rules of my game, which is that I was permitted to give her difficult and challenging problems and was more interested in her ways of attempting to solve them than in the correctness of the answers. She also did not know that, according to the norms, her counting level was at least as good as that of other first graders.

My immediate reaction to her discomfort was to reassure her, to let her know that she was not a failure. At this point, the goal was not to get her to produce more, so I did not use the neutral "keep going." Instead, I used a form of praise: "Oh, wow, you counted real high."

The clinical interview contains many attempts at comfort like this – one might say acts of kindness. At the same time, there is a tension between the desire to reassure and the need to avoid focusing on the correctness of response. On the one hand, the interviewer wants the child to know that he or she is doing well, if only because of effort; on the other hand, the interviewer does not want the child to focus on the correctness of each response and to feel inhibited in making errors. The tension arises because one way to comfort is to tell the child that the answer was correct.

The statement "Oh, wow, you counted real high" was delicately perched between reassurance and information about correctness. The tone was clearly approving and comforting, but the message was perhaps ambiguous. What I wanted to say was that Toby did not fail even though her every answer may not have been correct. She was a success in that she counted as far as she did, even with some errors.

And strictly speaking, "you counted real high" might be interpreted as saying exactly that. But the statement could have been interpreted as "you counted *accurately* real high." I was walking a fine line between the desired reassurance and giving the child more information than intended concerning the correctness of response.

In any event, as a "clinician" I saw that Toby was made uncomfortable by her perceived failure, and I tried to comfort her as best I could.

Episode 6: Hypothesis Testing

At the same time, as a "cognitive theorist" I developed a hypothesis about Toby's counting. Recall that she first encountered difficulty when she was asked to count in the 80s: "87, 88, eighty niiiiiine." I knew that "decade transitions" – that is, going from 59 to the new decade, 60, or from 89 to 90 – are especially difficult for children. They learn quickly that once one has entered a new decade – whether 30 or 80 – the correct procedure is to add on the 1, 2, 3, . . . that are already well known. The problem is to say the new decade. Once you figure out what comes after 89, you can easily go further. But what comes after 89?

Faced with this dilemma, children usually make a sensible guess – a guess based on a sensible rule. After "thirty-nine" comes "thirty-ten." And what could more naturally follow "eighty-nine" than "eighty-ten?"

Believing that Toby would be likely to make "errors" of this sort, I set out to test the hypothesis.

> H: What if I tell you some numbers now and you tell me what comes
>   next. OK, like if I said, 1, 2, . . . , you would say . . .
> T: 3.

Note that I used the technique of beginning with a very simple example that the child is likely to find easy and in fact let the child solve it.

> H: OK. 57, 58, . . .
> T: [Jumps in quickly.] 59.

H: OK . . . ah . . . 68, 69, . . .

T: [Hesitates a little.] 70.

H: Aaaahhh . . . 84, 85, . . .

T: 86.

H: . . . 87, 88, . . .

T: 89.

H: 89, . . .

T: Eighty-tennnn . . .

H: Uh-huh [Encouraging.] . . . eighty-ten . . . what's next?

T: [Looks up as she thinks and then shakes her head to indicate that she does not know the answer.]

H: OK . . . 98, 99, . . .

T: [Looks up and thinks for a little bit.] A hundred.

H: Very good. A hundred and eighteen, a hundred and nineteen, . . .

T: [Quietly.] A hundred and twenty.

H: A hundred and eighty-eight, hundred eighty-nine, . . . T: [She hesitates and then shrugs her shoulders; she smiles a bit. She starts to play with the sleeve of her shirt.]

H: OK . . . those are really big numbers, I mean that's very very high.

Several aspects of the interaction are worth noting. One is that I used experimental procedures to examine the hypothesis concerning decade transitions. That is, I manipulated the variable of "decade transition," giving Toby some problems in which the decade transition was critical (e.g., 68, 69, . . .) and some in which the decade transition was not critical (e.g., 57, 58, . . .). This was a true experiment (of a limited sort): Toby was both the "experimental group" (of one) and the "control group" (also of one). Note that I messed up the experiment a bit by giving her "87, 88, . . . " rather than "88, 89, . . .," which I had intended to do. But I quickly adjusted by simply repeating her "89," which did not seem to disrupt the flow.[15]

Two minor motivational points: I again did not criticize Toby for her "incorrect" answer, and in fact repeated "eighty-ten" as if it were correct and asked for the next response. Also, at the end, I tried again to comfort her by using the same kind of remark made earlier: "Those are really big numbers, I mean that's very very high."

Episode 7: Exploration and Pressure

Now that I had established that Toby could count reasonably well, I decided to increase the level of difficulty with some related tasks. I thought that I would explore what she could do with simple series of numbers.

H: Can you count by twos? 2, 4 [She nods.], 6, . . . , keep going.
T: [As if reciting a song.] 2, 4, 6, 8, 10, 12 [Hesitates at 12, long pause.].

It seemed as if Toby did not know what came next. I put her on the spot by saying nothing and letting her sit in silence. Her arm disappeared into her sleeve and there was a long pause.

H: What do you think comes after 12? 10, 12, . . .

Again I paused and let her sit in silence. She could only shrug.

H: 15?

I gave her this wrong answer to see if she would grasp at any straw. She nodded slowly, as if to indicate tentative agreement; but she was clearly not sure of herself. At this point it would have been easy and reasonable to conclude that she did not know anything about sequences of 2.

An observer might conclude that I had made a mistake by placing Toby under considerable pressure. On several occasions, I let her stew in a failure that she clearly recognized and found uncomfortable. I did this to discover whether she could persist in dealing with a difficult problem and come up with a strategy for overcoming the failure. The danger in my approach, of course, was that I might discourage and demoralize her. Was I going too far? Using my "clinical" judgment, I didn't think so.

Episode 8: The Rules of the Game and Competence

In the educational system, children are not often enough encouraged to think. In far too many schools, children learn that mathematics, and other subjects too, do not make a great deal of sense, and that getting the "right answer" involves memory or the use of some arbitrary procedure. For example, a good deal of the elementary mathematics curriculum is often devoted to the memorization of number facts. The child learns to respond quickly, correctly, and without thinking to number fact problems ("How much is 8 + 9?") presented on flash cards or the computer equivalent thereof (as 8 + 9 flashes on the screen, the child must type in the correct answer to prevent a rocket from blowing up something or other). Indeed, I believe it is no exaggeration to say that children may learn from repeated experiences like these the following lesson: Mathematics is that subject in which one is expected to obtain the correct answer quickly and without thought (which can be considered cheating).

Suppose that this is so (and there is some evidence to support the idea).[16] Suppose that children are often discouraged by teachers from thinking about school mathematics and other subjects. As Waller (1932) put it: "it seems likely that the intelligence which the schools reward most highly is not of the highest type, that it is a matter of incomplete but docile assimilation and glib repetition rather than of fertile and rebellious creation" (p. 24). One result may then be that in dealing with clinical interview problems children either do not try to think (because original thinking is discouraged) or are reluctant to express their ways of thinking (because they could be "wrong"). Putting it another way, as a result of the kind of discourse learned in school, children may end up looking a lot less smart than they really are.

This has enormous implications for the clinical interview. It means that the interviewer has to get the child in touch with his or her "natural intelligence" and to realize that it is acceptable *not* to play the school nonthinking game. As Binet and Simon (1916) put it: "the surest and most direct means for judging the intelligence of a child is to put questions to him, to make him talk. . . . one questions him in such a way as to solicit a personal reply, a reply which does not come from the book. . . . Freed from the constraint of the class, certain minds open, and thus one makes unexpected discoveries. . . . it is the spontaneous reflections of the child which indicate his intelligence" (p. 308).[17]

This point of view influenced my interview with Toby. I interpreted her initial success ("2, 4, 6, 8, 10, 12") as rote memory, and her subsequent failure as indicating that she had never been expected to understand the logic of the series. Further, I expected that she might be able to solve the problem if she were encouraged to think about it. You might say that in the spirit of Vygotsky, I was trying to understand her potential developmental level. I therefore introduced a new rule of the game: If you don't know the answer, try to figure it out.

> H: Maybe. How could you figure it out? Suppose you do 10, 12, . . . How could you find out what comes next?
> T: [She shrugs.]
> H: You know like what comes . . . well after 12 is what? Is . . .
> T: 13. [Quietly, but with confidence.]
> H: 13 . . . after 13 is . . .
> T: 14.
> H: OK . . . now how, if you're counting by twos, and you're at 12 . . .
> T: 15 . . .
> H: Yeah . . .
> T: . . . 18 . . .
> H: Uh-huh . . .
> T: . . . 21 [Nods and smiles as she says this.] . . . 24 . . . 26 . . .
> H: Uh-huh . . .
> T: . . . 28 . . . 31 . . . 34 . . . [She nods as she says each number.]

Now this was quite a surprise. Given the encouragement to "figure it out," Toby seemed to enter easily into the new form of discourse. And in doing so, she demonstrated a surprising degree of competence – more than she might have otherwise exhibited. Her "mistakes" (12, 15, 18, 21, 24) showed that she was capable of thinking; it is not easy for a first grader to produce a series increasing by threes. Indeed, her mistakes were more interesting and creative than her initial success, which was limited to the mere parroting of what was probably meaningless material (2, 4, 6, . . . , 12).

As time went on, Toby mastered the lesson that her job was to "figure things out," and indeed, she took great pleasure in doing so.

For example, much later (in the seventh minute) I asked her to solve a certain addition problem and she got the correct answer.

H: How did you know that?
T: I counted before you asked. [Very proud of herself.] I knew you were going to ask me that!

In other words, Toby had used a sensible strategy – counting – even before I asked her how she solved the problem. She knew that the interview was about thinking and that I would ask her about it. Indeed, she seemed to figure this out rather quickly and to enter into the spirit of it with great gusto. Of course, we may ask about the extent to which this is generally true. How easy is it to get children to understand the new form of discourse underlying the clinical interview?

Another interesting question is whether the very focus of the interview changes the child's normal cognitive orientation. Does the clinical interview bias the child toward thinking? Does the new mode of discourse *produce* new forms of mental activity on the part of the child?

The answer seems to be that at least on some occasions, the clinical interview changes the phenomenon it intends to study and in this respect partakes more of the spirit of Vygotsky than of Piaget, who wished to examine the child's "natural mental inclination." We might say that interviewer and child take an excursion through the Zone of Proximal Development. As Cole (1991) puts it: "Clearly, aspects of cognitive performance that once were attributed to psychological processes within individual children emerge as joint accomplishments between people, that is, as socially shared" (p. 405).

Episode 9: Introspection and Expression

In the previous episode, it was clear that Toby was thinking. But what was she up to? At first, her series involved threes, but then she seemed to shift to twos (24, 26, 28) before returning to threes (28, 31, 34). The flexibility of the clinical interview had allowed me to discover something, but I wasn't sure what it meant.

Consequently, I attempted to focus Toby's attention on how she "figured it out." I wanted her to introspect about her method and to report it to me. Research suggests that this is a very difficult task for young children.[18]

> H: OK, now say you're at 31, and you say the next one is 34, how did you know that 34 comes next?
> T: 'Cause I was counting by [Holds up two fingers.] um . . . this . . . I was skipping two of them.

At this point, Toby was visibly excited. I interpreted this as indicating that she had succeeded in finding a sensible method for solving a problem, was happy that it worked (at least she thought it did), and was thrilled both that I was interested in her thinking and that she was competent at solving problems. Indeed, I think that this was the turning point of the interview. Now she knew what I meant about figuring out a problem in a sensible way that she had created (as opposed to using a method that was imposed by the teacher and that seemed to make no sense). And she enjoyed solving problems in this way.

But I wanted her to be more explicit about her method of solution. After several nonessential things transpired,[19] I encouraged her again to express her thought.

> H: Tell me out loud how you do it. So, suppose you had, what was it, 31? [She nods.] How would you do it? Tell me out loud how you would think to yourself.
> T: [Jumps in quickly; looks straight ahead into space.] I was like, thinking like . . .
> H: Yeah, like how?
> T: . . . 31, 32, 33, . . . [Turns to look at me.] I was like talking to myself.
> H: Ah-hah . . . so what did you say to yourself when you were talking to yourself?

A very good question, if I must say so myself.

T: I was saying . . . I was like skipping two, and then saying the next one, and then skipping two and saying the next one. [She gestures with her hands as she explains.]

H: Ooooo-K, so if you're at 31 you'd go . . .

T: 34 . . . [Nods.]

H: 'Cause you skipped . . . 32 and 33. [She nods slowly.]

At this point, she had said everything she was going to say about her problem-solving method. I made a mistake, however, and for a while kept pressing her to say more. I will spare you the details (although you can find them in the transcript, given as an appendix). In retrospect I can't imagine what else she could have said. In any event, she was so happy about what she was doing that the badgering did not upset her. Finally, I summed up.

H: Ohhh . . . OK, OK . . . so you're using two numbers in the middle there, right? [She nods.] OK, very good.

Note that Toby was eventually able to express her method of solution. At first, she had trouble with the language of my request, "Tell me out loud how you would think to yourself." The words "think to yourself" seemed to present difficulties. Eventually she interpreted them as "I was like talking to myself" and got the idea that she was supposed to tell me what she said when she was talking to herself.

The clinical interview seems to involve giving the child practice in introspection, in understanding the language of cognition, and in expressing thought. At least one first grader was capable of profiting from these lessons fairly quickly (roughly at the 6-minute point of the interview).

At the same time, the child does not master the tasks of introspection and expression in one trial. Indeed, Toby struggled with these activities throughout the interview. Later (during the eighth minute), she solved 5 + 3, and I asked her how she did it.

H: OK, do it out loud, how do you, you know when you count these things, how do you . . .

T: I wasn't counting. I was figuring it out.

H: Figuring it! How do you figure it?

T: Like, you're thinking . . .

H: Yeah . . .

T: All different things . . . but . . . um . . . you think, um, that . . . you think it.

H: Uh-huh . . .

T: . . . what's going to come next.

H: OK, how . . . can you think that out loud for me? If somebody didn't know how to do it and you were trying to tell them . . .

T: I was like trying to help them.

H: Uh-huh, how would you help them?

T: I would like help them and try to explain it.

H: Could you explain it for me then?

T: What?

H: 5 + 3?

T: There's 5 . . .

H: Right . . .

T: . . . and 3 . . .

H: Right . . .

T: So that altogether makes 8. [Again, she gestures with her hands to the animals on the table.]

H: OK, but how do you figure out that it makes 8? How do you figure out that it makes 8?

T: 'Cause, um, when you think, you're like thinking about it . . .

H: But what do you think?

T: I think what's going to come next.

Later on (during the 11th minute), she was given a problem involving imaginary carrots. She said that as she was solving the problem, she had "3 in my head."

H: OK. When you have them in your head, do you have a picture of the fingers in your head, or do you have a picture of the carrots, or what do you have in your head?

T: It's like it's blank but I'm thinking about it . . . I'm thinking about it.

H: Uh-huh . . . when you're thinking, are you sort of saying the numbers to yourself . . . is that what you do?

This was probably a leading question. I should have asked her what she was thinking about it. Moral: interviewers make mistakes.

T: Uh-huh . . .
H: . . . by sort of saying the numbers to yourself . . . it's not so much pictures you have there . . .
T: No.
H: . . . but . . . yeah . . . you're saying the numbers . . .
T: But I think a lot of different things . . .

At this late point in the sequence, I finally described the purpose of the interview.

H: Right . . . right . . . OK . . . You see, what I like to do is try to find out how kids think about these things, so if you could tell me as much as you can about how you think, that would be good, OK? Let's do some new ones and you can tell me how you think about those, OK?

You might argue that I waited too long to do this, that I should have discussed the purpose at the outset. On the other hand, now she had the experience to understand what I meant by asking her to "tell me as much as you can about how you think." So maybe it was sensible to wait.

Episode 10: Construction and Competence

I also wanted to investigate Toby's understanding of informal addition, a basic mathematical concept.

H: Now, we're going to do something a little different, OK? [She nods.] We have two friends here that you looked at before . . . [I put two small animal figures on the table.]
T: Ohhh, they're so cute. [She was very excited about working with the animals.]

H: [After some irrelevant conversation.] OK what is this? [Points to one of the animals.]

T: Rabbit.

H: Uh-huh, rabbit and . . .

T: A squirrel.

H: A squirrel. OK. Now rabbit had 5 carrots. We're going to make-believe rabbit has 5 carrots and squirrel has 3 carrots. OK? [She giggles.] What's so funny? A squirrel likes carrots?

T: Nuts. [Giggles.]

H: Yeah well, this squirrel likes carrots. OK? All right . . . so rabbit has how many carrots? [Pause.] 5, remember he had 5, and squirrel has . . .

T: 2.

H: 3, OK . . . so rabbit has 5 carrots, squirrel has 3 carrots. How many do they have altogether?

Note that I took care to remind Toby of the basic facts of the problem I presented.

T: 7.

H: 7! How did you know that?

T: I counted before you asked. [Very proud of herself.] I knew you were going to ask me that!

H: You knew that! Ohhh . . . how did you count?

T: I counted like, there were 7 . . .

H: No, 5 and 3; tell me how you do it.

Again Toby got the terms of the problem wrong. She now wanted to transform it into 7 and 3.

T: 5 and 3. I counted 7, I counted 3. [Uses hands to gesture toward each animal; looks at me.]

H: 5 and 3 . . . can you do that out loud for me, how you get 7?

Note that I had given her another reminder.

T: I thought, like, 7, I was thinking, 7 + 3 and I got 10.

H: You got 10! 7 + . . . How do you get ten if you do 7 + 3? I mean do
   it out loud for me; count out loud for me.

T: I had 7 . . .

H: Uh-huh, and then what do you do?

T: I have 3, so that makes 10. [She gestures that she counts on her
   fingers.]

H: Oh, you do it on your fingers? [She nods.] OK. Can you do 5 + 3
   for me now?

T: 8.

At the outset, Toby did not want to deal with *my* problem, 5 + 3. I
do not know why, but she insisted in transforming my problem into
something else. I resisted this. I insisted that she do 5 + 3. But she
resisted too. Eventually, by sheer persistence, she transformed the
problem into what she had in mind, namely 7 + 3, and got the right
answer. Then, having done what she wanted to do, she allowed herself to consider *my* problem, 5 + 3, and easily solved it! If I had
judged her ability by her initial performance on my problem, I would
have concluded that she was not very competent.

It is a general rule of constructivism that children often do not deal
with the interviewer's (or teacher's) problem. Instead, they construct
and attempt to solve their own version of the problem. Moreover,
they often believe that what they have in mind is what the adult had
in mind.

If this is the case, then the interviewer must attempt to understand
the child's formulation of the problem and adjust the questions ac-
cordingly. In a sense, interviewer and child have to negotiate the
content of the interview.[20]

Episode 11: Thinking and Accuracy

I gave Toby a simple mental-addition problem.

H: How much is 3 + 4?

T: 6.

H: Uh-huh, how did you know that?

T: I was like thinking and counting . . .

H: Thinking and counting at the same time? Can you do that out
   loud for me, how you do 3 + 4?

T: I had 3 in my head . . .

H: Uh-huh . . .

T: . . . and I had 4 in my head . . .

H: Uh-huh . . .

T: . . . so I had 3 + 4 . . . [She again uses her fingers to count.] 3, 4, 5,
   6, 7 . . . 7.

Note that Toby initially made an error but, when asked to describe
the method of solution, managed to get the right answer. This sort of
thing happens frequently in the course of the clinical interview. Some
initial errors seem to result from sloppiness. The child tries to retrieve
a number fact too quickly or calculates an answer carelessly. But
explaining a strategy to another person forces the child to slow down
and to consider carefully what he or she is doing. And when this
happens, the child easily corrects trivial mistakes.

In brief, my hypothesis is that engaging in the introspection and
expression required by the clinical interview promotes care and accuracy in thinking.

Episode 12: Exploration and Openness

After a while, Toby volunteered that in class the students work
with a "robot book."

T: [W]e have this robot book, and that's how you do it, you see, you
   have all different math . . . it has a robot and, um, there's math on
   it.

I thought I would explore what the robot book was all about. Was it
the teacher's method for introducing drill and practice?

H: Can you show us what's in your robot book?

T: We like have high numbers up to 10 – that's all we can go up to,
   like . . .

H: Show me . . .

T: 5 + 4 . . . [She wrote the 4 under the 5.]

H: Um-hm . . .

T: . . . equals 9, but they don't have the line . . . no line. [She is referring to the line that would conventionally be written under the 5 and 4.]

H: No line?

T: No, and they don't write this [meaning the answer]; you have to solve it.

H: You have to solve it . . . ?

T: Yeah, like, ummm, I'll write one . . . that you have to solve! [Excited by her idea.]

H: All right, I'll try.

T: This one's easy for you.

H: I don't know . . . I'll try . . . 5 + 5 . . . you want me to do it?

After describing some details of the robot book, Toby revealed how comfortable – even intimate – her relationship with the interviewer had become. She was bold enough to propose exchanging roles with the interviewer, a prospect that she clearly found very exciting. Now Toby was to be in charge, setting the agenda, asking the questions. "I'll write one . . . that you have to solve!"

To an adult this may seem like a small and insignificant bit of banter. But usually it takes some daring and imagination for a 6-year-old child to propose a basic alteration in roles – that is to say, in power relations – with respect to an adult. Toby, however, clearly felt quite at ease with me and knew that I would not be affronted or threatened by her proposal. In the space of 17 minutes, she had progressed from bewilderment and reserve to understanding the rules of discourse and achieving a significant degree of comfort with the interviewer.

But more than comfort with me was involved. First, Toby could not have proposed the role reversal unless she had some idea of what "playing interviewer" was all about. She had learned not only her role in the game but something of the interviewer's too.[21] Second, I think she was able to assume the interviewer's role because she had learned that it was not harsh, domineering, or threatening. For Toby, interviewing was fun. She did not have to step too far out of character to act as an interviewer.

So not only had Toby and I achieved a degree of comfort; she had gained some understanding of interviewing and found it a comfortable and indeed enjoyable activity. As we shall see next, Toby saw school activities in a very different light.

For a while, I tried to discover what was involved in the robot book. Although the details are of little interest, Toby's general views of schooling are worth noting.

> H: I don't understand what the robot is.
> T: OK, it's like a book . . .
> H: Yeah.
> T: . . . and it has math in it to help you with it. [She showed how she solved a robot book problem.] . . . See that's how you do it . . . and if you get a mistake, she writes this [a sad face], and if you correct it, she does that [happy face].

I then asked her why the problem was written in a certain way.

> T: They do it different ways. They do it any way they want.

I then suggested that the problem might be written in that form for a certain sensible reason.

> T: It . . . no, they try to make it, um, tricky.
> H: Tricky . . . they try to trick you? [She nods.] How do you like that? [She smiles.] Why do they try to trick you?
> T: Because they want to make sure you know your math very well.

From experience in the classroom, Toby has acquired a view of mathematics education – *her* mathematics education – that might be paraphrased as follows. To help the child learn mathematics or to assess knowledge of mathematics ("they want to make sure you know your math very well"), the teacher (or the textbook) presents problems which are both arbitrary ("they do it any way they want") and deceptive ("they try to make it, um, tricky"). From the child's point of view, the teacher's role is to create obstacles, to present meaningless tasks, to trick, and then to reward the child's success with praise or punish failure with disapproval.[22]

Now of course it is shocking that the child should come to believe that this is what the learning of mathematics (or anything else) is all about. It is even more shocking that a teacher (and I don't believe she is unique) would act in ways that would lead Toby to believe this. What is interesting from the point of view of the clinical interview is that Toby would reveal this to me. At this point in the interview, her openness was striking. We had achieved a rapport so strong that she could share her perception of teaching and textbooks as deceptive and learning as meaningless. The education game as Toby saw it was certainly different from the interview game!

Her openness extended to what might be considered personal ignorance, failure, or inadequacy. A short while later, we were discussing how she might solve a problem like 20 + 100.

> T: . . . [T]wenty . . . plus . . . a hundred . . . [She writes "a hundred" as "00."] There's something like that and you have to figure it out . . . a hundred and twenty . . . so a hundred and twenty, so plus and you have to write the answers down here . . . I don't know . . .
> H: You don't know how to do it?
> T: I don't know how to do it.
> H: Let me give you a couple like that, OK? Suppose that . . .
> T: 'Cause I don't know the high numbers all that much.

Toby had learned that in the clinical interview she could freely reveal her thinking, including her ignorance. Such a strategy would not make a great deal of sense in a classroom in which the teacher's goal was to trick her.

Episode 13: Toby's Farewell

After about 37 minutes, the interview was at an end.

> H: It was hard work, but you did very well. Did you enjoy it?
> T: [Nods briefly and looks me straight in the eye.] Who are you?
> H: Who am I? [Everyone laughs, and so does Toby.] At what level do you mean that, Toby?

T: Why do you want to know about different things that children know?

H: I see. You know why we study children? We try to find out how they learn math so that we can help them learn math if they have trouble.

Toby nodded and the interview was really over. The boldness of her question confirmed that we had accomplished something important.

MAJOR FEATURES OF THE CLINICAL INTERVIEW

Several major themes emerge from the interview with Toby. We will consider first the interviewer, who combines the roles of researcher and clinician.

The Interviewer as Researcher

As researcher, the interviewer engages in four major activities, each of which demands the continual construction of theory.

EXPLORATION

In the spirit of Piaget, the interviewer is always alert to the possibility that the child may employ distinctive modes of thinking, and that her construction of reality may take an idiosyncratic turn. Given this general constructivist assumption, the interviewer must be open to exploration. Open-ended questioning may reveal that the child holds unexpected concepts about the nature of the world (as when Toby believed that the teachers "do it any way they want" and make it "tricky"). If the child answers in a way that makes no sense from the adult's point of view, the interviewer must attempt to discover the logic behind the child's response. Perhaps the child's answer does make sense, but with a *different question*, a question which the child thought the adult was asking (as when Toby persisted in answering the question 7 + 3 when I wanted her to solve 5 + 3). If the child's answer is wrong, perhaps it is the result of an "incorrect" but still interesting pattern of thought (as when Toby created a series increasing by 3 rather than 2). Similarly, the child may use words in a distinctive but essentially correct manner – for example, *mostest* may mean "equal large amounts," as in "they both have the mostest." The interviewer cannot discover things like this if he or she employs only a predetermined set of questions. The interviewer requires the intellectual and methodological flexibility to follow the child's thought wherever it leads. Sometimes the interviewer needs to ask open-ended questions; sometimes the interviewer can explore simply (or not so simply) by observing with great care. In both cases, the interviewer is an interpreter of hidden meanings and the goal is entering a possibly distinctive mind.

Unfortunately, much of our research and practice seems to lack the spirit of exploration. Researchers' worlds are too often impoverished, limited to the "variables" and measures of conventional research; and practitioners are wedded to the standard categories of diagnosis.

HYPOTHESIS TESTING

Exploration is balanced by hypothesis testing. The interviewer continually considers hypotheses about why the child does what she does. Some hypotheses derive from previous research, as when I attempted to discover whether Toby would experience difficulty at the "decade transitions" (e.g., going from 79 to 80), a phenomenon studied by several researchers (see, e.g., Fuson, 1988). Other hypotheses may be suggested in the course of the interview (as when I conjectured that in the 2, 4, 6, 8 problem Toby was sometimes counting by twos and sometimes by threes).

The interviewer then attempts to test the hypotheses by whatever means possible. On some occasions observation of the child's behavior suffices. The child may spontaneously reveal her strategy (as Toby did when she proudly announced, "I counted before you asked. I knew you were going to ask me that!"). On other occasions, the interviewer conducts miniature "experiments" within the clinical interview. Even though involving only one subject, these are true experiments: They investigate the effects of different levels of an independent variable, under the experimenter's control, on the child's response (as when I compared Toby's response to nondecade transition terms like 57, 58, ? with her response to decade transitions, like 68, 69, ?). We do not usually think of the clinical interview as an experimental method, but it often is.

ESTABLISHING COMPETENCE

Another major activity of the interviewer is establishing the child's competence. The interviewer continually attempts to determine whether the child's response expresses the limits of his or her competence, whether it is "the best he or she can do." Thus when Toby did not seem able to extend the series 2, 4, 6, . . . beyond 12, or when she did not seem able to solve 5 + 3, I did not accept her initial failure as a clear indication of a lack of competence. In one way or another, I continued to probe, changing the terms of the problem, rewording the question. And in both cases, my efforts succeeded in revealing some degree of competence. She could extend the series and she could add the numbers. It is of course important to explain why so much effort on my part was needed to establish the competence, but the fact remains that at the end of the process Toby exhibited some skill and knowledge. Without the efforts at establishing competence, the child would have appeared to be rather dull. And indeed she too would have got that impression about herself.

A good deal of research that claims to demonstrate children's incompetence can be interpreted as merely proving the experimenter's failure to employ methods sufficiently sensitive to elicit the child's competence.

THEORIZING

The interviewer is always thinking, theorizing. He or she has in mind expectations about what children of a given age are capable of doing (Toby should be able to count beyond 10 but will have difficulty at decade transitions), ideas about how children go about solving problems (first graders usually add by some form of mental counting), and concepts suggested by various theories (children construct their knowledge). To explore, the interviewer must be guided by ideas which allow him or her to make sense of what is observed. As Piaget noted, beginning observers "are not on the look-out for anything, in which case, to be sure, they will never find anything"

(Piaget, 1976a, p. 9). To test hypotheses, the interviewer must not only create them in the first place but devise appropriate experiments for testing them on the spot. To establish competence, the interviewer must develop conjectures about factors that might interfere with the child's expression of competence and again on the spot must develop new methods of questioning and testing designed to overcome the difficulties.

Doing a good clinical interview is very difficult. It is much harder than conducting predetermined experiments or giving a standard test. The interviewer is constantly engaged in creating and testing theories – theories of the individual child, but theories nonetheless.

The Interviewer as Clinician

The interviewer is also a clinician. To understand the child's thinking, the interviewer must at the same time assess the child's emotional world. The interviewer is not a "cognitive scientist" but a psychologist. Successful interviewing demands a monitoring of the child's feelings (is Toby getting bored or anxious?), an understanding of the child's motives (is Toby just trying to tell me what she thinks I want to hear or does she really believe that answer?), and an evaluation of the child's personality (Toby has enough self-esteem that she will not be devastated by my telling her that she made a mistake). The ultimate focus of the interview may be primarily cognitive, but its method is clinical in the best sense – not in the sense of focusing on pathology but in the sense of great sensitivity to and understanding of the *individual.*

The flexibility of the interviewing technique demands sound clinical judgment, that is, a theory of the individual. For example, my goal as an interviewer is to have the child work hard at the task, which will help me to uncover true competence. How I go about doing this, however, depends on my theory of the individual child. In most cases, I will want to put the child at ease, to make the child feel comfortable and confident. I will not tell the child that a mistake has been made. But in other cases, I might do just the reverse. I might employ a deliberate strategy of making the child feel a little uncomfortable, of having the child realize that mistakes have been made.

109

This might be useful, for example, in the case of a child who seems competent but is a bit overconfident or sloppy. In this case, the child might benefit from the perhaps uncomfortable realization that his or her success cannot be taken for granted and that careful attention to the task is necessary.

A degree of discomfort may be helpful in producing effort; it may be devastating. Sometimes criticism spurs the child on to greater accomplishments; sometimes it produces inhibition. It all depends on the individual child. And to theorize about that individual child the interviewer must act as "clinician."

The Child

In the clinical interview, children initially see the adult as powerful, believe that the interview operates according to the rules of the classroom, and have limited ability in introspection. But all that can change.

VIEWS OF THE ADULT

Most children have had no experience with the clinical interview. They therefore enter the interview with expectancies of several types. First, they probably focus on the interviewer's status as an adult. For the young child, this generally means an adult who is powerful and knowledgeable and who must be obeyed. Older children are somewhat less docile, but in general they defer to adults, especially strange ones. Second, children may focus on the interviewer's status as "doctor," if he or she was introduced in those terms. Unfortunately, this means that many children, unfamiliar as they are with the PhD, the EdD, let alone the PsyD, tend to see the interviewer as a medical doctor who just might enjoy sticking needles in their arms. Third, children may focus on the ethnic difference between themselves and the interviewer, if such exists. Children too are not color-blind, nor do they lack prejudices. An interviewer of a different ethnicity may scare them or inhibit them or even render them speechless.

THE INTERVIEWER AS TEACHER

Most important for the conduct of the clinical interview, I think, is children's tendency to place the interviewer in the category of teacher, or at least to believe that the rules of classroom discourse apply to the interview. Although fortunately there are many exceptions, this usually means that children expect to be "tested" about what they know, that they had better not reveal ignorance, that right answers are good and wrong ones bad, that they had better do what the adult tells them to do, that they should not think too much, and that the less said the better. To some extent, these attitudes are an accurate reflection of what goes on in the typical classroom. They may also result partly from the constructive activities of the egocentric child. Young children tend to see things in black and white, in terms of good and bad; they do not dwell on subtleties and may suffer from a harsh superego. Whatever their origins, the child's rules of discourse are quite different from, even opposed to, what is required by the clinical interview.

THE PROBLEM OF INTROSPECTION

At the same time, young children are often not adept at introspection and its expression. As Piaget and others have suggested, young children are not skilled at analysis and description of their thinking, particularly when it involves complex problem-solving activities (by contrast, they can always tell you when they are hungry or don't like something). So when the interviewer asks them to describe how they solve a problem, or what they are thinking, they are confused on several levels. They need to learn to examine their thinking, to conceptualize it, and to find the words to describe it to others. Each of these is of course a difficult task. What is going on in my head now? Am I thinking, imagining, wondering? And what words do I use to describe this activity to someone else? Thus Toby, even after she had learned that the game was to describe thinking, had a difficult time talking about it. As Toby put it at different times: "I was like, thinking like . . . . I was like talking to myself . . . I wasn't counting, I was figuring it out . . . . Like, you're thinking. . . . All different things . . . but . . . um . . . you think, um, that . . . you think it. . . . [My head] it's like it's blank but I'm thinking about it . . . I'm thinking about it."

111

And of course, these natural difficulties in introspection and its expression are heightened by the fact that introspection is so seldom encountered in the typical classroom. American teachers (in contrast to Japanese) seldom even use the word *think* in their classroom discussions (Stigler & Perry, 1990). Too often, classrooms are places for doing the right thing, not for thinking. Is it any wonder then that Toby had difficulty expressing her thoughts?

TRANSFORMATIONS

But the interview is not static. For various reasons to be discussed below, the child's view of the adult and of the rules of discourse, and even the child's abilities, may change in the course of the interview. For one thing, as the interview proceeds, the adult may become less threatening, less of a traditional authority figure. At one point, Toby even started to ask me questions.

The interviewer may even come to be seen as a source of rewards. After all, the interviewer pays considerable attention to the child's every word and gesture. And children like to be paid attention to. Indeed, they seem to find it especially gratifying to have an adult take their thinking seriously. Many adults do not seem to know or care what children think. Perhaps they do not realize that children really do have independent thoughts, sometimes different from the adult's. Or perhaps they believe that, after all, children should be seen and not heard. The interviewer is unusual in that he does seem interested in the child's thought. By the end of the interview, Toby was positively preening when she was able to tell me, before I asked, how she solved a problem: "I counted before you asked. I knew you were going to ask me that!" To some extent this indicates that Toby was simply attempting to please an adult, this time perhaps a rather odd one who rewarded her for talking about thinking. No doubt. But Toby's pleasure seemed to stem from an additional source: She seemed to experience pleasure in the very act of learning and expressing what she thought, or in knowing that she could have thoughts. Perhaps for her it was like opening a new toy.

Toby also seemed to learn new rules of discourse. She learned that the interview was not the kind of talk one might hear in her classroom. In the interview, the goal was to solve problems in sensible ways and to discuss one's thinking, which in turn was seen as more important and interesting than the mere right or wrong answers. In the interview it was no shame to be wrong. (Of course, we could regard wrong answers in the same way Tevye, in *Fiddler on the Roof*, views poverty: "It's no shame to be poor, but it's no great honor either.") In the interview, the goals are thinking, self-examination, and self-exposure. Conversation revolves around and supports these goals.

And as all this took place, Toby's affect changed. She was no longer wary of the strange adult or afraid to make a mistake. She seemed to enjoy herself more, to feel proud, to get excited. At the 31-minute point, she refused a break. The session was characterized by an enjoyment that seemed to stem from the honest work of problem solving and introspection. The contrast with schooling can only enhance the clinical interview's attractiveness.

The Relationship

Two processes seem to underlie the relationship that is established in the clinical interview between interviewer and child. One is that they learn to talk to each other. The child learns the new rules of the game, and the interviewer attempts to learn the rules of the child's game. Both need to develop their communicative competence.[23]

Perhaps even more important, interviewer and child develop a relationship of trust and mutual respect that permits an intimacy centered on the child's thought. The child knows that she will not be penalized for making mistakes and that the interviewer has a real interest in and respect for how she sees the world and solves problems. Of course, different interviewers and children develop trust and intimacy in distinctive ways. That is the "clinical" part of the clinical interview. But the relationship is central. It is worth quoting Gruber a second time on this matter. "[I]f you think of what [Piaget] did with children, it was thanks to the great respect he has for what they say. . . . Piaget respects the child. He genuinely wants to understand the child for what he is" (in Bringuier, 1980, p. 69).

CONCLUSION

In the lengthy, freewheeling clinical interview of the type we have reviewed, interviewer and child learn to communicate with each other and to develop trust. The child sharpens, or even acquires, the ability to introspect and express thinking. In the process, the child's thinking may develop and become more careful and accurate. Together, interviewer and child explore and expand the limits of the child's knowledge. In the process of interacting with the child, the interviewer develops an interpretation or a series of interpretations that help provide a new perspective on the child's thinking. Just as the child's thought is influenced by the interview, so is the interviewer's. The clinical interview can produce in the interviewer a jolting realization that the child's mind is indeed distinctive – a world of its own.

CHAPTER 4

Not a Cookbook: Guidelines for Conducting a Clinical Interview

"I say *talk* to them. Let them talk to *you*. And from their conversation always, somewhere, you will find a clue. . . . You say there was nothing in those conversations that was useful. I say that cannot be so."

Hercule Poirot, in Agatha Christie, *The Clocks*

I hope that by now you are convinced that in the right hands (mouths? minds?) the clinical interview can truly help us to enter the child's mind in a sensitive manner. At the same time, you should realize that the method is extremely difficult to use. It takes great skill and insight to monitor the child's motivation, to reword questions, and to invent discriminating experimental tests, especially when all of this needs to be done "on-line" (or, as we used to say, on the spot). But the difficulty of the clinical interview must not be allowed to detract from its value for research or practice. Many scientific methods take months or even years to master – "reading" x-rays, using a microscope, performing surgical procedures.[1] Does this mean that the methods are unreliable or "unscientific"? No. Good things are often hard to do.

In this chapter, I offer guidelines – general principles – for the conduct of the clinical interview. (Some of these principles are unique to the conduct of the clinical interview. Some will also prove helpful as guidelines for *any* form of testing with children.[2]) What follows is not a cookbook. It does not tell you exactly what to do and when to do it. Conducting a clinical interview is not like preparing a simple recipe. William James's maxim concerning the teacher's art applies equally well to the psychologist's use of the clinical interview: "An intermediary inventive mind must make the application, by using its originality" (James, 1958, p. 24). Your "inventive mind" must apply the guidelines creatively, "by using its originality," responding to the demands of the particular situation confronting you. You need to use your head, to do what seems to make sense at the time with a particular child in a particular context. You need to feel free to ignore the "rules" if necessary.

This chapter begins with a discussion of the "state of mind," or orienting framework, with which you should begin the interview. After describing what this involves, I present guidelines for interviewing. For the sake of convenience and clear exposition, they are given in the following order: preparing for the interview, recording the interview, establishing and monitoring motivation, assessing thinking, establishing competence, and determining learning potential. The order of presentation is not meant to imply that these activities occur in a strict sequence. The interviewer monitors motivation virtually all of the time; establishing competence alternates with assessing thinking. The interview is not linear; it is a complex swirl, a pattern woven of many strands of interviewer and child activity.

STATE OF MIND

The interview is a state of mind as much as it is a particular set of questions and techniques. The interview demands a distinctive approach to science and practice. The interview should be based on an understanding of the child as an autonomous constructor of knowledge and on an active stance toward theory and assessment. Considerations like these do not play a significant role in standardized testing and assessment.

Recognize the Child's Autonomy

Different motives lead researchers and practitioners to enter the child's mind. The researcher values enlarging the body of psychological knowledge; the practitioner wants to help the individual child to function more effectively. To accomplish these goals, the interviewer must begin the task with fruitful assumptions and expectancies about the child's thinking. The interviewer should begin with the proposition that the child's thought is the product of a genuine attempt to make sense of the world and to create meaning.

This of course is the general constructivist hypothesis. The child's attempts may succeed or fail; her constructions may be similar to or different from our own; she may exhibit "strengths" as well as "weaknesses." The key point is that the child's constructions have an integrity: They are "honest" and autonomous attempts to cope. You should therefore enter the interview with a view of the child as an active constructor of knowledge. Even if – or rather, *especially* if – the child has been experiencing difficulty with schoolwork, don't assume that she simply knows nothing, has learned nothing, is cognitively incompetent. Assume instead that you are dealing with a child who like all other children is engaged in an attempt to construct a view of the world and means for dealing with it.

Why assume these things? Not only are they "true" (or at least they are currently our best understanding of children's intellectual function), but your expectancies make a difference. If you begin your work as interviewer with the assumption that the child does not construct knowledge but simply absorbs (or fails to absorb) it from others, then you are unlikely to realize that what seems deficient and possibly bizarre nevertheless serves some useful function for the child, and may even result from sensible thought.

An example: Believing that the child knows only what is taught, you observe that the child gets 13 as the answer to $13 - 6$. What can you conclude? She must be poorly motivated, guessing, stupid, or learning disabled. Given this nonconstructivist expectancy, you may entirely miss the fact that she has employed a sensible strategy to solve the problem and indeed believes she is doing exactly what the teacher has taught. (The teacher said, "Always subtract the smaller number from the larger." By this logic, $6 - 3 = 3$ and of course 1 take away nothing is 1, so the answer is 13.)

Furthermore, if you believe that she is poorly motivated, guessing, stupid, or learning disabled, you are then unlikely to follow up sufficiently on the child's thinking to see where and how it makes sense. You are unlikely to take her work seriously and to appreciate and then investigate the sense it might make. Indeed, your basic assumption is that it makes no sense; it is some kind of deficit. The outcome of your approach, which I would term a lack of "respect" for the child's constructions, is that you are unlikely to gain her trust. And if trust is lacking, why should the child reveal her personal constructions? If the child does not believe that you take her thinking seriously, she may be reluctant to tell how she really got the answer to $13 - 6$. Under these circumstances, it is easier for the child to assume that she is wrong or stupid, and to try to figure out what you would like her to say, than to expose what she is really thinking.

Remember when Toby insisted on solving her problem (how much is $7 + 3$?) rather than my simpler problem ($5 + 3$?). If I had not been willing to assume that she was engaged in some sensible activity, I would not have learned that she could in fact add numbers like these with some skill. The interviewer's initial assumptions and expectancies are crucial. In the absence of a view of the child as an autonomous constructor of knowledge – a form of respect – and the resulting mutual trust,[3] the interviewer will likely miss what is of value in what the child says, and the child is unlikely to say very much of value. If you are not prepared to see the child's competence, the child may not display it.

Be Active, Creative, and Take Risks

Standardized testing generally involves a more passive stance than does the clinical interview. In general, the tester is required to present only a specific, prearranged set of questions; the clinical interviewer develops new queries, on the spot, in response to the child's answers. The standardized tester must treat all children in the same ways; the clinical interviewer attempts, at least to some degree, to treat each child as an individual. The standardized tester focuses mainly on the child's response; the clinical interviewer has the more complex task of homing in on the thinking that produces the response. The standard tester focuses on the child's typical performance; the clinical interviewer attempts to elicit the best that the child can do. In general, administering a standardized test requires less thought, skill, and effort than does conducting a clinical interview. Indeed, standardized testing puts the pressure on the child; the clinical interview puts it on the interviewer.

A more positive way of saying this is that the clinical interviewer (whether researcher or practitioner) must adopt an active stance. The cognitive aspect of the clinical interview requires that the interviewer be prepared both to test hypotheses concerning the child's thinking and to explore it. The clinical aspect of the clinical interview requires that the interviewer be sensitive to the child's personality and affect and learn to develop methods for treating the child as an individual. In short, unable to take refuge in an existing test's easy theoretical assumptions about thinking and its superficial approach to "rapport," the interviewer must act as the kind of "intermediary inventive mind" described by William James. Unlike standardized testing, clinical interviewing is not passive and safe. The clinical interview involves risks; it requires both clinical sensitivity and scientific creativity.

PREPARING FOR THE INTERVIEW

Conducting a clinical interview is not entirely a spontaneous process. What may seem extemporaneous, fluid, and indeed easy is in reality the result of a long process of preparation and training. The interviewer needs to begin with insight into cognitive developmental processes and knowledge of norms; needs to have available tasks and problems; and needs to arrange recording and setting.

Don't Go on a Fishing Expedition Without Your Theoretical Rod and Tackle

There is a paradox in the clinical interview. On the one hand, the interviewer's goal is sensitivity to the child. The interviewer wants to have an "open mind" in order to discover what is in the child's mind. The goal is to learn how the *child* thinks and how the *child* constructs a personal world. The danger is in imposing adult categories, in forcing the child's responses into a predetermined, adult mold. The ideal question is "How did *you* solve that problem?" not "Did you solve the problem in the way *I* taught you or the way *I* do it?"

119

On the other hand, to discover something about the child's cognitive construction, the interviewer must have some ideas about what to look for, some notions about the forms children's thinking may take. Lacking concepts for interpreting the child's behavior and explanations, the interviewer is likely to overlook what is important and to focus on what is trivial. As Piaget put it, novice interviewers often "are not on the look-out for anything, in which case, to be sure, they will never find anything" (Piaget, 1976a, p. 9).

The paradox then is that to be truly "open," the interviewer's mind must be prepared. The open mind cannot be an empty mind.

What does this mean for you? Before interviewing, you must know as much as possible about what you want to study. Read the literature; you must adopt, at least provisionally, a theoretical framework with which to interpret your observations. As pointed out earlier, the successful interviewer takes an active stance, interpreting, theorizing, trying to make sense of what the child does and says. The standard tester need only rely on the theory implicit in the test.

Keep Meaningful Norms in Your Head

One particular kind of idea that the interviewer needs is norms. The developmentalist needs to know that 4-year-olds are unlikely to say the word *unlikely* or that almost every 12-year-old knows how to spell *spell*. The clinician needs to know that a particular instance of anger is extreme at age 8 but not at age 5. In the absence of such norms, the child's behavior in an interview (or outside it) is likely to be uninterpretable. The interviewer may not be able to decide whether the child's response indicates mental retardation, normality, a creative effort, or a sign of emotional disturbance.

Sometimes useful norms are available in the published literature. If you are interested in moral judgment, you can learn from the existing research that "moral realism" is a phenomenon characteristic of 4- to 6-year-olds and that "moral relativism" does not emerge until much later. Or if you are interested in the child's understanding of a particular word, you may be able to obtain precise normative information from certain published tests or other databases.

The interviewer cannot always rely on published norms concerning the topic of interest. For one thing, if the interviewer's topic is new, relevant norms are unlikely to be available. For another, even if norms do exist, they may be of little value if they are based on faulty methods. For example, poor children score lower on just about any standard test than do middle-class children. These are the true norms for standard tests, but standard tests are flawed in ways described earlier and do not necessarily indicate anything important about poor children's real abilities. More sensitive methods of assessment often yield a different picture (Ginsburg, 1986a). So in some cases the norms should at least be taken with a grain of salt.

In cases in which norms are unavailable or of dubious value, the interviewer must rely on informal norms, acquired in homely ways. Such norms usually involve imprecise expectancies, a kind of approximate statistical knowledge: *Most* 4-year-olds act this way but *usually* 7-year-olds don't. Such norms are more often acquired from everyday experience over a long period of time than they are from explicit data presented in scientific publications. Informal norms are a key part of what is often called *intuition* or *practitioner's knowledge.*

Whether norms are explicit or implicit, and whether they are acquired from everyday experience or from the scientific literature, interviewers, like testers, cannot do without them. Therefore, you must follow two courses of action: Read the literature to find out what researchers have learned about what children normally do. But also, because the published research literature is sometimes exceedingly narrow, running to fads of interest largely to a small group of researchers, you have to get to know children informally, in effect immersing yourself in the relevant culture. In research, there is no substitute for hands-on experience, for getting your hands dirty. Both the literature and your experience will help you to get norms into your head.

Norms and ideas are not enough, however. You also need to have available some tasks with which to begin the interview. Depending on what happens, you may decide not to use the tasks, or to modify them; but you should have them available to start with.

Prepare a Protocol With Which to Begin

Before beginning, you need to work on a rough plan for the interview, including a list of tasks and questions you will ask. Let's say you are interested in the child's conceptions of the teacher. Your protocol should reflect the several dimensions of your interest in this topic (the teacher's goals or basic approach, skill at explaining, attitudes toward individual children, fairness, knowledge, patience, and the like) and should describe methods for engaging the child in a consideration of these topics (e.g., asking the child to discuss what her teacher did in the last lesson, asking about a hypothetical situation involving teachers and students, or asking such questions as "What do you remember most about your teacher from last year?").

In a sense, your protocol is similar to a standard test. You may employ all of the questions on your protocol with all of the children you interview. But, of course, you do not limit yourself to the protocol: You feel free to engage in flexible questioning.

Once you are thoroughly familiar with an area, your protocol may be largely in your head, and you may not need to write it out. In any event, don't go into an interview "cold."

Use Theoretically Meaningful Tasks but, if in Trouble, Cast a Wide Net

Ideally, questions and tasks should stem from your theoretical concerns, from the research findings in the literature, and from your informal observations. But often the beginning interviewer has difficulty in developing appropriate questions and tasks. In this case, you may find it useful to base interview questions and tasks on questions in existing standard tests or similar materials.

Suppose you are interested in studying the student's conception of American history. You might begin by using the questions given in the student's textbook. They may be ambiguous or require modification, or they may even not make a great deal of sense. Nevertheless, they are a useful way to get started, and you can easily follow up on them once you get the student's initial response. Similarly, you can build interviews on items from various standard tests. If you are interested in mathematical thinking, begin with some questions from a standard mathematics achievement test. If you are interested in comprehension, begin with some items (suitably reworded and disguised) from an IQ test. Indeed, standard test items served as a basis for some of Piaget's early work. In *Judgment and Reasoning in the Child*, Piaget used the absurdity items from the Binet test as the basis for intensive clinical interviews on logical thinking (e.g., "I have three brothers: Paul, Ernest, and myself") (Piaget, 1964).

Prepare Specific Tasks With Which the Child Can Engage

Tasks should not be vague and unclear, leaving the child uncertain about what the question is and what needs to be done. Instead, tasks should present problems with which the child can grapple. Tasks should be focused and complex enough to engage children in extended bouts of thinking. (This is also a useful goal for the constructor of test items.)

Suppose that you want to investigate children's understanding of written texts, for example, stories. One approach would be to say, "Tell me how you understand a story." But this is much too vague and will not get you very far. Instead, it would be far more effective to have the child read a particular story and to ask specific questions designed to illuminate the process of comprehension of that story. "What was the first thing that happened in the story? What did Roger think about Penelope? How did you figure out that Roger didn't like her?"

Suppose you are interested in children's understanding of addition. Do not simply ask, "How do you add?" A more effective approach would be to present the child with an addition problem to be solved and then to ask about the methods just used in dealing with those specific numbers. This situation gives the child the opportunity to think about something "concrete" and to introspect about mental activities transpiring in the immediate present.

The general rule is to make the task "specific." This can be accomplished in many different ways, in part depending on the topic and the developmental level of the child. Piaget discovered early in his career that it is often useful to provide children, especially young ones, with problems involving concrete objects. Thus, if the goal is to understand the child's concept of "larger than," the interviewer might devise problems involving sticks of various sizes. Concrete objects may help the child to *see* what the problem is and also may externalize the child's thinking processes. That is to say, the child's actions on the objects, which the interviewer can easily observe, may reveal key aspects of her strategies.

For example, to determine which is larger, one child carefully places two sticks side by side, making sure that both have a common base; another child puts them side by side but ignores the base. The placement of sticks suggests that the first child is considering several dimensions of the problem (what Piaget calls "coordination of relations"), whereas the second child is focusing on only one of the relevant dimensions (what Piaget calls "centration"). In this case, each child's arrangement of sticks gives a fairly solid indication of strategy and concept. The interviewer can then ask appropriate questions to gain further information concerning each child's ways of thinking about "larger than."

Literal concreteness is not required; it is not always necessary to employ real objects. What is important is to make the problem *specific* and *focused*, something into which the child can sink her (mental) teeth. For children at some developmental levels, oral or written stories introduce sufficient specificity, and one does not have to illustrate them with dolls and props. Thus, ever since Piaget's original work (Piaget, 1962), investigations of moral judgment present children with dilemmas expressed in story form (Damon & Hart, 1992). Similarly, if the goal is to investigate the understanding of school mathematics, it is quite appropriate to present third- or fourth-grade children with written problems which do not involve objects, manipulatives, stories, and the like. Such written problems are specific: They capture what most children deal with on a day-to-day basis in school.

In general, employ specific tasks that engage the child in familiar, everyday activities.

Vary the Tasks

Children can easily get bored with problems that seem to repeat themselves. In general, children do better – they are more interested and more open – with a variety of problems than with minor variations on the same theme. Therefore, try to vary the types of problems you give, the materials, the characters in stories, the types of response the child is required to make. (Again, this is also a useful goal for the constructor of test items.)

Suppose that you are investigating moral judgment, with a particular interest in the child's ability to determine guilt on the basis of intention. To make sure that what you observe represents a consistent pattern of thought, you need to present the child with several problems, all of which need to involve situations in which intention is pitted against accident. Thus, you might use a story, like Piaget's, in which a child breaks one dish on purpose, whereas another child breaks five accidentally. Who is more guilty? If intention is considered important, the child will consider the first child more guilty than the second; if on the other hand, the child takes a "realist" stance, focusing on concrete outcomes, then the second child is more guilty because more real damage was done.

In developing stories of this type, introduce variety. Clearly it would not be a good idea to vary the story simply by changing the number of dishes in each case. A better approach would be to create stories describing different types of damage. An even more effective tactic would be to develop some stories in which intention is contrasted with concrete outcomes that do not necessarily involve physical damage at all (e.g., stories comparing lies with inaccurate reports of fact). Vary the menu.

Prepare Both Open-Ended and Focused Questions

Although effective tasks tend to be specific, productive questions should at first be open-ended. (This of course is not a typical characteristic of test items.) Tasks should engage the child in thinking; questions should encourage the child to describe it as fully and accurately as possible. In particular, questions should not bias response; they should not be leading; they should not restrict answers. At first, questions should be open-ended, giving the child freedom to respond and allowing the expression of personal ways of thinking, of the child's world view. Avoid questions that require or permit a yes or no answer. Questions in open-ended form are more likely to provide insights into the child's thought than questions that can be answered by a simple yes or no. "Tell me how your teacher treats you" allows for far more spontaneous expression than "Is your teacher fair?"

Depending on what you discover in the child's responses to the open-ended questions, you can introduce a series of more focused, directive questions to examine specific hypotheses about the child's thought. In general, the sequence of questions should proceed from general to more specific queries. Liben (in press) recommends that implementing such a sequence can be facilitated by a simple checklist designed to help the interviewer keep track of which questions have been asked and which should be asked. The interviewer needs to remember what the child said in response to the first, open-ended question and then whether specific follow-up questions in fact have been asked.

Get the Equipment Ready

Once you have decided on the tasks, make sure that you have readily available all of the equipment which the child might need in the course of the interview: paper and pencil, blocks, toys, whatever is likely to be required. There is nothing worse (well, almost) than stopping an interview to hunt around for a toy or a block for a certain task. By the time you have found the equipment, you may have lost the child's interest.

Book a Room

The interview, like a standard test, should take place in a reasonably comfortable place that is quiet, free of distractions, and well lit. Often this is not possible. I have interviewed in the school nurse's room, in corridors, in large closets. Frequently children walk by, shouts can be heard in the background, the school loudspeaker system blares announcements from the principal, and the room is cluttered and hot. It is a testament to the power of the clinical interview that these potential distractions seldom detract from the success of the interview. Children often find the clinical interview so interesting that they are oblivious to the distractions.

The arrangement of seating is an interesting issue. I usually find it effective to sit side by side with the child, or perhaps at right angles to the child. This has several advantages. The main one is that it may signal a less authoritarian relationship than does sitting opposite. Also, it makes it easier for me to read what the child writes (although some interviewers, like teachers, quickly learn to read material upside-down). On the other hand, sitting side by side has at least one disadvantage. It makes it harder for interviewer and child to see each other's face and thus to pick up signs of affect and the like. Sit where you feel most comfortable. The seating arrangement will not make or break the interview.

RECORDING THE INTERVIEW

As we have seen, an interview is an extremely complicated and elaborate form of interaction. There is no way that the researcher or practitioner can accurately remember everything that occurs in this free-flowing discourse between two persons. The interviewer needs to record the interaction in a form useful for her purposes, whether they involve research or practice. The recordings will eventually need to be "reduced" (annotated, categorized, or even scored) in a convenient and theoretically useful way.

How do you record what happens in such a complex interaction so that you can remember and then use what is important? For purposes of research, audio recordings are often adequate. Use a simple cassette recorder with a 90-minute tape, one side of which will usually be long enough to record your interview with one child. It is usually most efficient to use a separate tape (or at least side of a tape), clearly labeled and dated, for each child, so that it is clear where a new interview begins.

If you have the equipment and facilities, you may wish to use a video camera. This introduces complications: You need a camera operator and you need to put the child at ease about the whole process of videotaping. Nevertheless, videotape provides some real advantages. It shows the context – what you were doing and what was going on in the background. It shows facial expressions, movements, body postures, giving a glimpse at some of the nonverbal means of expression, which cannot be captured on audiotape (like Toby placing her hand in her sleeve) and which may be vital for understanding the child's meaning and motivation. And of course, whether you use video or audio, save all of the child's written work. These productions too can provide insight into the child's thinking.

For some research purposes, you may find that neither audio- nor video-recording may be necessary. Instead, you may simply code aspects of the interview as they occur. Preliminary interviews or available theory may allow you to home in on – and to code – particular aspects of the child's thought. Suppose for example, that you are interested in the child's ability to make transitive judgments (if $a > b$, and $b > c$, then $a > c$). In the course of the complex interaction that takes place during the clinical interview, you may use a reliable coding scheme to identify, on the spot, four different strategies that children may employ to deal with transitivity problems. You may note only whether and when the child uses any of these strategies and ignore anything else that takes place in the interview. (Of course, you could also perform such coding after the interview by examining a video- or audiotape.) Perhaps highly directed coding sounds limiting, and it is. But in this case, it is entirely appropriate to the research goal, which is, not to explore, but essentially to test specific hypotheses.

Some authorities recommend that practitioners too make audio or video records of interviews and also prepare careful transcripts (Garbarino et al., 1992). This is certainly desirable, but in my experience, it is impractical. Practitioners usually do not rely heavily on audio- or videotapes. For one thing, as a practitioner, you seldom have time to review them. In general, you will want to take careful notes about the child's performance, either during the interview (which is very hard to do) or immediately after the interview (in which case you will probably forget some interesting material). You may wish to supplement these notes with audio or video recordings, which may be useful as a backup in case your notes leave some issue unresolved or in case you later want to investigate something you did not think of at the outset.

ESTABLISHING AND MONITORING MOTIVATION

In their early work on intelligence testing, Binet and Simon (1916) gave the following, generally sensible advice on motivating the child:

> The attitude to be taken in regard to the child is delicate; first of all there must be goodwill; one must try to remain in touch with him; excite his attention, his self-respect; show satisfaction with all his replies, whatever they may be, encourage without aiding, without suggesting. . . . Avoid disturbing the child by fixedly regarding him. Naturally, one will not fall into the ridiculous error of teaching him; it is a question here of ascertaining the state of his mentality, not of teaching. (p. 295)

As I have argued earlier, the requirements of standardized administration make it difficult for the tester to accomplish Binet and Simon's goals. If, following the logic of standardized administration, the tester must behave in a substantially similar fashion toward all children, then it may be difficult to establish "goodwill" or "remain in touch with" or "excite . . . attention" in *a particular* child. Indeed, contrary to Binet and Simon's advice, to reach a particular child, it may be appropriate, once a good rapport has been established, to show *dis*satisfaction with a response – it all depends on the context and circumstances. Establishing rapport requires treating children as individuals; it means doing different and special things for different and special children.

This is not easy, and it involves more than deploying a set of particular techniques, like showing "satisfaction with all his replies." Instead, establishing rapport and motivating the child require a demanding clinical sensitivity, which we shall now explore.

Establish Trust

The general goal is not simply to put the child in a good humor or to encourage relaxation or compliance with the interviewer's de-

129

mands. Rather, the goal should be to create a special relationship between interviewer and subject, a relationship of trust. The clinical interview requires a special form of intimacy. The child needs to learn that it is safe to reveal her mental activity, a private and protected domain.

In school, the child is often criticized for answers or beliefs; they are judged right or wrong. In standardized testing, the child knows that she is being evaluated. The end result, the child believes with some accuracy, will be a judgment about "dumbness" or "smartness." Under these circumstances, the best policy is to play it safe, to give the answers that the teacher or tester seems to want, and to hide one's ignorance.

In the clinical interview, the interviewer must attempt to overcome these attitudes. The child must come to believe – hopefully because it is true! – that the interviewer respects the child's mental activity and that no harm will come from revealing it. The focus is not on right and wrong answers or on smartness and dumbness. Instead, the interview can be a kind of celebration of the child's mind. The child needs to understand that the process of introspection and its expression might be interesting, informative, and sometimes enjoyable. What is needed is something deeper than "rapport." It is an intimate relation of trust, a relationship that cannot be accomplished by a simple tactical maneuver of the type attempted by the administrators of standardized tests.

Make Informal Contact

Children are usually interviewed in schools or clinics. Under these circumstances, most children, especially young ones, are likely to cast the adult in the role of teacher or doctor. Most likely the child must imagine that if the adult is in a school, he or she can be expected to do school-like things; if in a clinic, doctor-type things. All in all, these are very reasonable inferences. (After all, the interviewer may even be called "doctor," and the child is unlikely to distinguish between the MD and PhD.) And simply saying, "We will play some games today," will not change the child's expectancies about the adult's behavior and role.[4]

130

You want to establish a very different kind of relationship. You want to convince your Toby that you do not want to play prototypical teacher or doctor; that is not the only game in town.

The first step might be to get to know the child on an informal basis. (This I did not do with Toby.) Stop by the classroom; spend some time with the children in the playground; play games with them. This will not only help the child to see you as less threatening but will also teach you something about the child's life in her ordinary surroundings. What is the school really like? The teacher? The child's peers? Surely such information is particularly valuable for the clinician and the school psychologist. Don't see the child only in your office!

Explain the Purpose of the Interview

It is hard to explain the purpose of a clinical interview, especially to young children. After all, it is an unfamiliar form of discourse, a game which they are not likely to have played before. Nevertheless, you must make an effort to communicate that the focus is on thinking, not merely on correctness of the answer. You need to establish that you are interested in how the child solves problems or thinks about things, and that the interview does not involve evaluation in the sense of taking a test that results in a grade or score. No doubt, the child will not understand everything you say. He might wonder why an adult would want to know what he is thinking. The child may not even believe a good part of what you say. He will come to an understanding of the interview only after having some concrete experience of it. At the same time, you will have accomplished a great deal if only you get across the general attitude that you respect the child enough to try to explain what you are about.

Suppose that you are a practitioner whose goal is to explore the child's learning difficulty in reading. You might introduce the interview by saying, "I work with children to help them read better. I would like to talk with you to find out how you do your reading, how you think about reading. If I can find out, I might be able to help you with it."

By contrast, if you are a researcher interested in reading comprehension, you might say something like "I study how children learn to read. I would like to talk with you about how you understand stories. If I find out, I might be able to help kids learn to read better. Of course, what you do here with me won't affect your grades or your report card."[5]

Whatever you say, make it simple and honest.

Use the Child's Language

Try not to sound formal and stuffy. Don't use fancy words. Instead of "Now I would like to examine your reading comprehension," say "Let's talk about what this story means." Indeed, in talking with a child, try to use her language, even it is "wrong." The child may say "take away" instead of "subtract" or "bad" instead of "guilty." Swallow your pride and sense of propriety and do the same yourself. Don't use adult, technical terms. Pick up on the child's language and ask "Who was the baddest?" instead of "Which child was the more guilty?"

There are several reasons for doing this. The primary reason of course is that speaking the child's language can put the child at ease and help her to understand what you are saying. This approach is not possible in standardized testing, but you can take advantage of it in the clinical interview. A secondary reason is that it is another way of signaling that you accept the child's way of doing things. So say what you long ago learned not to say – talk child-talk – if it will help you to understand what the child knows.

Put the Child in the Role of Expert

In his early work on moral judgment (specifically, the rules governing social interaction in games), Piaget used the technique of playing novice to the child's expert. Piaget claimed that he did not understand how to play marbles and that he needed the child to explain the rules of the game.[6] (In fact, this was not true. Before beginning the research, Piaget studied the game of marbles, becoming an expert himself.) The child was then the expert and could with authority and pleasure transmit his wisdom (only boys were studied) to the adult novice.

You can implement this approach in several different ways. One is to say that you are trying to learn about how children think about some topic – their homework, their ideas about animals, etc. – and you need help. Another is to ask the child to offer a make-believe explanation of some topic to a younger child. "Suppose that you want to explain to your younger brother why a tree is alive. How would you do that?" Or "Suppose you wanted to teach a younger kid the best way to do his homework. What would you say?"

Of course, putting the child in the role of expert means that you have to accept the role of novice. This is more or less the reverse of what happens in standardized testing. But that is as it should be: In the clinical interview your goal is to learn something from the child, to understand the child's constructions; the goal is not to determine whether the child's thought conforms to your standards.

Begin With an Easy Task

You want the child to feel confident, to believe that success is likely; you do not want the child to be threatened by failure. This of course is especially true if, as a practitioner, you are interviewing a child who has been experiencing academic or emotional difficulty. Therefore, begin with a task on which the child is likely to succeed. (Of course, you should avoid my mistake, in the interview with Toby, of *announcing* that the task will be easy. Failure under these circumstances can only make the child feel worse.) Using whatever information you have available (school records; published norms; your internal, subjective norms), choose tasks that ought to be relatively easy (but not so trivial as to appear "babyish"). Do not begin by placing the child in a failure situation. If the child seems to have trouble with the initial task, change it right away; make it simpler so that the child can succeed without too much trouble.

Similarly, if you wish to interview the child about emotionally charged issues (e.g., beliefs about what it means to be classified as "learning disabled"), begin with neutral material; do not probe the sensitive areas until a trusting relationship has begun to develop.

After you have put the child at ease with an easy task, you may wish to increase the difficulty of problems. But once you have hit upon what is too hard for the child, return to some easy problems to allow the child to conclude the interview with an experience of success. (This procedure is similar to the approach of some standardized tests, like the Binet IQ test, which begins with items that norms predict are appropriate for the child's age level, then moves to more difficult items to establish the point where the child consistently fails, and finally returns to relatively easy items so that the child can exit on a note of success.)

Be Warm and Supportive

Children are often placed in the subordinate position of being judged by an adult. That is one of the basic conditions of childhood, and they are fully aware of it. In schools, children are frequently tested, and no doubt they must at first find it hard to distinguish between an ordinary test and the clinical interview. Is it an exaggeration to suppose that, despite the adult's disclaimers, all children must at some point in the clinical interview fear that the adult is testing, evaluating, indeed threatening, their intelligence – their very goodness? I think not.

Of course, there are dramatic individual differences in children's fear of testing, a fear to which they assimilate the clinical interview. Some children, particularly those from the upper middle class, are prepared for testing and may become accustomed to it. Some children may see it as an opportunity to demonstrate their prowess.[7] For other children, evaluation can be a terrifying experience. For example, testing must produce great anxiety in the child who has experienced only failure in school and who has been treated as incompetent in the classroom. Or, to offer another example, imagine the feelings of a child from a "different" culture, a child uncomfortable with schools and not accustomed to testing, who is examined by a strange adult, an adult unfamiliar with the child's culture or even language. Is it not natural for this child to perceive testing (and the clinical interview) as threatening, to perceive evaluation as *de*valuation?

Like testers, interviewers must try to counter these feelings and to allay the child's anxiety. You can do several things to help. First, you must attempt to empathize with the child's feelings. Try to understand how the child must feel about the interview. Don't assume that the child automatically sees it as an enjoyable or even nonthreatening experience.

Second, you can try to be warm and supportive. Show that you recognize that the child is distressed and act in a comforting manner. Remember that you are dealing with a child who is likely to feel threatened.

Third, your initial description of the interview as having a purpose other than evaluation may help. But remember that it is not enough simply to tell the child what the interview is all about. You have to prove it in word and deed.

Fourth, in many cases you can let the child know that she has not been singled out because of poor academic performance or general stupidity but that *all* (or most) children in the class are being interviewed. Of course, sometimes you cannot say this in honesty. Often the practitioner does test particular children precisely because they are doing especially poorly in school. In this case, the best policy is to acknowledge that fact openly. "Your teacher thinks that you are having trouble with reading. I'm going to talk with you about reading so we can try to figure out how we can help you." (Note the focus on the improvement of teaching, not on a disability in the child.)

All these things can help – empathy, warmth, explanation of the interview, and telling the child that others are in the same boat. But you also have a secret weapon. The very fact that you as an adult attend respectfully, the fact that you show an interest in the child's thinking and ways of looking at the world – all of this relaxes the child and enhances motivation. The interviewer's style can help the child to get past the initial anxiety and to respond with genuine enthusiasm. Indeed, observation suggests that in the clinical interview, both interviewer and child are more relaxed and "human" (in the sense of engaging in a genuine social interaction, in a real conversation) than they are in the testing situation, where the child is often defensive and the adult, playing at scientific inquisitor, is stiff and authoritarian.[8]

Encourage Effort

You want to make sure the child is attending to the tasks you present, is working hard, and is trying to deal with them in a serious way. The major way to encourage such motivation is to praise the child for effort, for engagement, for thoughtfulness. Of course, you can't do this just once at the outset and then ignore the issue; you have to keep working on it. Throughout the session, you need to use phrases like "I'm glad you're trying so hard" and "that was a good way to think about it." Certainly you should put more emphasis on praising effort and thoughtfulness than on rewarding correct answers (or punishing incorrect ones). In general, you do not want to say, "That's good. That was the right answer." Such an approach diverts the child's attention from thinking; indeed, it reinforces the tendency to worry about *the* right answer. Similarly, it is generally not a good idea to say, "No. That's the wrong answer." This may devalue the child's method of solution, which in fact may be quite sensible.

On the other hand, there are important exceptions. I am reluctant to say that you should *never* tell the child that an answer is right or wrong. Sometimes, particularly in the case of children who are smart but careless, it may be useful to acknowledge the child's failure in a very explicit fashion. "That was wrong. I know you can do it. Try again."

Furthermore, children usually know when their answer is wrong,[9] so that your saying it comes as no surprise. They feel uncertain; they know they have used an inappropriate method of solution. The adult's failure to say, "that's right," in effect confirms that the child was wrong. The adult's statements "you're trying very hard," "that's a real hard problem," or "that's a good way to think about it" all may provide some comfort but may not remove from the child's mind the self-imposed stigma of being wrong.

Under these circumstances, a more honest (for both participants) and effective approach might be to acknowledge explicitly both the failure and the effort or thoughtfulness. "I saw you were having a hard time with that one, but that's OK. I'm more interested in how you solve the problems than in whether you get them right or wrong." Or "You got that one wrong. But that's a hard problem that most first graders don't get. Anyway, what's more important is how you think about it."[10]

How much encouragement is needed? Unfortunately, as in the case of many other aspects of the clinical interview, the answer is: It depends. Some children require a good deal of encouragement and praise; others do not. Some may even require some pushing or other forms of pressure. Individual differences in motivation are enormous among children at the same age. The "clinical" aspect of the clinical interview requires that you judge on the spot how much encouragement and how much pressure are appropriate for the individual child.

Monitor Affect

Throughout the interview, you must constantly monitor the child's emotion. You need to be aware of the child's anxiety, delight, interest, boredom, and the like. Of course, you may use this information in various ways. For example, you may wish to lessen the anxiety of a child who is failing or conversely to increase the pressure on another who is not trying hard enough. But whatever the goal, it is important to be aware of the child's emotional state.

Often, the child's beliefs, feelings, and attitudes will emerge spontaneously in the course of the interview. Sometimes you may need to probe to learn about them. "How does it feel when you don't know the answer or when you can't solve a problem?" "Is it cheating if you count on your fingers?" "What does your teacher think when you do that?" "How did you feel just now when you got that answer wrong?" "What kinds of problems do you find easy?" "Hard?" "What are you having trouble with in school?"

Encouraging the child to understand and express feelings about learning should be a key aspect of education. It is very difficult for all of us to say, "I feel lost and confused," "I don't understand," or "I feel bad because I don't know this." On some deep level, we must feel that our missteps in the course of learning signal deep personal inadequacies. Beginning in childhood, we need to learn to understand, express, and place in perspective feelings like these. The clinical interview can provide children with some assistance in doing this.

Encourage Verbalization

You should not assume you know what the child is thinking. You certainly don't want to put words into the child's mouth; indeed, you want to take words out of the child's mouth. Your goal is to help the child to express as much as possible about her own thinking, to say as much as possible about her concepts and methods.

There is an obstacle, however. Some children learn from experience in the classroom that the teacher is not particularly interested in their thinking; the children's job is to produce the right answer, which is essentially how the teacher thinks about the issue. Some children also learn that they should not volunteer information, let alone their personal views, opinions, and ways of thinking. It is much safer to try to figure out what the teacher wants them to say.

The clinical interview promotes a different kind of discourse. You have to encourage the child to verbalize as fully as possible in response to questions about her thinking, concepts, and ways of conceptualizing the world. The clinical interview can be successful only if the child is willing to expose her ways of thinking, to reveal her personal and private ways of dealing with the world. As I indicated earlier, this requires considerable trust. In effect, you have to convey the message: "Please tell me everything you can about what you are thinking. The correctness of the answers is not what's most important to me; I want to know how you get the answers."

As we saw in the case of Toby, children may need to learn what you want and how to do it. This is not the sort of discourse that takes place in many classrooms. You have to keep asking the child to explain how she got the answer to a given problem: "How did you do it?" "Explain how you got that answer." "How did you think that through?"

Dealing With "Difficult" Children

From the interviewer's point of view, children may be "difficult" in several ways. Some children are extremely shy and reluctant to interact with the interviewer. I once interviewed a 4-year-old, Kate, who at first refused to talk with me at all. I circumvented the difficulty by using her mother as a channel for communications. After listening to my question, the child whispered the answer in her mother's ear, and the mother then conveyed the response to me. After a time, Kate's whispers became louder and louder, so that I could hear them, and gradually I convinced Kate to whisper louder still and eventually to do away with her mother's echo. No doubt this approach was extreme, and in many cases the parental channel might be unavailable or ineffective. But gentle patience, persistence, and approval usually suffice to put the shy child at ease and encourage some degree of communication.

A second type of "difficult" child is one whose cultural background does not permit or encourage children to speak freely with adults, or at least with "different" adults, those from another group. What to do in this case? One approach, of course, is to use an interviewer from the child's culture or at least one who is familiar with it. Often, however, this may not be possible or practical. Patience and empathy can solve the problem in many cases. After all, communication between very diverse groups is possible; we are not (at least not yet) impossibly balkanized. Sometimes, it is necessary to resort to unusual measures. For example, the culturally different child may be more comfortable in a group situation in which friends are also being interviewed. A group interview is difficult to carry off but at least can serve as a point of entry. Perhaps after a while the child will become comfortable enough to agree to participate in an individual interview.

Very rarely you will encounter a child who is boastful and vain, an obnoxious show-off. With such a difficult and sometimes uncooperative child, the best policy is basically patience and clear focus on the process of problem solution, not on the child's putative talent or giftedness. One child, Ronald, began the interview by announcing that he was "G and T," not even bothering to explain that he was labeled, as I later found out, as "gifted and talented." I would have labeled Ronald a pain in the neck. In any event, we eventually got along well enough by focusing on the task, not on how smart he considered himself to be. To Ronald I had to convey the message: "I'm not interested in your correct answers – of which no doubt there are many – but in your ways of thinking about them." It also helped that I deliberately put him in situations in which he would fail. This seemed to induce some humility, caused him to stop putting on airs, and got him to approach the problems with care. Now in general I do not of course advocate presenting children with problems intended to make them fail. But in Ronald's case of runaway arrogance, the strategy made sense. In the clinical interview, the major rule is that *it all depends.* This brings us to our next topic, the "clinical" in the clinical interview.

The Priority of the "Clinical"

Individual differences among children abound, and you as interviewer therefore have to treat each child in a unique way. That is both the strength of the clinical interview and its major weakness. It is hard to treat each child appropriately, each according to her needs. Doing it requires real "clinical" skills. In this context, "clinical" judgment does not mean proffering diagnoses of pathology; rather, it means being sensitive to the nuances of individual needs. That is why we should be proud to talk of the *clinical* interview. Researchers are often not trained in clinical judgment but I think they should be; practitioners are usually assumed to possess keen clinical insight but some could sharpen their skills in this area.

Clinical judgment means that technique must vary according to the individual child. To get some children to attend carefully and devote full effort to the task, it is simply necessary to ask them once to pay attention. Other children require such frequent reminders that the interviewer might appear guilty of badgering the child. Technique may also vary according to the individual interviewer. An interviewer may be more adept at using one technique than another, just as a baseball pitcher may be more skilled at throwing a fastball than a curve.

Some children profit from a good deal of structuring; others require an open-ended approach. Some children need gentle encouragement; some children need to be told to work harder. Some children profit from failure; others fall apart when they experience it. Some children do well when the interviewer persists on a particular topic (as I did with Toby's counting by twos); other children do better when the interviewer switches to a new problem. Some children do better with a slow pace; some with a faster one.

140

So I repeat: It all depends. And being a good clinician is knowing how it all depends and what to do about it. Now how can one learn to become a good clinician of this type? That is a question for the next chapter.

ASSESSING THINKING: WHAT DOES THE CHILD KNOW?

We come now to the heart of the clinical interview: examining the child's thinking. On some occasions, your goal may be discovery; on other occasions, hypothesis testing. But in both cases, you must always interpret the child's behavior and develop hypotheses about the child's mental life. The interviewer – whether researcher or practitioner – is a theorist. Why did the child make that response? What did he mean by that statement? Although it is vital to interpret, don't leap to conclusions.

Don't Discourage the Child's Way of Solving Problems

Children often solve problems in unorthodox ways. Much of the charm of Piaget's work lies in showing that children see the world differently from the ways we do, and that their conceptions make a certain amount of sense. Yes, the sun does seem to be following us around when we walk. Yes, $12 - 4$ does equal 12 if you cannot subtract a larger number (4) from a smaller one (2) and if you don't understand "borrowing." In school, children may solve problems in ways that the teacher did not teach. The child may not memorize the answer to $5 + 4$ and instead figure it out by reasoning that it must be one more than $4 + 4$. Indeed, the teacher often may not approve of the child's personal methods for solving problems, as is often true in the case of arithmetic by finger counting.[11]

What to do? The first commandment is not to belittle the child's ideas. Almost invariably they make some sense – from the child's point of view. The child constructs these ideas in an attempt to understand, to create meaning. You must help the child to realize that you accept and even value her methods of solving problems, even if they

141

are unorthodox. Your first goal is to find out how the child thinks. Even if you may later wish to teach the child another method, you first need to find out how the child spontaneously approaches the task, and you need to make the child feel that what she does has value (which is tremendously motivating for the child). Later, you can use what you learn about these personal ways of thinking to help the child move beyond them to something more effective.

Don't Assume That a Wrong Answer Is Wrong or That a Right Answer Is Right

Sometimes, when the child gives what seems to be an incorrect answer, it may be the result of an interesting line of reasoning, a result of assumptions different from those which motivated your question. Indeed, the child's "wrong" answer may really be the "right" answer to a different question, a question you did not ask.

For example, 4-year-old Dorothy[12] was asked, "Is a pencil crooked or straight?" She replied, "Crooked." To the interviewer's question, "How do you know that?" she replied, "Because it is bumpy and bends around the ends." Subsequent questioning revealed that she knew that most of the pencil is straight; only the ends are different. Her answer "Crooked" was the correct response to the question (which was not intended or asked!) "Are the ends of the pencil straight?" In that sense, her wrong answer was not wrong.

Similarly, when the child gives a correct answer, don't assume that the reasoning behind it is sound. Dorothy was told: "Listen carefully and tell me if the sentence I say is a good or bad sentence. 'Tom's sister haven't been shopping today.'" She replied, "Bad sentence." The interviewer asked, "Why?" Dorothy replied, "Because they didn't have food to eat for dinner." In other words, Dorothy seemed to think that the sentence was bad, not because it was grammatically incorrect, but because it would lead to an unfortunate result, namely nothing to eat for dinner.

If wrong answers can be right, and right answers wrong, what is an interviewer to do? The solution is: Look beneath the answer to understand the thought that produced it.

Ask the Fundamental Question

One way to accomplish this is to ask the child how he solved the problem. The fundamental question of clinical interviewing is "How did you do that?" Of course, this generic question may be varied in many ways to accommodate different children, different ages, and different situations. Here are several ways to ask children how they did it:

"Can you do it out loud?"
"How did you figure that out?"
"Can you show me how you did it?"
"How do you know?"
"How would you show it?"

Some children are unwilling or afraid to display their personal ways of solving problems. The teacher may have told them that their way is wrong or babyish, and so they are reluctant to talk about it. Or they may generally try to please adults by saying whatever it is that adults seem to want to hear. In cases like these, you have to communicate that you really want to learn about the child's ways of thinking. One way to do this is to say, "Can you now show me a different way to do it?" Or "Show me a new way." Or even "Do it a different way from how you do it at school."

Another approach to an uncommunicative child is to ask her to discuss examples of other children's work. "Here is how another kid in your class solved the problem. Here is what he said about how he did it. . . . What do you think about that?"

Shh!

On some occasions, a very important interview technique is to say nothing. Ask no questions. Do not rush the child or probe constantly. For example, when Toby counted by twos up to 12, apparently by rote memory, and could not go on, I simply waited for her to continue. It seemed like an eternity but was in fact only about 10 or 15 seconds.

143

This made her uncomfortable, I think, but had the virtue of conveying the message that I expected her to work hard at the problem and come up with a solution.

Doing nothing is of course harder for interviewers than doing something, especially when (as I have advised) they are attempting to take an active role in following up on the child's thought. But the child needs ample time to think and work out her methods of solution (and she needs to *learn* to think carefully if she doesn't already do it). The child needs to learn that you are not interested solely in quick, correct answers but take seriously, and indeed encourage, her attempts to think things through.

The danger in this tactic, of course, is in putting the child on the hot seat, making her uncomfortable. Here clinical judgment again comes into play. You have to decide whether the particular child can take the pressure and will profit from your silence. If the answer is yes, then just wait, and then maybe ask the question again before going on to something else.

Echo and Reflect

On some occasions the Rogerian technique of "reflection" may suffice to elicit interesting material. Instead of asking directly, "How did you do it?" or the like, you simply repeat or echo the child's last statement. For example, at one point Toby told me about her "robot book": "No, you see, we have this robot book, and that's how you do it, you see, you have all different math . . . it has a robot and, um, there's math on it." My response (partly because I did not know what she could be talking about) was a simple reflection: "So a robot book you have in class, and it has math on it?" Similarly, later on, Toby said, "Yeah . . . you could count them or count them with your fingers, but the teacher doesn't want you to count with your fingers," and I echoed, "She doesn't want you to count with your fingers?"

This approach is not appropriate at the beginning of the interview, when the child does not know that the focus is on exploring thinking, but it may be useful after you have already established the "rules of the game" and may have asked the "How did you do it?" question more times than may seem comfortable.

Ask for Justifications

Another way to elicit the child's thought processes is to ask for a proof that the answer is right or that the belief is correct. "How could you prove it to me?" "How could you make sure you are really right about that?" Asking in this manner for justifications does not require the child to introspect about the thought processes she used to obtain the solution or come to the belief. Rather, the request encourages the child to think about the issue, perhaps for the first time. Perhaps the child simply learned by rote memory that 2 + 2 is 4; now she has to figure out why that might be true. Perhaps the child did not realize that the magnitude of the damage was the factor determining a judgment of guilt; now she must explain to another the grounds for the judgment. Or perhaps the child does not know that she attributes life to any object that moves; now she must explicitly consider the criteria for a judgment of life. In general, a request for justification says to the child: "You may not have thought about this before, but think about it now."

Of course, such a request may not elicit from the child an account of the methods by which the problem was in fact solved. In Piaget's terms, the child's response may not be a "spontaneous conviction." The child may begin to think about the issue for the first time and produce new justifications. Of course, although new, these may be interesting and may provide insight into how the child now thinks about the issue, not how she did in fact come up with the solution or belief in question. In Piaget's terms (1976a, p. 11), the current justification is a "liberated conviction" which reflects the child's "natural tendencies of mind."

Explore

The interviewer begins with theoretical notions about the ways in which children think about certain problems: for example, that the young child sees inanimate objects as "alive," possessing minds and thoughts. But often the child responds in unexpected ways; her answers do not fit the interviewer's existing categories. According to the

145

child, the toy is not exactly alive, but it is not exactly a nonliving object either.

What to do? The strength of the clinical interview is that it allows the interviewer to explore the child's way of thinking, even if it is unusual or unexpected, even if it does not conform to the interviewer's hypotheses. After all, the ultimate issue is not what the interviewer has in mind; it is what is on the child's mind. So if the child does or says the unexpected, explore it. Follow the child's response wherever it leads. If the child uses an unusual method to solve a problem, don't worry about whether it fits your category; find out as much as you can about what the child did. If the child gives an unconventional reason for doing something, ask for an explanation and explore the underlying logic.

Help the Child to Introspect

As we saw in the case of Toby, the clinical interview may involve giving the child practice in introspection and its expression. After all, most children are not accustomed to examining their mental processes and talking about them. Even the most willing and cooperative child may have difficulty in talking about thinking. You need to help the child to observe her internal states and express in words what is observed. Indeed, the child needs to learn a new, shared vocabulary of the mind, a vocabulary that can make public what is ordinarily private. You and the child need to agree on what you both mean by *thinking* and *ideas*, and the like.

Of course, none of this is easy. As we have seen, many writers (Flavell et al., 1995; Piaget, 1976b) claim that young children in particular find it hard to introspect, and psychologists have disagreed for at least a century on the meaning of mentalistic terms like *mind* and *thinking*.

Observe

Despite your best efforts, some children may not say (and cannot learn to say) very much about their thinking. However, there is more to the clinical interview than recording and evaluating answers to questions and other verbal material. A major component of the clinical interview is observing the child's behavior very carefully for whatever clues it may offer about thinking. You can get useful information by observing how she is using her fingers when she does math, what she says when she whispers to herself, or what parts of a story she attends to when she reads. Look also at the child's facial expression and gestures; note pauses and pace; "paralinguistic" cues can convey meaning.

So, look carefully. Children's behavior often reveals a good deal about their thought.

Experiment

The interviewer can also learn about a child's thought by experimentation. A true experiment involves manipulating the "independent variable" (while holding other factors constant) and observing its effects on the "dependent variable," the subject's response.[13] Thus, you feed three different doses of a drug to an animal and observe the effects on learning to traverse a maze. If the animal learns the maze most quickly when the dose is high, you can conclude that dosage affects learning.

The clinical interview also involves experiments in the sense that the interviewer often presents planned variations on a problem, observes their effects on the child, and from this information makes inferences about response. At key moments, the interviewer introduces critical problems or experimental variations to decide among various hypotheses. For example, suppose that the child seems to believe that things are alive if they move. She does not tell you this directly, but that is your hunch. One way to check it is to determine whether the child attributes life to several different kinds of objects, some of which move (a car) and some of which don't (a candlestick). Movement then is the independent variable and judgments of life are the dependent variable, and you have performed an experiment (faulty as it may be)[14] to determine the relation between the two.

Piaget relied often on such experimental techniques, perhaps because he did not believe that children are proficient at introspection. Thus, in the case of conservation, Piaget varied the physical arrangement of two objects that were in some way equivalent (in length, volume, etc.) and determined whether these variations affected the child's judgment of their equivalence. The child did not have to say much about her reasoning; she needed only to indicate whether the two objects were the "same" or not. So don't rely solely on the child to tell you what she is thinking. Discover how she reacts to key variations in problems.

Consider next several "don'ts" – interview sins which should usually (with reference to the clinical interview, never say *never*) be avoided.

Don't Talk Too Much

The child should do most of the talking, not you. Of course, you have to be active, asking penetrating questions. But you should spend most of your time listening to what the child has to say and observing. If you are talking more than the child, something is wrong.

Don't Ask Leading Questions

Phrase your question in a neutral way so as to avoid suggesting an answer. "The golden rule is to avoid suggestion" (Piaget, 1976a, p. 13). Don't say, "Did you get the answer by . . . ?" Say instead, "What did you do to get this answer?" Don't say, "Which line of candies has more?" Say instead, "Do both lines of candies have the same number or does one line have more?"

Suspend the Tendency to Correct and Teach

As an interviewer, you must refrain from correcting and teaching (in the sense of providing direct instruction), except under certain circumstances to be described when we consider children's learning potential. Don't say, "No, you're wrong; this is how to do it." (And don't show your disapproval of an incorrect response by grimacing, scowling, or rolling your eyes.) Remember Binet and Simon's (1916) advice: "Naturally, one will not fall into the ridiculous error of teaching him; it is a question here of ascertaining the state of his mentality, not of teaching" (p. 295).

Of course, teaching the child is not always "ridiculous." It is certainly not ridiculous for the teacher to teach the child, and it is not ridiculous, under certain circumstances, for the interviewer to provide hints and even systematic assistance in order to explore what Vygotsky (1978) has called the Zone of Proximal Development (the child's learning potential, a topic to be discussed below). Also, it is sometimes useful to correct the child's misunderstanding of something unessential so that you can go on to the real issue. For example, if the child forgets the name of a character in a story, feel free to tell it to her, so that you can explore the issues the story is designed to cover. At the same time, you should not forget that your major goal is to determine how the child achieved the incorrect answer, not to correct her thinking (which in fact might have been very sensible). If your goal is to discover how the child in fact solved a problem, try not to teach.

Of course, there are exceptions to every rule – at least, to every rule of interviewing. Suppose that you discover that a child lacks some concept or is employing a seriously flawed strategy. Suppose further that the child realizes that there is something amiss and looks to you for help. Under these circumstances, can you refuse to help? Refusing may constitute an unethical violation of the trust you have established with the child. You know the child needs help and the child knows it too. How can you refuse to help? One simple solution is to tell the child that you still have some questions to ask but later on will provide help in the needed area.

In brief, focus on the child's thinking, not on correcting errors or teaching. Help the child later.

ESTABLISHING COMPETENCE

Two situations commonly arise in the course of an interview. The first is that you have been interviewing a child who has not been performing very well. You have made every effort to ensure that the child is well motivated. You have begun with easy problems, you have been encouraging her, and you have been supportive. You seem to have established a good relationship with the child and feel that the interview is going well. But she gives wrong answers and seems to employ immature strategies of solution. At this point your question is whether you have adequately assessed the child's competence. Is this the best she can do? Have you already reached the limits of her knowledge?

In the second situation you have also succeeded in laying the groundwork for a good interview. The child is motivated, she gives a correct answer, and she even describes a reasonable strategy for getting it. But you have the feeling that her success is more apparent than real; she may be "in over her head." She may not really understand her answer or the means for obtaining it. Your question here too is whether you have adequately assessed the child's competence. Does the correct answer really indicate an underlying understanding? Does she really understand the methods she used to get the correct answer?

In both cases, you want to find out whether the child's performance accurately reflects competence. Is the failing child capable of a higher level of performance? Several methods are useful for investigating this issue: rephrasing the initial question, changing the task, repeating and reviewing problems, and probing. Is the second child's success genuine? You may find out by employing countersuggestion.

Consider first the possible "false negative," the child who has done badly but may possess an underlying competence.

Rephrase the Question

If the child does not seem to know how to deal with one of your questions, perhaps saying "I don't know" or using an immature strategy, what can you conclude? Perhaps the failure merely indicates that the child has misunderstood the question and therefore is not dealing with the problem you wanted to pose. Or to put it another way, perhaps you have not yet succeeded at finding a good way to communicate with the child. Perhaps you haven't yet found the right question.

Why might the child misunderstand? One reason is that language is often ambiguous, particularly when it is used out of context, as is usually true of our language of testing and interviewing. Test items or interview questions usually refer not to real events in context, but to abstractions, to imagined events. We ask, "Which is bigger, a dog or a cat?" but no animal is in the testing room (and of course the generic dog or cat exists only in imagination as a prototype). Reality and context typically enter only in the form of stories. These may be realistic, but they are not real. The child being interviewed is not *in* the story; she must imagine it.

Under these conditions, there is room for a good deal of misunder-standing – or at least different understanding – on the part of the child. Indeed we might wish to coin a new word for this phenome-non, namely *diff-understanding,* in which the tester or interviewer poses one question but the child understands it as a different one and hence responds with a "mistake" to the original question (but not to the question as interpreted by the child). No doubt the term *diff-understanding* will not catch on, but it makes the important point that children's mistakes may make a certain kind of sense. Your first task therefore is to determine whether the child has understood the ques-tion in the way you intend. Does the child know what aspects of the problem you would like him or her to deal with, or did the child diff-understand?

One way to find out is simply to ask him or her to repeat the question, or better still reformulate it. Suppose you point to the writ-ten numbers 12 and 34 and say, "Add these numbers." The child gets 10. You then ask, "What was the question I asked you? Tell me in a different way." Or "Tell me what I'm asking you to do."[15] The child says, "You asked me to add these up, so I did 1 plus 2 plus 3 plus 4." The answer indicates that the child diff-understood.

Another approach is to rephrase the question. Suppose you say, "The cat is big. The mouse is small. Which animal is big?" The child cannot give an answer. Hypothesizing that the child does not under-stand the word *animal* but really does have the concept of *bigger,* you then rephrase, saying, "Which one is bigger than the other?"[16] Per-haps this question will manage to tap the child's understanding of relative size.

Misunderstanding or diff-understanding is always a possibility. Hence, when you are preparing basic problems before the interview, try this exercise: Think of three or four ways of rewording each basic question. Of course, during an actual interview, you will not enjoy the luxury of a quiet interval in which to create and contemplate various alternatives. The exigencies of the clinical interview demand that you develop rewordings on the spot, in immediate response to what you believe to be the child's particular ways of misunderstanding or diff-understanding the question.

So if the child does not seem to understand your question, rephrase it. If the child does not seem to understand the problem, present it in a different way. Because you are not engaged in standardized testing, you should not feel bound by the constraint to present the same (objective) problem to all children. You can, indeed should, treat each child differently. Do whatever it takes to have the child understand the problem – that is, to make it subjectively equivalent for all.

Change the Task

You may even wish to change more than the wording. You may change major features of the problem itself, making it different or more specific or more concrete. Instead of asking about classification in the abstract ("Are there more cats or more animals?"), use objects to demonstrate and ask questions about them. Embed the problem in a context. Instead of asking whether this line is longer than this, tell a story about two fishing poles and embed your question about length in that.

At the same time, remember that children differ in their "preferences" for certain kinds of tasks. In general, children will do better with concrete manipulatives than with written problems. But the reverse may be true too: A few children will prefer abstract mental problems to manipulatives. (One of my daughters genuinely enjoyed memorizing number facts.)

The moral is that you never know what will work; be flexible enough to try almost anything.

Repeat and Review

Suppose that you have asked the "How did you do it?" question in an attempt to uncover the child's thought. You cannot just sit back and relax, expecting the child to provide you with full details about her thought. Indeed, the child's response is likely to be incomplete, unclear, or ambiguous, and you should not necessarily believe everything that is said. The child may *seem* to indicate that the sun is alive. But does she really believe this? Is the wording of the reply ambiguous? Is the answer a fluke, indicating nothing significant about her competence? You have to clarify the child's remarks; you must obtain additional evidence in order to make sound interpretations concerning competence.

What to do? One approach is to repeat the problem and to ask the child to explain more carefully, and slowly, how she solved it, what she thought about it, etc. You can say, "I didn't quite understand what you meant, so let's do the problem over again and this time, try to tell me again how you are doing it. Let's go over it more slowly this time."

Another approach is to present the child with several similar, but not identical, problems in order to determine whether the child exhibits the same behavior or offers the same explanations in all cases. You should attempt to "replicate" findings within the clinical interview, to establish the reliability of the child's response. In general, your interpretations gain in plausibility to the extent that your data – that is, your interview observations – indicate that a particular behavior or thought process can be reliably observed.

Probe

Another approach to resolving ambiguity is to ask further questions, to probe, to dig deeper, all in an effort to clarify the child's response and to gain deeper insight into her thought. You need to say things like "What did you mean by that?" "Tell me more," and the like. Keep up the chase until you have gathered enough evidence to make a plausible interpretation of the child's behavior, or until the child seems to have nothing more to say (or at least is unable to add anything informative).

But don't push the child to the point of making her feel uncomfortable or stupid. Some children eventually get fed up with numerous requests for explanation. Thus, when repeatedly asked, "How did you get the answer?" 6-year-old Sam[17] protested: "I just did. From my brain. From my mind. From my brain and my mind and everything else." And finally, "You told [asked] me too many times!"

Offer Countersuggestions

Finally, consider the "false-positive," the case of the child who *seems* to have done well but may not really possess the competence suggested. She got the right answer; she used a reasonable strategy. But several aspects of her behavior may make you suspicious about whether she really understands. Perhaps her responses seem to be parroted; perhaps she answers with a questioning tone; perhaps she exhibits uncertainty with shrugs of the shoulder or body language; perhaps her answers seem tentative.

If you suspect the child's answer is superficial, challenge it. This can be done in one of at least two ways. The first is to present a countersuggestion, that is, a verbal contradiction of what the child has just said. In the conservation of liquids problem, the child is first shown two identical glasses, both filled with liquid, and judges that the amounts are the same. Then liquid from one glass is poured into another, taller container. Does the child recognize that despite this visible transformation, the amounts still remain the same? Suppose that a child seems to succeed at this problem, arguing that both glasses of liquid have "the same to drink." Using countersuggestion, you can say, "No, this one has more to drink because it is taller." Or "I just saw Sarita, and she said that the taller one has more. What do you think about that?" In this situation, the child who really understands conservation will stick with the answer and even explain it; the child whose response is superficial may well accept the wrong answer merely because you suggested it. Indeed, the ability to resist counter-suggestion should be considered an important criterion for demon-strating true understanding.

Another kind of countersuggestion involves the use of extreme examples. Suppose the child says that the taller and shorter glasses have the same amount to drink. Show her a very wide, flat glass contrasted with a very tall, thin one, a narrow tube. Will she still maintain her belief in the face of so striking a contrast? Or suppose the child says that intention should determine culpability, not amount of damage. By this logic, the boy who broke 10 dishes accidentally is less guilty than the girl who broke just 2 in the course of an intentionally mischievous act. But then offer this extreme example: Suppose that the virtuous boy broke 100 accidentally, whereas the naughty girl broke only 1. Is the boy still less guilty? If the child maintains her judgment about the priority of intention despite this extreme example, her belief seems to rest on a solid foundation.

Countersuggestions are effective but should not be undertaken until you have developed a comfortable and trusting relationship with the child.

DETERMINING LEARNING POTENTIAL

As we saw in chapter 2, Vygotsky broadened the approach to assessment by introducing the notion of the Zone of Proximal Development (Vygotsky, 1978). The basic idea is that the child's intelligence should not be considered only in a static fashion, as some kind of fixed attribute or mental operation in isolation from social context. If the child acting alone cannot solve a problem, perhaps she will overcome the difficulty when provided with some form of social support. In Vygotsky's view, it is vital to focus not only on the child's "actual developmental level as determined by independent problem solving" but also on the child's "level of potential development" in a facilitating social context (p. 86).

How can we use the clinical interview to measure this kind of potential development? Providing "adult guidance," as Vygotsky suggested, seems to involve a continuum of techniques that range from minimal "hints" to overt teaching (direct instruction). Even a simple rephrasing of a question can be said to provide a "hint," as can placing a problem in a concrete context. Indeed, such forms of adult assistance are integral to the classic Piagetian clinical interview. And direct instruction (which Piaget avoided, and Binet and Simon termed a "ridiculous error") certainly is one way to provide adult guidance.

For purposes of exposition, we now consider hints and teaching as separate categories. But do not forget that they are points on a continuum and that forms of adult assistance may partake to some degree of both. At one extreme, how does the child perform only with the minimal help provided by hints? Under these conditions, does she more or less spontaneously reorganize her thinking to deal with the problem? At the other extreme, how does she respond to more directed, but brief, teaching? Does she assimilate it well, thus indicating that she can profit from instruction in this area?

Provide Hints

Hints do not "give away" the answer. They provide information that is only indirectly relevant to solving or thinking about the problem. If the child responds quickly and successfully to hints, at least two interpretations are possible. Either the child "already knew" the material and the hint simply helped her to access it, or the child was already close to knowing the material and the hints merely provided a slight impetus to complete the process. In both cases, the hints show something about the child's potential developmental level, not just her actual, current, static level.

Here are a few examples. A child is told a story about a farm and the various animals living on it (Newcomer & Ginsburg, 1995).[18] The child is then asked, "Why don't the pigs live in the house?" If the child cannot answer this question, it is rephrased: "Why do the pigs have to live in the pigpen? Why won't they let the pigs live in the house?" The first question merely asks for an explanation of the pigs' absence from the house; the rephrased question implies that humans do not let pigs live in the house for some good reason, which it is now the child's job to discover. If the child still cannot answer, the following hint is given: "What do you know about pigs? Are they clean? Do they smell good? Would you like a pig to live in your house? Why?" Note that the hint doesn't directly provide the answer (that humans don't want pigs in the house because they stink, etc.). Instead, it places the question in the context of the child's experiences and raises all of the relevant issues.

In another question the child is asked whether it is true or false that all flowers are roses. If the child is wrong, the hint is: "Think about the flowers you have seen. Can you name some flowers? Are they all roses?" If the child says no, then the original question is repeated. Again, this hint does not give away the answer. Instead, the original question is simply related to the child's relevant experiences, which of course should be relevant to answering it.

Teach

Teaching (direct instruction) provides information that is directly relevant to solving the problem. If teaching is effective, then at least some degree of learning potential has been demonstrated. Consider an example involving simple arithmetic (Ginsburg, 1990). The child is first asked to determine "in her head" whether 32 is closer in value to 24 or 62. Judgments like these require a kind of "mental number line." If the child is not successful, a hint is provided: "Try to do it by counting. See if that will help." Note that this is quite indirect, simply pointing the child to a relevant strategy. But suppose that does not work. Then the interviewer says: "You can tell how close they are by trying to count. We can count from 24 to 32 like this: 24, 25, . . . , 32. Twenty-four is not too far away from 32. But think about how long it would take to count from 32 to 62. Try it. It's really far away." In this case, considerable information is provided: The child is shown how to count to solve the problem and is even shown how to do this particular mental number line problem. If the child is successful on this and similar problems, we will have learned something about her learning potential: Although she requires considerable adult assistance, she is capable of learning a rather abstract procedure involving the mental number line.

Traipsing Through the Zone of Proximal Development

Many examples of adult assistance do not fall neatly into the categories of hints or teaching. Here is an example.

At age 4 years 10 months, Max was asked to "draw a person" (an item from a well-known intelligence test). He drew a line on the answer sheet and said, "I can only draw that."[19]

I: What is that?

M: A line.

I: What does a person look like? You are a person, what do you have? What are your parts?

Max pointed to his head and said "head."

I: Right, you have a head.

Max then ran his hands over his legs and said "legs."

The interviewer asked if he could draw a head and he drew a circle. Interviewer and child then proceeded along these lines with the major parts of his body. He ran his hands over his legs, arms, and head, as if trying to feel his limbs in their entirety in order to be able to visualize them enough to reproduce them on paper. In this way, he was able to draw the major parts of a person. When he finished this he exclaimed: "I drawed a person! I knew I could draw a person."

The degree to which this example illustrates hinting or teaching is difficult to determine. But whatever the precise mix, the procedure seems to reveal something valuable about the child's competence.

EPILOG

Even the most experienced interviewer never conducts a completely successful interview. In a sense, you never finish the interview. You always wish that you had said something different. You always think of something that you could have said. You almost never learn as much as you would like about the child. But even if your interview is imperfect, as it must be, you are likely to learn something about the child's mind, and the child might too.

CHAPTER 5

Evaluating Clinical Interviews: How Good Are They?

American authors, who love to do things big, often publish experiments made on hundreds or even thousands of persons; they believe that the conclusive value of a study is proportional to the number of observations. That is only an illusion.

Binet, in Cairns, "Phenomena Lost"

Questions about the objectivity, reliability, validity, and replicability of findings – the standard issues of scientific research – will continue to be asked, but answers will take a form consistent with the new perspective rather than with the outworn mainstream model.

Mishler, *Research Interviewing*

This chapter is necessarily heavier and more technical than the rest, because evaluating the clinical interview requires some specialized "psychometric" concepts and arguments. I try to present the technical material in as clear and simple a way as possible, so that beginners can understand it. More advanced students can, I think, profit from the somewhat novel view of reliability and validity presented here. Of course, those already convinced of the method's value may wish to skip the chapter entirely and proceed to the next.

THE NEED FOR EVALUATION

I have tried to make as strong a case for the clinical interview as possible, arguing that it can be a valuable method for both research

159

and practice. For many purposes, the clinical interview seems to be more powerful than the traditional, standardized methods of psychology, specifically tests and controlled laboratory tasks. Indeed, I have argued that the importance of these paragons of the "scientific method" in psychology has been overblown: They are the emperor's new clothes. Yet every method, including the clinical interview, suffers from limitations and weaknesses that must be acknowledged, understood, and confronted. Indeed, the potential dangers of a human measuring instrument like the clinical interview are obvious. A technique which draws so heavily on the interviewer's imagination, ingenuity, and sensitivity, and which demands judgment quickly rendered, is clearly delicate, fragile, and easily susceptible to error. Think of how many things could go wrong in a given interview! Leading questions, intimidation, failure to pursue important leads, misinterpretations of the child's responses – these are only some of the potential dangers.

So the task now is to evaluate the clinical interview. How good is it? Can it be as powerful as I claim? In traditional psychometrics, to ask whether a method is "good" is to inquire into the extent to which it meets the criteria sanctified by the holy trinity of objectivity, reliability, and validity. Was the test instrument administered in the same way to all? Was the scoring criterion clear and employed carefully, so as to elicit agreement among raters? Were the responses stable? And do they correlate positively with related measures? But as the epigraph from Mishler heading this chapter maintains, the old framework of psychometrics is "outworn," at least for certain purposes, and its assumptions have come under increasingly heavy attack. At the end of the 20th century, we all agree (well, almost all) that scientific method does not operate in a mechanically "objective" manner, free of theoretical preconception, unburdened by values, untouched by social influence, and leading inexorably to certainty and the ultimate truth. A confident and cheerfully simpleminded positivism is no longer our methodological god and guide.

Although the new methodological age challenges positivism and scientism with new insights from the "phenomenological-interpretive perspective, . . . constructivist epistemology, feminist methodologies, poststructuralism, postmodernism, and critical hermeneutics" (Schwandt, 1994, p. 130) – what a mouthful! – we should avoid being seduced by the rhetoric. Yes, the "goodness" of the clinical interview needs to be evaluated differently from the "goodness" of traditional methods, but the clinical interview does need to be evaluated. We need to employ the clinical interview, or any other method, with rigor. We must insist on critical examination of the clinical interview, an evaluation that is sensible and sensitive and at the same time champions "objectivity." By this I mean simply that as a scientific method, the clinical interview should yield interpretations that are "rationally warranted, reasonable, or defensible – that is, well founded rather than groundless opinions" (Toulmin, 1982, p. 115, quoted in Eisner, 1991, p. 51).

I start with the basic assumption that the clinical interview needs to be as "objective" as possible. The method should respect evidence and employ it in a judicious manner and should not be subject to the whims, biases, or fantasies of individual investigators. Its interpretations should be scrutinized: Not all of them are equally valid, useful, sensible, or acceptable. "Objectivity, though the term has been taken by some to suggest a naive and inhumane version of vulgar positivism, is the essential basis of all good research. Without it, the only reason the reader of the research might have for accepting the conclusions of the investigator would be an authoritarian respect for the person of the author" (Kirk & Miller, 1986, p. 20). Surely the aim of the postmodernist and critical psychology manifesto is not to supplant the rigidity of traditional science with the terrorism of fanciful opinion.

There is another, and more important, reason for striving for objectivity. Remember Binet's critique of the "alienists," who used idiosyncratic techniques to assign diagnostic labels to children experiencing difficulty in school. Lacking objectivity, their methods resulted in a good deal of harm to many children. We do not want the clinical interview to produce the same result.

Therefore, in this chapter I examine the goodness of the clinical interview, asking how one can determine the extent to which a particular use of the method can be considered objective and the extent to which it can be said to yield reliable and valid information. My effort at evaluation will be based on modern conceptions of objectivity, reliability, and validity (e.g., Delandshire & Petrosky, 1994; Messick, 1989; Moss, 1994) – conceptions I believe to be appropriate to the special characteristics of the clinical interview.

Up to this point, I have been referring to *the* clinical interview, as if it were one technique. But as we have seen, there is no one clinical interview. For different purposes, the method takes different forms, each of which must be evaluated by appropriate criteria. I therefore consider the effectiveness of three different uses of the clinical interview: exploration, focused research, and intensive study. I also discuss the issue of whether different criteria need to be applied to the evaluation of the clinical interview for purposes of research and practice. I argue that research and practice differ less than we ordinarily suppose, so that the same reformulated notions of objectivity, reliability, and validity can be used to evaluate the clinical interview in both cases.

I should tell you from the outset, however, that my "evaluation" is based on very little empirical evidence. The clinical interview has seldom been studied, perhaps because psychology has not considered it a legitimate method and perhaps because we have not known how to study it. In any event, my discussion is largely speculative, centering much more on what ought to be known about the clinical interview than on what is known.

EXPLORATION

There is little disagreement concerning the value of using the clinical interview for purposes of exploration in both research and practice. In research, exploration involving the clinical interview (or other methods, like observation) may be used for several purposes. One of these is to develop and refine one's hunches, ideas, and hypotheses. Suppose that the investigator has the suspicion that children develop notions about how schools function and what it takes to be successful in them. Suppose further that the available research literature provides little guidance concerning the nature of these ideas. What to do? The investigator develops a few general questions which are then used as the basis for free-floating interviews with children. The intent is "emic," in the sense of attempting to appreciate the child's point of view, to allow the categories of analysis to emerge from the data, and to avoid (as much as is possible) imposing the researcher's preconceptions on the investigation. In a bootstrap operation, the initial interviews are used to suggest categories for analysis; further questions are developed to test hypotheses; and the cycle repeats itself several times, eventually resulting, if the work is successful, in a gradual refinement of the categories, hypotheses, and questions.

Exploration thus conceived is much more than discovering whether a particular task the researcher has devised "works" with certain children. Rather, it is discovering how the children "work" and then devising tasks to assess the processes involved. Indeed, exploration is the approach that a constructivist *must* take in initiating research. If children construct worlds that are in some ways idiosyncratic and different from the adult's, then the researcher must attempt to "enter the children's minds" in order to grasp that separate reality.

How can one judge the goodness of the clinical interview when used for purposes of exploration? There is widespread agreement that the traditional criteria of objectivity, reliability, and validity do not apply in this case. This is so because exploration does not involve measurement in the sense of obtaining information about some clearly defined psychological characteristic. Instead, exploration is all about the search for ideas that can be investigated. And if this is the case, one judges the exploration solely on the basis of its success in stimulating the creation of both good ideas and research designed to investigate them. The proof is in the pudding of theory and data, not in the following of some finicky guidelines of proper research etiquette.

Most investigators are likely to concur that in exploration, almost anything goes. Yet my impression is that not enough researchers appreciate the real value of exploration and know how to engage in it. They pay lip service to the argument that exploration is a good thing, a desideratum of research, but seldom devote to it the effort it requires. They seldom write about it to any extent; they seldom train their students how to do it. They see exploration as "fooling around"; it is not serious scientific work. Theirs is the unfortunate view that the essence of "scientific" research is the endgame, the formal study, the context of verification, not the context of discovery that leads to the endgame and indeed makes it valuable and possible. But both exploration and validation – both discovery and verification – are essential. And if researchers downplay exploration, they are in danger of getting caught up in the technicalities of method and in the ephemeral fads of research activity. They are also in danger of relying too heavily on a sometimes myopic research literature and of becoming smugly oblivious to realities that can be ascertained – indeed, they often hit you over the head – from exploratory interviews and observations.

Researchers should use the clinical interview to explore, to immerse themselves in the data, and to attempt to develop ideas and categories responsive to the data of children's worlds. After all, this was a vital part of Piaget's approach, and it was very successful. (In the last chapter, I present a simple exercise for helping students to do this.)

Practitioners need to do the same thing, and more. Like the researcher, the practitioner needs to develop a theory and test it. The main difference between the two is that the practitioner's theory attempts to explain the *individual* child's functioning, not the functioning of children in general. The researcher attempts to generalize to all children, or at least all children of a certain age or type; the practitioner is not interested in generalizing beyond the individual child who is being assessed and then (hopefully) helped. But both researcher and practitioner create theories and use evidence to test them (Ginsburg, 1986a).

Practitioners should be as open as researchers to new theoretical insights. Practitioners should not limit themselves to employing existing analytic systems in order to impose preconceived diagnostic categories on the child (he or she is "learning disabled" or has low "reading aptitude" and the like). Instead, good assessment requires sensitivity to the distinctive problems of individuals. And often exploration will allow the practitioner to glimpse a reality different from that described by the limited world view of standard diagnostic categories. Perhaps, for example, the child's difficulty in mathematics is caused not by low aptitude but by a misunderstanding of some material poorly explained by the teacher (Ginsburg, 1997).

Practitioners can also use the exploratory clinical interview to obtain background information about the children being studied: their interests, the nature of the work they are doing in school, the material they find easy or difficult. Children's responses to open-ended questions about these matters may help the investigator to get the "lay of the land" – that is, the children often reveal a good deal about their personalities and motivation, their cognitive styles, the language they use, and the degree to which they are introspective and expressive. Information of this type may help the practitioner to conduct an effective assessment and may bear at least indirectly on the child's problems.

One evaluates the practitioner's explorations, not by the criteria of standard research, but by success in generating insights into the child's functioning. The practitioner's explorations are successful to the extent that they lead to interesting and testable hypotheses concerning the children being assessed.

In brief, one of the great benefits of the clinical interview for researcher and practitioner alike is the promotion of an exploration that can lead to sensitive insight into others' minds.

FOCUSED RESEARCH

In recent years, use of the clinical interview in a relatively focused form has become increasingly prevalent and acceptable. In this section, I first describe basic aspects of this use of the clinical interview and then present some information on its reliability and validity.

The Method

The clinical interview is used in focused research something like this: Perhaps as a result of exploratory investigations, or simply in response to an existing research literature, the investigator wishes to examine some particular concepts or strategies in the population of interest. Perhaps the researcher wishes to know whether children's theory of mind develops along certain lines, whether concepts of justice are general or tied to particular contents and contexts, or whether children employ certain strategies in evaluating scientific evidence. The researcher devises key tasks to be used as the basis for an interview or, better still, uses available tasks and then delineates clear definitions of the concepts or strategies under consideration. All children receive the same tasks and the children's behavior is always evaluated in terms of the concepts and strategies of interest to the investigator.

All this is very similar to what usually transpires in standardized testing or in conventional "laboratory" research. The key difference is that use of the clinical interview involves individualized patterns of questioning. Although administering identical tasks to all subjects (at least at the outset), the examiner is free to question each subject in a relatively flexible and deliberately nonstandardized fashion, using the various probes and contingent methods characteristic of the clinical interview. So although all subjects may at first be asked, "What makes this toy car go faster than that one?" the subsequent line of questioning may vary to some degree for each child. But because the investigator needs to evaluate responses in terms of preestablished categories, the variability in questioning is not likely to be extensive. If the investigator must decide whether responses are of Type A, B, or C, then certain common questions are likely to be employed across subjects. The need to categorize in limited ways constrains the flexibility of the examiner, with the result that this type of clinical interview may differ little from the traditional approach employing standardized administration.

We see then that in focused research using the clinical interview, the initial task is standardized and a uniform scoring system is employed. But the method of administration of the task is deliberately nonstandardized and may vary *to some extent* across subjects. And of course the resulting data – the children's behavior and responses to questions – are complex and sometimes difficult to evaluate by means of a uniform scoring system.

An example of this approach is provided by D. Kuhn, Garcia-Mila, Zohar, and Anderson (1995). In this microgenetic study, individual children and adults were repeatedly presented, over a period of some 10 weeks, with four complex problems, two in the physical domain and two in the social. For example, one problem involved determining what factors (e.g., size, weight, depth of water) influenced the speed with which different toy boats moved down a tank of water. (The problem is analogous to the scientific-reasoning tasks introduced by Inhelder & Piaget, 1958.) Throughout the course of the study, a controlled form of interviewing was employed to analyze subjects' methods for investigating the causal structure of the phenomena in question and to uncover their causal theories. "The interviewer asked a range of questions ('What are you going to find out?' 'What do you think the outcome will be?' 'What have you found out?') but provided no direction or feedback. . . . By means of probes used as necessary, it was made clear to the subjects that the task was to identify the causal relations operating in the specific database being examined" (D. Kuhn et al., 1995, p. 25). In brief, the interviewer had available several basic questions, along with probes, and was free to use them "as necessary" (i.e., with flexibility) in order to investigate subjects' theories and strategies of solution.

Liben and Downs (1991) have developed an organized system for probing children's responses to open-ended clinical interview questions about maps. The interview was devised to see first what children identified spontaneously in maps (rivers, roads, etc.), but then, if children failed to comment on a particular feature, a series of increasingly specific probes was employed (e.g., "What do you think this might be?"), and finally, if all else failed, the examiner inquired into a specific possibility ("I think maybe this could be a _____. What do you think?").

Practitioners sometimes take a similar approach. One example is provided by a system of "organized probes" – a highly structured and limited form of clinical interviewing (Ginsburg, 1990) – used in conjunction with standardized testing of children's mathematical abilities. The general idea was that after administering the standardized Test of Early Mathematics Ability (or TEMA) (Ginsburg & Baroody, 1990), many examiners would find it useful to probe further into the thought processes that produced the observed performance, particularly in the case of errors. Many examiners find this difficult to do because they have not had training or experience in assessing students' thinking. Consequently, I tried to provide examiners with a structured and comfortable procedure for probing the strategies and concepts underlying students' responses to the TEMA.

To illustrate, in the case of concrete addition, the basic TEMA question is: "Joey has two pennies. He gets one more penny. How many does he have altogether? If you want, you can use your fingers to help you find your answer." (As the questions are asked, the examiner shows the child the numbers of pennies involved.) Under conditions of standardized test administration, the examiner may or may not learn from the child's overt behavior what problem-solving process was employed.

The organized probes help the examiner to determine whether the student used such procedures as counting on the fingers, mental counting, or memorized number facts. Three types of probes are available for this item, and the examiner is free to use them as necessary. The first is: "It's OK to use your fingers. Put your hands on the table and show me how you do this. Tell me out loud what you are doing." This encourages both externalization of the strategy in behavior and thinking aloud. In response, some children who had previously thought that it is improper or even cheating to use the fingers breathe a sigh of relief and show the examiner their finger-counting procedure or tell about it. A second question is: "How did you know the answer was _____?" In this case, some children say, "I know that 3 and 2 is 5 because I just knew the answer. I learned it." If the answer was given quickly, the child's explanation may be a good indication of the use of memorized facts. A third question is: "Why does 6 pennies and 2 make _____ altogether?" In response to this question, some children say, "It had to be 8 because I know that 6 and 1 is 7 and then 1 more must be 8." Here the use of a reasoning strategy is evident. These probes are analogous to the sorts of relatively controlled interviewing employed in research, as described earlier.

Reliability and Related Issues

How does one evaluate focused-interview methods or probes? The traditional psychometric criteria of reliability are useful for organizing our thinking about this issue. From a psychometric point of view, the basic questions are these: Do independent observers agree on their categorization of interview responses? Do different interviewers produce the same types of responses in individual children? Are responses to a clinical interview stable over time or across children? In examining these issues, we should keep in mind that the reliability of the clinical interview cannot be established *in general.* The clinical interview refers, not to a particular measurement device, but to a general approach, which takes different forms for different purposes. Therefore, just as one must determine separately the reliability of each individual test, so it is necessary to determine the reliability of the clinical interview as used in each particular investigation. Whatever the evidence, we will not be able to conclude that *any* use of the clinical interview is reliable to some degree. Instead, we may conclude from the evidence only that the clinical interview *can* achieve some level of reliability under certain circumstances.

INTER-OBSERVER RELIABILITY

Suppose that I do a relatively focused clinical interview to determine whether a child uses a realistic form of moral judgment ("He is guilty because he broke a lot of cups even if he didn't mean to.") or a relativistic form of moral judgment ("He is guilty because he deliberately broke one cup."). In doing the interview, I use the same basic set of questions ("Who is more guilty? How do you know? Why is he more guilty?" etc.) but I have the freedom to vary them a bit and to probe as necessary. Children's responses to these types of questions will vary to a considerable degree, especially when they explain why a particular child is guilty. Given the variability of questions and the complexity of response to "why?" questions, one basic issue is whether independent but knowledgeable observers agree on what they see in such data. To what extent do they agree in their categorization (coding) of the data? Does an independent observer see realistic moral judgment where I do? This is the classic issue of inter-observer reliability.

Research shows that the clinical interview can achieve acceptable levels of inter-observer (or inter-rater) reliability. A clinical interview study of arithmetic strategies in second-grade students showed: "For the ADDITION section agreement on accuracy was 100%, for strategy / error codes, 96%. In the MENTAL ADDITION section, agreement on accuracy was 99%, on strategies, 93%, and for errors, 81%. Overall agreement (all sections combined) was 99% on accuracy and 94% on process components" (Jones, 1986, p. 53).

In a clinical interview study of moral judgment regarding abortion,

169

50% of the interviews were coded by independent raters. Inter-observer agreement on mode of reasoning (moral, personal, mixed) was 89% (Smetana, 1982). Similarly, independent ratings of a sample of 16 interviews centering on adolescent–parent conflicts resulted in kappa reliabilities ranging between .89 and .93.

Clearly, the clinical interview *need* not be deficient with regard to inter-observer reliability (although like any other method it *can* be if used poorly).

ALTERNATE-FORM RELIABILITY

Alternate-form reliability usually refers to a situation in which the question is the extent to which two apparently equivalent forms of the same test yield the same results. Does IQ Test Form A yield essentially the same score as IQ Test Form B? The analog in the case of the clinical interview is the extent to which two independent interviewers, both examining the same child, come up with the same results. If I interview Eileen and so do you, do we agree that she uses Strategy X and not Strategy Y?

To my knowledge only one study directly investigating this issue has been performed. In the study of arithmetic strategies described earlier, one interviewer examined all of the 69 second graders, and a second interviewer examined a sample of 10 of the same children (Jones, 1986). The goal was to identify the written and mental-addition strategies which the children employed. The interviews were taped and independent judges coded the interview results using transcripts of the videos and the students' written work. (As we saw earlier, there was a high degree of inter-rater agreement on this categorization.) The relevant question concerning alternate-form (or, better still, "alternate-interviewer") reliability is the extent to which the two independent interviewers of the same 10 children produced similar strategy categorizations. The results showed that coefficients of agreement ranged between .70 and .92 on different categories (Jones, 1986, p. 55).

INTERNAL CONSISTENCY

Suppose that a test contains several items designed to measure the same trait. The issue of internal consistency refers to the extent to which the child responds in the same way to all items. The analog for clinical interviewing is something like this: Suppose I give the child several problems which are essentially the same in structure (e.g., several moral dilemmas involving lying) and conduct a clinical interview concerning the child's concepts or strategies of solution. Does the child use the same strategies in response to all of the problems?

Again, I know of only one investigation dealing with this issue, the study by Jones (1986). She found that the internal consistency of items measuring arithmetic strategies (like writing numbers as they sound, as in the case of 201 for *twenty-one*, 404 for *forty-four*) was relatively high, with an alpha coefficient of .81 (p. 41).

TEST–RETEST RELIABILITY

If you take an achievement test on Day 1 and then again on Day 2, your scores ought to be about the same. You could not have learned enough in the short time interval between the two testings to improve your performance significantly. Similarly, if a clinical interview shows that on Day 1 you use Strategy X, presumably a second clinical interview on the next day, before you have had much relevant experience, ought to show that you continue to use Strategy X. This is the issue of test–retest reliability. Jones found that test–retest correlations for various categories of arithmetic reasoning ranged from .60 to 1.00 (p. 55).

DOUBTS ABOUT RELIABILITY

The clinical interview can achieve acceptable levels of internal consistency and test–retest reliability. But is such consistency desirable? Not necessarily. Suppose that children do not respond in consistent ways to different interview items. They use one strategy on one item and another on a second. Or they respond in one way on Day 1 and another on Day 2. In at least some cases, this may not imply any inadequacy in the interview method. The inconsistency may simply be an accurate measure of the lack of stability in children's strategy use – a phenomenon stressed in recent theorizing (Lemaire & Siegler, 1995; Siegler, 1988). Even Piaget, who intended to investigate basic and enduring cognitive structures, observed considerable *décalage*, or unevenness, in children's behavior (Piaget, 1971). In brief, low internal consistency or test–retest reliability may say more about the true state of the child than about the reliability of the measuring instrument.

Consider next the perils of alternate-interviewer reliability. Suppose that a child uses a different strategy in response to each of two independent interviewers. Does this mean that the interviewers are inconsistent or that they have measured correctly the child's true inconsistency? These interpretations may be hard to disentangle from one another. Or conversely, suppose that both interviewers find that the child uses the same strategy. This kind of reliability may be spurious: A broken thermometer may always produce a reading of 65°. "'Quixotic reliability' refers to the circumstances in which a single method of observation continually yields an unvarying measurement. The problem with reliability of this sort is that it is trivial and misleading. . . . Americans, for example, reliably respond to the question, 'How are you?' with the knee-jerk 'Fine.' The reliability of this answer does not make it useful data about how Americans are" (Kirk & Miller, 1986, p. 41). For these reasons, good agreement between independent interviewers may be suspect. For example, both may be biased, all too ready to read certain interpretations into the data.

How can one guard against bias of this sort? The reliability coefficient itself, and the kind of data that go into calculating it, are of no help in this regard. Other types of information are necessary to investigate the possibility of this type of bias: for example, information concerning the types of questions the interviewer asks (were leading questions employed?) and the ways in which they are asked (tone of voice? intimidating manner?). This issue will be discussed in greater detail later when we consider the evaluation of the clinical interview used for purposes of intensive study.

GENERALIZATION

One very striking phenomenon involving the clinical interview is that the *qualitative* results can show remarkable consistency across children. It is often possible to generalize results quite widely. "What's so remarkable is that the answers show an unbelievable convergence" (Piaget, 1976a, p. 25). Use of the relatively focused clinical interview can elicit highly similar responses across a wide range of subjects living under dramatically varying conditions. Asked to explain, in the conservation problem, why a short row of seven objects has more than a longer row of seven objects, different kinds of children consistently answer, "because you spread them out!" This kind of regularity is especially remarkable when it is observed in children of drastically different cultures. For example, Opper's research shows that "in many cases Thai and Malaysian children's arguments [concerning classification] are virtually identical to those of Swiss children" (Ginsburg & Opper, 1988, p. 131).

Similarly, Inhelder points to the consistency of qualitative results across varying problems: "Each theme is studied via a considerable number of different experiments which complement one another" (1989, p. 215). Thus, the results for the conservation of number are generally similar to those concerning the conservation of continuous quantity, and this too indicates a high degree of generality of qualitative phenomena uncovered by the clinical interview. In non-Piagetian studies, the same type of generality can be observed in studies of mathematical thinking in the school setting. Children in the Ivory Coast, in Africa, describe their arithmetic strategies and "bugs" in virtually the same words as American children (Ginsburg, Posner, & Russell, 1981).

The bottom line is this: The clinical interview can reveal consistent results involving the processes of thinking across a wide range of children and across different (but theoretically related) tasks.

REPLICABILITY

The issue of reliability can be approached in a basic way by asking whether clinical interview results can generally be replicated. This is a broader and more fundamental question than the narrow and technical issue of test–retest reliability. The question of replication refers to the core issue of whether clinical interview results can be obtained by any qualified, independent observer. The answer is that the clinical interview method has had a good history of replication. Indeed, clinical interview results – particularly Piaget's – are among the most replicable *in all of psychology.* Any competent investigator interviewing a child anywhere in the world can replicate Piaget's basic conservation results or moral-judgment findings. By contrast, it is difficult to replicate some of the basic laboratory findings concerning conditioning and learning (Kimble, 1961).

Undeniably, the clinical interview can produce replicable results. Many would maintain that replication is the key test of scientific method.

CONCLUSIONS

If the intent is to use the clinical interview in a focused manner, to measure constructs identified by previous research or pilot study, then at least two independent observers should agree on categorizing the results. Inter-observer reliability is crucial. The very limited amount of available evidence suggests that inter-observer reliability for the coding of clinical interview results can reach high levels. This should come as no surprise. Since the early days of IQ testing, psychologists have been adept at devising coding schemes for relatively complex material (like responses to comprehension questions on IQ and other tests).

Furthermore, at least under certain circumstances, the other forms of reliability – alternate-interviewer, internal consistency, and test–retest – can reach conventionally acceptable levels. It is possible for different interviewers to identify the same processes in a given child. It is possible for the clinical interview to reveal consistent use of strategy in the child. And it is possible for a second interview to identify the same processes as the first.

At the same time, there is reason to believe that these forms of reliability are not necessarily crucial criteria for sound research. The meaning of these forms of reliability and the necessity for their use are in doubt. If the investigator is dealing with strategies that normally vary within individual children, then alternate-interviewer reliability, internal consistency, and test–retest reliability should not be expected to reach high levels. Furthermore, high alternate-interviewer reliability may indicate only a common bias, not accuracy in measurement. To investigate this issue it is necessary to go beyond traditional psychometric measures to consider such matters as method and manner of questioning.

Two other forms of evidence are relevant for assessing the clinical interview's reliability. One is that the results of such interviews can be widely generalized across groups of children and tasks. The second is that clinical interview studies have had an excellent history of replication. The possibilities of wide generalization and replicability are good recommendations for the clinical interview.

Validity

As I have repeatedly pointed out, the clinical interview is a delicate process, difficult to implement with sensitivity. It should come as no surprise then that the clinical interview is likely to be less "reliable" than a conventional intelligence test. But this is a small price to pay if the clinical interview produces deeper insight into thinking than does the reliable but theoretically uninteresting IQ instrument. Perhaps the very factors which degrade the reliability of the clinical interview – the flexibility of the interview procedure and the complex responses it elicits – are precisely those that enhance its validity.

Consider now the evidence concerning validity. Can the clinical interview compensate for its difficulty and relative unreliability by yielding improved "validity"? Can the clinical interview provide "valid" measures of the phenomena under investigation? Can the clinical interview produce its claimed payoff: insight into the child's thinking?

In examining these issues, we should keep in mind that, as in the case of reliability, the validity of the clinical interview cannot be established *in general*. Validity must be determined in connection with each use.

CONTENT VALIDITY

Suppose that the goal of a clinical interview is to measure the child's use of syllogistic reasoning. Perhaps the first question to ask concerns the "content," or "face," validity of the interview. Content validity "provides judgmental evidence in support of the domain relevance and representativeness of the content of the test instrument, rather than evidence in support of inferences to be made from test scores" (Messick, 1989, p. 17). Thus, to establish content validity, the interviewer needs to determine whether the tasks presented to the child seem to be reasonable and representative syllogism problems.

Usually, establishing such content validity is easy. In fact, content validity seems so obvious in the clinical interview that interviewers do not bother to deal with it in an explicit way.

But establishing content validity is insufficient. Although the problems may indeed involve syllogisms, the question is whether they provide evidence allowing reasonable inferences concerning the child's syllogistic reasoning. Devising problems with appropriate content is only the first step toward the goal of examining the child's thought.

The situation is analogous to a classic problem in educational research. Interested in comparing the effects of different methods of teaching reading, the experimenter randomly places some children in a "whole-word" instruction group and other children in a "phonics" instruction group and then measures reading proficiency as the outcome. But the results of the experiment, whatever they may be, are hard to interpret, because the experimenter has no information about whether the children actually read by means of the method taught in their respective groups. On the surface, the instruction in both groups had a clear "face validity"; but this is not sufficient to answer the basic question of whether the instruction had its intended *psychological* effects. Without evidence of this type, the outcome measures – whatever their apparent content validity – cannot be interpreted meaningfully and the experiment is useless. (Unfortunately, a good deal of Method A vs. Method B educational research takes this unsatisfying form.)

CRITERION VALIDITY

A second type of validity usually considered in psychometric analyses is "criterion" validity, both predictive and concurrent. The question is the degree to which the measure in question – here the clinical interview – is correlated with some relevant behavior, either at the present time or in the future. Thus, to what extent does the reading achievement test score correlate with the teacher's current grade or predict success in a later English literature class? Does the airplane-flying test predict success at flying airplanes either now or in the future?

Consider again the example of the clinical interview designed to investigate syllogistic reasoning. Suppose that children's success at syllogistic-reasoning tasks in the clinical interview is positively correlated with current or future success at mathematics problems that seem to require syllogistic reasoning. Such evidence would not make us unhappy; it is consistent with the hypothesis that the clinical interview designed to measure syllogistic reasoning does indeed measure it.

So far as I am aware, evidence concerning the concurrent or predictive validity of the clinical interview is lacking. This is not, however, a great handicap, because such evidence is likely to be tangential at best. Suppose that the clinical interview on syllogistic reasoning does indeed correlate with success on certain types of mathematics problems. This result would be ambiguous unless we were certain that the clinical interview did indeed measure syllogistic reasoning and unless we were also certain that the mathematics problems did indeed require syllogistic reasoning for their solution. But we do not yet know whether the clinical interview in fact measures syllogistic reasoning – indeed, that is precisely what we want to discover! – and we also do not know whether the criterion measure (here the mathematics problems) indeed requires syllogistic reasoning. Therefore, an observed empirical correlation between the clinical interview and the math problems would be very difficult to interpret; it could provide only very indirect and weak evidence relevant to the validity of the clinical interview.

CONSTRUCT VALIDITY

The third and most important type of validity discussed in psychometric analyses involves what is usually called "construct" validity. This is "based on an integration of any evidence that bears on the interpretation or meaning of the test scores" (Messick, 1989, p. 17). Of course, certain types of evidence are especially useful for interpreting test scores. "Possibly the most illuminating of all [forms of evidence] are direct probes and modeling of the processes underlying test responses, an approach becoming both more accessible and more powerful with continuing developments in cognitive psychology" (p. 17). In other words, the most important evidence is not whether the test consists of apparently relevant problems (content validity) or whether test results correlate in sensible ways with other tests or criteria (concurrent and predictive validity). The key evidence is internal to the testing situation itself: Does the child's behavior in response to the test questions or to additional probes provide direct evidence concerning the thought processes in question?

Messick's theory provides a valuable perspective on evaluating the clinical interview. From his point of view, the primary issue is whether the clinical interview provides clear and direct evidence concerning the operation of the cognitive processes under investigation. In the case of syllogistic reasoning, the interviewer first needs to be clear about what is meant by syllogistic reasoning and then needs to be able to point to specific behaviors of the child indicating that syllogistic reasoning was in fact employed. "Validity is an integrated evaluative judgment of the degree to which empirical evidence and theoretical rationales support the adequacy and appropriateness of inferences. . . . [A]lthough there are many ways of accumulating evidence to support a particular inference, these ways are essentially the methods of science" (Messick, 1989, p. 14). In other words, the evaluation of the validity of the clinical interview is simply a special case of the appraisal of scientific research: The basic question is whether the body of evidence as a whole is coherent and convincing in pointing to the operation of the specified cognitive processes.

In practice, this is not difficult to do in the focused clinical interview. The interviewer usually begins with a fairly clear notion of the cognitive process in question (syllogistic reasoning or mental addition or realistic moral judgment); devises relevant problems (with clear content validity); and then specifies certain kinds of behaviors in the child that indicate the use of the cognitive process under investigation. Thus, the examiner may specify that the child is considered to use syllogistic reasoning when he or she can fulfill several conditions. One is to solve problems of the type "Socrates is a man; men are mortal; is Socrates mortal?" Another is to make certain kinds of verbal statements ("I know Socrates is mortal because if he is a man, and if it is true that all men are mortal, then he *must* be mortal too."). A third is to respond to probes in certain ways. Thus, if asked, "Now what if all men had green hair. Would Socrates also have green hair?" the child should answer in the affirmative and should also indicate explicit awareness that syllogisms can operate under counterfactual conditions. A fourth condition might be that the child makes spontaneous remarks indicating understanding or use of syllogistic reasoning. Thus, if after the first question ("Socrates is a man; men are mortal; is Socrates mortal?"), the child proclaimed, "Of course, and if men were immortal then Socrates would be too," one could adduce further evidence that the child understood syllogistic reasoning.

In brief, the *internal* evidence that is at the core of the clinical interview – solution of key problems, observed behaviors, responses to probes, spontaneous verbalizations about thought process – is the key to construct validity. Indeed, the evidence provided by the clinical interview is the perfect example of the web of evidence necessary for making judgments about validity. In general, the typical focused clinical interview provides more direct and relevant information concerning the measurement of cognitive processes than any standard test of which I am aware. In the clinical interview, one *sees* the child thinking ("I added them in my head"; "equals means the end is coming up"). In the typical standardized test, one makes indirect inferences about children's thinking based on assumptions about what this test measures and what that test measures and what some degree of association between them might mean. If this is the case, which method, clinical interview or test, would you consider the more "scientific"?

DOMAIN VALIDITY

Clearly the clinical interview can provide useful information concerning children's thinking. But it is possible that clinical interview methods are more effective – more valid – in providing information concerning some cognitive processes than others. That is, the validity of the clinical interview may be higher in some domains than in others.

Consider two cases. Clinical interview methods seem to be more useful for uncovering the sequential solution processes involved in various forms of thinking than for discovering the perceptual processes involved in reading a word. In the first case, children may be able to introspect that "first you take the top number, then you add it to this one . . . ," etc. But in the second case, they may say only: "How did I see it was *A?* I just saw it." Much more than that would be very hard for anyone to say. The processes of perception seem more deeply rooted in the unconscious than do the strategies of at least some kinds of thinking.

Further, it seems likely that even when children find it difficult to describe the processes behind their answer, they may be able to justify and explain those responses. Thus, given a simple number fact problem, the child might say, "I just knew that 4 and 5 is 9," and might be unable to say a word more about the method of solution. But if asked to justify the response, the child might say, "It has to be 9 because if you counted 4 more from 5, you would have to get 9." In this case, the child's responses are about two different phenomena: getting the answer and justifying its correctness. And the clinical interview seems more valuable in gaining insight into the second than the first.

We need to learn more about the different kinds of thinking that children employ and the effectiveness with which the clinical interview can provide information about them.

CONVERGENT VALIDITY

The results of the clinical interview need not stand alone. They can be related to, and can gain meaning from, a web of evidence obtained from various methods. Liben (in press) suggests that "interview methods call for follow-up studies with more focused tasks, that is, for the use of converging methods to determine if the conclusions suggested by interview methods are supported by different approaches" (pp. 15–16). For example, children's open-ended responses to a question like "What is a map?" may be followed by specific, standardized questions concerning features of particular maps, by sorting tasks which require children to make judgments about the maplike nature of various figures, and by tasks which require children to rate the similarity of maplike figures. All of these methods used together can help the researcher or practitioner to obtain deeper insight into children's thinking than can any one method alone. The clinical interview can play a key role in this process of multimethod research, and the web of evidence resulting from it may help to confirm the utility of the clinical interview method.

HISTORICAL VALIDITY

Next I propose another kind of validity, which might be called "historical" validity. By this I mean that one criterion for judging the success of a method is its long-term success in research. Piaget (and his colleagues and students)[1] used variations on the clinical interview method for many years in his research, and no one, I think, would deny that he and the field as a whole learned a great deal from it. The clinical interview has a substantial historical "track record" which should not be ignored. And of course in recent years other prominent researchers have employed the method (e.g., A. L. Brown, Campione, Webber, & McGilly, 1992; D. Kuhn et al., 1995; Resnick, 1989). So one legitimate answer to the validity question then is that we know the method can be valuable because Piaget and others have used it with great success over a lengthy period of time.

The Accuracy of Verbal Reports

The accuracy of verbal reports is a classic problem in psychology, dating back to the time when introspection was a major source of data for experimental psychology. Today there is debate as to whether "think-aloud" protocols can provide accurate accounts of adults' cognitive processes (Ericsson & Simon, 1993). What about children? In the clinical interview, children are often asked to describe in words their thought process. "How did you solve that problem? What did you do?" Consequently, evaluation of the clinical interview must also deal with the issue of the accuracy of children's verbal reports. To what extent can children report accurately on their cognitive activities?

Piaget himself was not sanguine about children's ability to report on their own thinking. In his early work, Piaget (1964) proposed that young children are incapable of introspection; later in *The Grasp of Consciousness*, he came to similar, although more elaborated and nuanced, conclusions (Piaget, 1976b). Recent research provides evidence consonant with this view. Preschoolers are "poor at recognizing that they themselves have just been thinking and at recalling or

181

reconstructing what they have been thinking about, even in situations designed to make accurate introspection very easy. These shortcomings are considerably less evident in 7–8-year-olds" (Flavell et al., 1995, p. v).

Piaget felt, however, that young children's difficulty in introspection did not cripple the effectiveness of the clinical interview. There were several reasons for his belief. The main one was that the interviewer does not rely exclusively, or even heavily, on young children's introspection as a source of evidence. Instead, the interviewer observes how children respond to key questions (e.g., "Do these have the same amount?" "Why does this one have more?"). In these cases, the interviewer employs verbal evidence, but it often does not consist of introspections. The child says, "This has more because it is spreaded out," which is a simple description of the objects' physical appearance, not an introspective account of the child's thinking. Furthermore, the interviewer attends to children's manipulation of objects and to the kinds of gestures they make. In effect, the interviewer is "using children's hands to read their minds" (Goldin-Meadow, Wein, & Chang, 1992, p. 201). The interviewer notes the facial expressions children exhibit, for they provide information concerning the firmness of conviction.

In short, to make inferences about the child's thinking, the interviewer employs a web of evidence – verbalizations, behaviors, judgments, expressions – in which introspection need not play a major role. Of course, the interviewer does not hesitate to examine introspection when it is offered, as it often is by older children.

Suggestibility

One of the dangers of the clinical interview, because it depends to so great a degree on human judgment and skill, is that the interviewer may unintentionally "put words in the child's mouth." Doing this obviously detracts from the validity of the interview (although consistent suggestion might conceivably enhance its reliability). Both common sense and research suggest: "In general, children are more susceptible to examiner and situational influences than are adults; in the examination of preschool children, the role of the examiner is especially crucial" (Anastasi, 1988, p. 38; see also Hughes & Baker, 1990).

No doubt suggestion can and does occur in the clinical interview, as in many areas of adult–child (or adult–adult) interaction. But how serious is the problem of suggestibility in the clinical interview, especially in the case of young children? Although little of the available research appears to deal directly with suggestibility in the clinical interview, some useful information is available.

Consider first research on an extreme case, namely the effects of suggestibility in interviews concerning memories of sexual abuse in childhood, a topic which has recently stimulated considerable controversy and attracted public interest. Researchers have found that children in this situation can indeed be influenced by interviewer suggestions and that preschoolers are more suggestible than older children. Several factors may be responsible for this, including "young children's general lack of knowledge and experience, their difficulty with deliberate recall, their lack of metamemory [awareness of their own memory strategies], their lack of sophisticated communication skills and their subsequent dependence on contextual cues and information, and their eagerness to do and say what they think is expected, particularly what is expected by adults" (Garbarino et al., 1992, p. 55).

Even in this charged situation, however, the power of suggestion is not total. Children are less likely to be suggestible at a time very close to the events that may have occurred. "A child's report is less likely to be distorted . . . after one interview than after several" (Ceci & Bruck, 1993, p. 18). Children are more likely to report abuse after a period of repeated interviews "when an interviewer pursues a single hypothesis about the basis of the child's difficulties, which entails leading and suggestive interviews" (p. 8). In brief, these results suggest that to exert their effects, adult suggestions need to be persistently applied over the long term.

The research also shows that in these extreme circumstances of examining possible abuse it is possible for skilled interviewers to avoid bias. "Interviewers who ask nonleading questions, who do not have a confirmatory bias (i.e., an attachment to a single hypothesis), and who do not repeat close-ended, yes/no questions within and across interviews, are more likely to obtain accurate reports from children. Interviewers who are patient, nonjudgmental and who do not attempt to create demand characteristics (e.g., by providing subtle rewards for certain responses) are likely to elicit the best quality reports from children" (Ceci & Bruck, 1993, pp. 18–19). Also, research seems to indicate that young children resist suggestions concerning events that are central to them. "In general, it seems that young children are least likely to be vulnerable to post-event suggestions when they are asked to recall events that they understand and know something about and that they find interesting or salient" (Garbarino et al., 1992, p. 57).

What can we conclude from this? Even in highly charged areas, interviewers can avoid suggestions, and children can resist them.

Of course, most interviews do not revolve around the horrible topic of abuse. Consider next the role of suggestibility in the more common and relevant context of schooling, a very different but still emotionally salient domain, in which children seem to be especially sensitive to adult influence. In school, children are often highly motivated to discover in the teacher's behavior clues for right and wrong answers. If the teacher frowns, then perhaps the child's answer is wrong and should immediately be changed. If the teacher raises an eyebrow, the child had better try a different strategy. Here is an example, from *How Children Fail* (Holt, 1982), about a classroom in which the teacher was examining her students on the parts of speech. The students' task was to decide in which column on the blackboard, labeled Noun, Adjective, and Verb, were words presented by the teacher to be written:

> There was a good deal of the tried-and-true strategy of *guess-and-look*, in which you start to say a word, all the while scrutinizing the teacher's face to see whether you are on the right track or not. . . . This one was more poker-faced than most, so *guess-and-look* wasn't working very well. Still, the percentage of hits was remarkably high. . . . Finally one child said, "Miss _____, you shouldn't point to the answer each time. . . . Well, you don't exactly point, but you kind of stand next to the answer." . . . [The teacher] was pointing herself at the place where she would soon be writing. From the angle of her

body to the blackboard the children picked up a subtle clue to the correct answer. (pp. 25–26)

Although Holt's reports are anecdotal, they have a ring of truth, and anyone who has been to school knows that such things can and do occur, even if it is not clear how pervasive they are in different kinds of schools. (In my experience, this kind of game playing is not entirely unknown even in the PhD defense!) But for our present purposes, the question is how such school-based suggestibility affects children's response to the clinical interview, which is typically conducted in a school setting. If they become adept at "reading" the teacher in order to get the right answer (a different kind of literacy from what the school intends!), do children try to outsmart the interviewer in a similar way? Do they engage in a kind of self-imposed suggestibility, in which they try desperately to base their responses on even the most subtle of signals from the unwitting interviewer?

Although there appears to be no research on this issue, I would suggest (perhaps a bad word in this context) that at the outset, many children, like Toby, probably do see the clinical interview as another instance of schooling and therefore probably engage in the kinds of defensive behaviors that seem to serve them well in classrooms. They play typical school games (like figure out what the adult really wants you to say) in the clinical interview. But if the interview goes well, these children learn, again like Toby, that the rules of discourse in the clinical interview are different from those in the typical classroom, and that it is not necessary to engage in traditional school games, among them self-imposed suggestibility. Under these circumstances, children learn new rules of discourse, which include a tendency to examine and describe one's own thinking and to avoid speculations about the interviewer's.

In brief, we have seen that suggestibility is a real phenomenon that can pose dangers for the clinical interview. First, research shows that when the interview topic is highly charged and personal, children's reports can be distorted. Second, common observation reveals that children engage in a kind of self-imposed and deliberate suggestibility in school, as a means to the end of pleasing adults and getting the right answer. But neither of these dangers need debilitate the interview process. In the first case, the closer in time the interview is to the topic under consideration, the less likely is the child to distort the memory of what occurred. Furthermore, even when the topic is abuse, skill in interviewing can reduce the likelihood of suggestion. And in the second case, the child's strong tendency to please teachers and other adults can be overcome by the introduction of the new rules of clinical interview discourse, as we have seen in the case of Toby. The bottom line is that a good interviewer can avoid the real dangers of undue suggestion and the distortions that stem from it.

Summary

The focused use of the clinical interview does not depart a great deal from the positivist approach of conventional psychological research. This class of methods can exhibit adequate inter-observer reliability: Independent judges can agree on their interpretations of the results, at least when previously specified and adequately defined categories are employed. Results can be replicated and generalized. The methods can exhibit adequate construct validity, particularly in their providing direct, internal evidence concerning the use of particular strategies or mental processes. The methods do not depend for their success on elaborate and accurate verbal reports, although these are in fact often provided by older children. And although suggestion is always a danger, interviewers can avoid it and children can resist it, at least when immediate and relevant content is involved. The focused clinical interview is more difficult to administer than a standardized test, but interviewing can be conducted with skill and can yield useful results. In brief, the focused use of the clinical interview should arouse little controversy.

INTENSIVE STUDY

The main question in this section refers to the objectivity of the clinical interview in the intensive study of the individual. What criteria should we employ to assess the objectivity of this type of clinical interview? How do we know when intensive clinical interviews have been successful? But first, consider a brief description of the nature of intensive study of the individual and then some misconceptions about it.

What Is Intensive Study?

Intensive use of the clinical interview falls into several categories: practice, research on individuals, aggregated research on individuals, and romantic psychology.

PRACTICE

Practitioners – clinicians, school psychologists, pediatricians, among others – may employ the clinical interview to obtain an understanding of their clients' thinking. Does the child think in an obsessive fashion? How well does the child understand the concept of plant life? How does the child conceptualize the nature and causes of the disease from which he or she suffers? In these cases, the practitioner's goal is to develop a theory of the individual – that is, to arrive at as complete an understanding as possible of this particular person in his or her individual and ultimately unique circumstances. The goal of such "intrinsic case study" (Stake, 1994) is not to develop general theories – that is the researcher's job – but to apply general theories so as to arrive at a deeper understanding of this individual in particular. And the goal of doing that is eventually (not necessarily during the clinical interview itself) to help the individual (e.g., to improve the mode of thinking, to promote more elaborate and accurate concepts, to deepen understanding).

Given the goal of understanding and of ultimately helping the individual, the clinical interview is used in a flexible and individualized manner. The practitioner often begins with exploration, follows up on whatever leads emerge, and then engages in intensive interviewing designed to shed light on the nature of this particular child's thought, concepts, and difficulties. The practitioner's interpretations draw upon the child's responses to the deliberately nonstandardized and individualized clinical interview. These data are unique and not directly comparable to those of other children. The basic question for the practitioner is how to use the clinical interview in the individual case with an adequate degree of objectivity.

RESEARCH ON INDIVIDUALS

In conducting research on individuals, the interviewer deploys the clinical interview in a highly individualized and flexible manner, much as was illustrated in the case of Toby, presented in chapter 3. The questioning is tailored to the individual; special tasks are employed; no attempt to standardize the approach is made.

Certainly the intensive study of individuals has had a long and distinguished history in psychological research, ranging from the early giants of the field – Darwin's (1955) account of his son's emotional development, Freud's (1963) case study of Dora, Binet's (1969) examination of his two preschool daughters' concepts of number, Piaget's (1952b) observations of his three babies' sensorimotor development – to contemporary accounts, like Bloom's (1970) detailed description of early language development, Gruber's (1981) study of Darwin's creativity, and Sacks's (1995) rich portraits of autism.

The goal of this kind of research is to "develop new concepts, elaborate existing concepts, provide insights, clarify complexity, and develop theory" (Peshkin, 1993, p. 25). In a sense, the researcher in this tradition is not interested in the individual per se but in developing general theory. Indeed, the researcher would abandon study of this particular individual if it did not lead to general knowledge. In "instrumental case study" (Stake, 1994), the case itself is of "secondary interest; it plays a supportive role, facilitating our understanding of something else" (p. 237).

This type of research provides a special kind of information. As Lewin (1935) put it, accounts of psychological process are "always to be derived from the relation of the concrete individual to the concrete situation" (p. 41). Moreover, one case can often provide great insight into psychological principles: "the importance of a case, and its validity as proof, cannot be evaluated by the frequency of its occurrence" (p. 42).[2]

Work of this type has aroused considerable controversy, particularly around issues of generality. How can one draw general conclusions from a single case or from a mere handful? My own view is that the historical record demonstrates the utility of this approach: Intensive study of the individual has taught us a great deal and presumably can continue to do so. Besides, there are dangers in aggregating data over individuals (Siegler, 1987). And also, think of how little we have learned from many large-scale, highly statistical studies.

In any event, the purpose of this chapter is not to debate the issue of whether to engage in intensive study of individuals (see Valsiner, 1986, for a review of that topic) but to evaluate the use of the clinical interview in such efforts. In recent years, the clinical interview has been used to good effect in studies of the individual. Thus, it has been used to detect key phenomena for further study (e.g., Erlwanger's [1975] description of certain "bugs" in Benny's approach to decimals); to examine the operation of a *system* of mathematical knowledge (e.g., my own examination of Peter's understanding of division [Ginsburg, 1971]); to establish the existence theorem with respect to a particular cognitive process (e.g., the demonstration by Cochran, Barson, & Davis [1970] that a child could invent a computational procedure as powerful as and in a way more sensible than the standard algorithm); and to identify new cognitive mechanisms (as in Baroody's [1984] case of Felicia, who displayed an interesting method for reducing memory load in calculation).

The goal of the next section is to evaluate the clinical interview as a tool for conducting such studies. Using the clinical interview in this manner presents both researcher and practitioner with a fundamental dilemma, namely how to balance radical sensitivity to the individual with "objectivity," the need to provide evidence ensuring that "our positions are rationally warranted, reasonable, or defensible – that is, well founded rather than groundless opinions" (Toulmin, 1982, p. 115, quoted in Eisner, 1991, p. 51).

AGGREGATED RESEARCH ON INDIVIDUALS

The obvious weakness of individual case study, using the clinical interview or any other technique, is its ambiguity with respect to generalization. How typical is the individual examined so intensively by means of the clinical interview? To what extent can the findings be generalized? Obviously, if the knowledge gained from the study is not in some sense general, then there was no point in conducting the research in the first place.[3] Even if it focuses on individuals, the goal of all research is to arrive at general knowledge.

One approach taken by researchers interested in generalizing case study results is to aggregate them. This is "collective case study. It is not the study of a collective but instrumental [case] study extended to several cases" (Stake, 1994, p. 237). The basic idea is to collect a group of individual clinical interview studies that all focus on roughly the same topic but that of course investigate that topic in ways tailored to the individuals and hence differ from one another in detail.

One example of this approach is a recent study (D. Kuhn et al., 1995) investigating the ways in which individuals coordinate existing personal theories with new evidence. The writers describe their approach as follows: "While suggestive, the group data reveal little about the patterns of strategy usage by individual subjects. . . . [Therefore], we turn to individual case study data. Each subject's record across the ten sessions was treated as an individual case study and examined with respect to patterns of knowledge acquisition, strategy usage, and strategy change. Case studies were then compared and examined as a whole to discern common patterns" (p. 75).

The aim of the aggregated approach is to exploit the sensitivity of the case study, relying heavily (but in the Kuhn et al. study not exclusively) on the clinical interview, while at the same time enjoying the benefits of comparisons involving a reasonably large number of subjects. Of course, this approach to the clinical interview, although attempting to cope with the problem of generalization, still must address the fundamental issue of objectivity. In any particular study, do the individual interviews which are to be aggregated meet the necessary standards of objectivity? There is little merit in forming generalizations based on suspect individual interviews.

ROMANTIC PSYCHOLOGY

Romantic psychology refers, not to a psychology of romance, but to a romance of a psychological nature – that is, a kind of aesthetic psychological portrait. A romance was originally "a fictitious tale of wonderful and extraordinary events" and later "real happenings and adventures as exciting and usual as those of such literature" (Friend &

Guralnick, 1960, p. 1263). The psychological romance tells the story of the fascinating "real happenings and adventures" of the mind, adventures as unusual and interesting as those of fiction. The psychological romance aims to produce in the reader not only an enjoyment of them but an empathic understanding of the mind capable of generating these adventures.

A. R. Luria, a student of Vygotsky, described the approach as follows: "Romantics in science want neither to split living reality into its elementary components nor to represent the wealth of life's concrete events in abstract models that lose the properties of the phenomena themselves. It is of the utmost importance to romantics to preserve the wealth of living reality, and they aspire to a science that retains this richness" (1979, p. 174). Luria's famous case study of an individual with incredible powers of memory did indeed attempt to "preserve the wealth of living reality" and to celebrate its wonder. Thus: "What impact did the various facets of S.'s memory which have been described have on his grasp of things, on the particular world he lived in? . . . Here begins an account of phenomena so amazing that we will many times be left with the feeling little Alice had after she slipped through the looking glass and found herself in a strange wonderland" (1968, pp. 72–73).

The clinical interview can be used to produce romantic tales of this sort. In another telling of the story of Toby (Ginsburg, 1996b), I tried to produce such a romance, the goal of which was in part educational: to help the reader achieve an empathic understanding of the fascinating ways in which children think about mathematics. The aim was not to offer new data, not to propose new theory, not even to help Toby; it was rather to tell an interesting and, I felt, important story. The interest of the story derived from the cognitive details – from Toby's concepts and constructions – but the main point was not to develop a new theory of these details but to tell an interesting story about them, to share my sense of wonder about Toby's mind.

As Luria pointed out, however, "romantic scholars and romantic science have their shortcomings. . . . Sometimes logical step-by-step analysis escapes romantic scholars, and on occasion, they let artistic preferences and intuitions take over" (1979, pp. 174–175). Consequently, the objectivity of the clinical interview must be as vital a concern for the practitioner of romantic psychology as for the researcher.

One common misconception concerning the intensive use of the clinical interview is that it must result in "qualitative" data. Not true. Detailed, descriptive data concerning individuals can be quantified, as done, for example, by Labov and Fanshel (1977) in their study of one person's psychotherapy. Similarly, it would be possible to quantify aspects of the clinical interview (e.g., the length of Toby's and my statements as a function of time in the interview setting); whether doing so would be *informative* is an unanswered question. In any event, we should be mindful of the simple proposition that qualitative research "does not imply a commitment to innumeracy" (Kirk & Miller, 1986, p. 10). The clinical interview can yield *both* qualitative and quantitative data.

Second, the intensive use of the clinical interview does not rule out the simultaneous use of other methods, including standardized tests, questionnaires eliciting factual information, and observations of behavior in everyday life. Both researcher and practitioner may well profit from knowing not only how the individual child constructs a personal reality but also how the child's performance ranks against peers', what have been the major events of the child's life, and what in fact the child does in the classroom. The clinical interview gives only one perspective; it affords only one type of "fairness." Other perspectives can broaden the researcher's view.

Third, the intensive use of the clinical interview should not be seen as implying a priority of the idiographic (the study of the individual) over the nomothetic (the attempt to develop general laws). Use of the clinical interview shows that a person's uniqueness cannot be understood without referring to what people have in common. The practitioner – or the researcher – cannot understand the individual event, the unique, without placing it within a larger framework. We saw earlier that the interviewer employs norms, often implicit but norms nonetheless, to interpret distinctive acts of the individual.

Without such norms, the interviewer does not know whether the act is interesting, distinctive, or worth examining.

Just as one cannot understand the particular without appeal to the general, so general laws are meaningless without the individual instance. "No general principles can ever be applied except to concrete and particular objects. The individual case stands at the gateway and terminus of generalized knowledge" (Allport, 1942, p. 150, quoted in Franck, 1986, p. 24).

Both researcher and practitioner engage in elaborate conceptual work, employing a general theory, based on many cases, to arrive at an understanding of the individual's uniqueness. Using Allport's terminology, we can say that the "idiographic" (the individual's distinctiveness) cannot be grasped without reference to the "nomothetic" (what is shared by the group). Franck (1986) puts it well: "Just as new idiographic knowledge of individuals may serve as a point of departure for extending and enriching our knowledge of laws of human nature, so may nomothetic knowledge of general laws of human nature make possible deeper and more trustworthy idiographic insights into individuals" (p. 32).

CONCLUSIONS

The clinical interview can be used in practice, individual research, aggregated individual research, and romantic psychology. The method involves both using general principles to understand the individual case and using the individual case to develop general principles. The method can result in both qualitative and quantitative data. It can be used alone or, preferably, in combination with other approaches. But in all cases we need to evaluate the method's objectivity, and it is to this topic that we turn next.

Evaluating the Intensive Clinical Interview

As used in intensive study, the clinical interview is a complex human-measuring instrument which cannot be evaluated according to many of the traditional psychometric criteria. This argument was introduced in connection with the focused clinical interview; but it is even more crucial in understanding the intensive clinical interview, so now I expand on it.

WHY CERTAIN TRADITIONAL PSYCHOMETRIC CRITERIA ARE NOT RELEVANT

Criteria like internal consistency and criterion validity are irrelevant when it comes to assessing the adequacy of the clinical interview. Consider the case of internal consistency. One scenario for the clinical interview is that over the course of a session, as familiarity with the interviewer and with the rules of the game increases, the child's responses may very well become transformed in a clearly positive direction. As we saw in the case of Toby, confidence and expressiveness may increase, with the result that the child exhibits far more competence as the interview proceeds than was displayed at the outset. This type of limited internal consistency is, rather than a problem for the clinical interview, a sign of its success.

Another scenario is that over the course of a session, the child uses various strategies to solve the same class of problems. Thus one first grader I observed began by using a counting-on method to solve a mental-addition problem ("4 and 3 is 4, 5, 6, 7") but later simply used memory of number facts to get the answer and later still used "derived facts" ("4 and 5 is 9 because I know that 4 and 4 is 8 and then just 1 more"). As mentioned earlier, Siegler and his colleagues (Lemaire & Siegler, 1995; Siegler, 1988) have stressed the importance of recognizing fundamental inconsistencies in children's cognitive activities. In cases like these, lack of internal consistency is not a psychometric problem: "Inconsistency in students' performance across tasks does not invalidate the assessment. Rather it becomes an empirical puzzle to be solved by searching for a more comprehensive or elaborated interpretation that explains the inconsistency and articulates the need for additional evidence" (Moss, 1994, p. 8).

Similarly, if we interview the child on two occasions, a day apart, and the child shows little consistency, can we conclude that the method is unreliable? Not necessarily. The child's behavior may again be evidence only of the kind of well-documented inconsistency in individual response noted above.

Criterion validity (concurrent or predictive) is also not a psychometric benchmark but an "empirical puzzle." Suppose that a child exhibits a particular type of moral judgment in regard to social situations. How can we "validate" this "response" against some external criterion (either concurrently or in the future)? The most obvious possibility is to examine whether the child shows a similar response to another moral-judgment task. But what type of task should we use? If we give the child a moral-judgment task from a different domain and there is little consistency, can we conclude that there is a lack of concurrent validity? Not necessarily. The child's behavior may be evidence only of domain-specific moral judgment; the child's thinking is tied to context (Smetana, 1995). The phenomenon is perhaps puzzling, but its existence is not a psychometric demerit.

In brief, lack of internal consistency or criterion validity may point, not to psychometric deficiency, but to an interesting empirical phenomenon to be explained. The clinical interview needs to be evaluated, not by the traditional psychometric criteria, but on its own terms. The task is to specify what they are, and that is what I now attempt to do.

FIVE WAYS TO EVALUATE THE CLINICAL INTERVIEW

Evaluations of the intensive use of the clinical interview in practice or research have seldom, if ever, been attempted. Consequently, this section, even more than previous ones, is almost entirely speculative. I draw on various writers' ideas, and offer some of my own, to propose ways in which any particular intensive use of the clinical interview *could* be evaluated.

I argue that an evaluation of the clinical interview should consider five issues: (1) Was the interview conducted in an adequate manner? (2) Did the child respond seriously to the interview? (3) Is the interpretation of the interview plausible and rationally derived from internal evidence? (4) Can the study be replicated? (5) Did the interview have beneficial effects on the child and on the interviewer?

Adequacy of implementation. The microscope is an essential tool for many biology experiments. How can its adequacy as a measuring instrument in a particular study be evaluated? One factor that must be included is consideration of the researcher's skill in using it. We would not take seriously a study based upon the findings of researchers untrained in microscope use or of skilled but inattentive or drunken researchers. In a sense, the "validity" of the microscope is a temporary function of the adequacy of its user. The microscope itself is potentially a fine tool for certain purposes, but this potential is contingent on the skill, knowledge, training, temporary mental state, and sobriety of the researcher.

A similar argument may be made concerning the clinical interview. It is potentially a fine tool for certain kinds of research and practice. But its successful use depends upon the skill of the interviewer. Evaluation must therefore examine whether the researcher or practitioner conducts the interview in an adequate fashion.

What does this mean in practical terms? When I evaluate interviewing skill, I review students' videotaped interviews, focusing on such issues as whether they ask leading questions, whether they are sensitive to cues offered by the child, whether they follow up on interesting statements, whether they make accurate observations of the relevant behaviors, and whether they accurately gauge the child's emotional state and respond to it appropriately. In short, I attempt to examine the student's interview in the light of the guidelines for interviewing described in chapter 4. Of course, I recognize that interviewing style must vary in response to the needs and characteristics of the individual child. Some children require more probing than others; some require more support and warmth than others. Nevertheless, I can usually tell when someone – a student or myself – has badly messed up a part of the interview.

Liben (in press) also makes the valuable point that part of the interviewer's expertise is "sophisticated knowledge of the domain" under investigation (p. 15). The interviewer should not forget that it is difficult, if not impossible, to conduct a good interview without deep understanding of the subject matter. Recall that Piaget undertook careful study of the game of marbles before interviewing children about it.

Adequacy of implementation can be evaluated in both positive and negative terms. One could imagine giving interviewers a positive score based on degree of sensitivity to the child, the use of good follow-up questions, and the like, or a negative score based on use of leading questions, bullying, and similar ineffective or harmful methods. As a guide to the evaluation of interviews, and the possible development of interviewer-rating schemes, Table 5.1 shows an abbreviated checklist form of the interview dos and don'ts.

Adequacy of response. It is not enough for the researcher or practitioner to do a good job in conducting the interview. For the interview results to be informative, two criteria need to be met. First, the child has to produce a response of some kind. And second, the response needs to be "genuine" or "engaged" in the sense of a serious effort on the part of the child. (This is where my analogy breaks down. Biologists using a microscope do not have these problems with their specimens.)

Imagine a situation in which the child remains silent and refuses to respond in any way, despite the interviewer's best efforts. Obviously this interview produces no useful information concerning the child's real mental state. Imagine a situation in which the child gives flippant answers, guesses, makes up absurd answers, tries to produce the response he or she thinks the examiner wants, tries always to please the examiner, or fails to attend and in general resists the interviewer's skilled efforts at getting him or her to engage with the problems presented. You might say that such a child is not serious about the interview, does not deal with the real issues of the interview, does not grapple with the material at hand. Such an interview may reveal a good deal about the child's motivational state and personality, but it is not informative with respect to the intended focus of the investigation, namely the child's thinking. An effective interview is one in which the data are "reliable" in the sense of *genuine* and *nonephemeral*.

Consequently, evaluation of the clinical interview must include an examination of the child's engagement. Again, one can imagine scoring the child's response in positive and negative ways. A nongenuine, ephemeral response may be characterized by stubborn silence, a snide smile, frequent changes of answers in response to countersuggestions, a lack of attention to the problems, listless tone of voice, a lack of affect, long delays in response, the presence of "romancing" (one of the indicators Piaget [1976a] looked for in his original work on the problem), or sighs of boredom. An engaged response may be

Table 5.1 *A checklist for the successful interviewer*

- Use meaningful norms.
- Begin with a prepared protocol.
- Use theoretically meaningful tasks.
- Understand the domain under investigation.
- Prepare specific tasks with which the child can engage.
- Prepare open-ended questions.
- Make informal contact.
- Explain the purpose of the interview.
- Use the child's language.
- Put the child in the role of expert.
- Begin with an easy task.
- Display warmth and support.
- Encourage effort.
- Monitor affect.
- Encourage verbalization.
- Show "clinical sensitivity" to the individual.
- Ask the fundamental question.
- Remain silent when necessary.
- Echo and reflect.
- Ask for justifications.
- Explore interesting leads.
- Help the child to introspect.
- Observe key aspects of the child's behavior.
- Rephrase the question.
- Vary the task when necessary.
- Repeat and review tasks.
- Probe unclear responses.
- Offer countersuggestions.
- Provide hints and other forms of help to establish learning potential.
- Conduct appropriate experiments.
- Encourage the child's way of solving problems.
- Avoid talking too much.
- Avoid leading questions.
- Avoid unnecessary corrections and teaching.

characterized by lively affect, a lack of hesitation in response, a use of child-language (rather than "canned" adult words) in response, focused attention, and fluent expression. An interesting research project might involve identifying response characteristics of children judged to be clearly engaged or not engaged in interviews.

Plausibility of interpretation. Perhaps the most important question to ask about the clinical interview is this: Is the interpretation of the interview plausible and rationally derived from internal evidence?

Many writers concur that "validity" is an issue of persuasibility of argument within a scientific community. The basic reasoning is this: Our "scientific" goal is the understanding of human behavior – the creation of theories and interpretations rationally derived from "objective" evidence. To achieve this goal, we accumulate various forms of evidence – observations, test scores, clinical interviews – which allow us to make plausible inferences and interpretations about behavior. "Validity" is basically convincing the community of scientists that our interpretations are rationally and sensibly derived from the weight of the evidence that we and others have collected. According to a contemporary authority: "Qualitative inquiry, like conventional quantitative approaches to research, is ultimately a matter of persuasion, of seeing things in a way that satisfies, or is useful for the purposes we embrace. The evidence employed in qualitative studies comes from multiple sources. We are persuaded by its 'weight,' by the coherence of the case, by the cogency of the interpretation" (Eisner, 1991, p. 39).

The issue then is whether interpretations derived from the clinical interview can persuade the scientific community. But note that "[w]hat is to be validated is not the test or observation device as such but the inferences derived from test scores or other indicators" (Messick, 1989, p. 14). Obviously, all clinical interview interpretations are not equally valid. A particular use of the clinical interview by a particular investigator may result in fallacious interpretations, just as an experimental psychologist might make faulty use of the experimental method or a biologist may produce an inaccurate reading from a microscope. Consequently, the issue is whether this *specific* use of the clinical interview results in persuasive arguments, not whether the clinical interview in all of its possible implementations is "valid."

Of course, some traditionalists will doubt that the clinical interview, because it violates the usual methodological canons, can result in persuasive interpretations concerning thinking. But according to the most profound theorist of validity, if the goal of our research or practice is understanding thinking, "[p]ossibly most illuminating of

199

all [types of evidence] are direct probes and modeling of the processes underlying test responses, an approach becoming both more accessible and more powerful with continuing developments in cognitive psychology" (Messick, 1989, p. 17). In other words, inferences concerning thinking are best derived from "direct probes" and from examination of the processes underlying response – exactly those procedures that are at the heart of the clinical interview. In providing a substantial web of evidence concerning the child's mind the clinical interview can indeed lead to plausible, "objective" interpretations and in fact has a better chance of producing them than do standardized methods of assessment.

Suppose that you grant that in principle clinical interview interpretations *can* be "valid" and indeed may have a better chance of being valid than those based on standardized test scores. The next question is: How do we know whether a *particular* clinical interview interpretation is valid? Consider three possible criteria: group derivation, internal evidence, and inter-interpreter reliability.

1. *Group derivation.* One possibility is that the validity of a clinical interview interpretation is enhanced by a consensual process of creation. Suppose that in deriving my interpretation, I had reviewed the videotape of Toby's interview with a group of colleagues and that through a process of discussion we arrived at a common interpretation, plausible to all members of the group. Of course, this discussion would take place under certain constraints. One is that all members of the group should be well trained in a common theoretical framework to be employed in interpreting the results. Most human behavior is so complex that it can be interpreted from many different points of view. An observer could examine Toby's interview from the point of view of language alone, or of personality. Or even if an observer restricts attention to the cognitive, he or she could examine Toby's Piagetian structures or her memory. If the observers diverge in their basic focus or theoretical framework, there would be no possibility of agreement on interpretations. So the first rule is that the observers must intend to focus on the same issues and to employ the same theoretical framework. They should not be naive as to the purposes of the study.

A second constraint is that the observers should be allowed to consider all of the available evidence. That is, they should be allowed to interpret behavior *in context*. Any particular verbalization may assume different meanings depending on the child's affect, the immediately preceding events, the relationship between child and adult, etc. Observers should not, as is common in some coding schemes, focus only on small bits of behavior – standing alone, they are uninterpretable.

A third constraint is that at various points in the process the observers would arrive at their interpretations independently, writing them down and committing to them, before discussing them with other members of the group, so as to preserve individual points of view and avoid group influence.[4]

In short, the group would engage in a process of "hermeneutic" debate. "A hermeneutic approach to assessment would involve holistic, integrative interpretations of collected performances that seek to understand the whole in light of its parts, that privilege readers who are most knowledgeable about the context in which the assessment occurs, and that ground those interpretations not only in the textual and contextual evidence available, but also in a rational debate among the community of interpreters" (Moss, 1994, p. 7).

In fact, that is more or less how the interpretation of Toby was derived. I reviewed the videotape with my seminar on clinical interviewing, with my class on the development of mathematical thinking, and with groups of teachers. Each time the tape was reviewed, I learned something from the reactions of students and teachers. Almost each time, someone would point to some bit of evidence that I had failed to notice ("Did you see how Toby looked unhappy there?" or "Did you notice that she said . . . ") or would offer an interesting interpretation that I had not thought of ("Well, maybe she was thinking about . . . ") or would challenge one of my interpretations ("No, that couldn't be right because she also said . . . ").

I am convinced that these kinds of "hermeneutic" discussions resulted in at least two outcomes. One is that my interpretation evolved over a period of time. It definitely changed. A second is that my interpretation improved. I was forced to take into account evidence that I had missed, to justify my interpretations, and to consider other views.

Now suppose that a clinical interview interpretation is derived in this manner. Would it persuade you? The answer is, not necessarily. There are several dangers inherent in such hermeneutic argument. One is that as a person in a position of power with respect to the students (although not really with respect to the teachers), I might have a disproportionate influence on the outcome of the discussion. That is, I might be fooling myself, manipulating the discussion so as to reinforce my own views. I suppose that is a possibility, and certainly the hermeneutic discussion would be more convincing were it conducted in a situation where one of the participants did not also dispense grades to the others.

But even that would not solve the problem. Groups are often swayed by a dominant member and can foster mutual delusion. Beware group-think. The group mind is not always rational or task oriented. (Think of adolescent clubs, political conventions, or faculty meetings.) Furthermore, agreed-upon interpretations are not necessarily good ones. Group process does not guarantee insightful outcome. Although patting themselves on the back to celebrate consensus, groups can be, and often are, wrong.

In brief, a hermeneutic process of developing interpretations may be helpful, and I believe it often is and should be encouraged. Nevertheless, dangers are inherent in the process, and a successful outcome is not guaranteed, so that we are still left with the problem of deciding how to evaluate the validity of a clinical interview interpretation.

2. *Internal evidence.* One solution is to examine how the interpretation is derived from the evidence internal to the clinical interview. If my interpretation is that Toby believes that the = sign involves an "operational" notion rather than an appreciation of equivalence, I must convince you that the weight of the evidence points in that direction. How to do this? I can refer to Toby's reluctance to accept as valid a written statement like $7 = 4 + 3$. I can cite her skeptical expression when she is presented with statements of this type. I can quote her verbalization, "It means the end is coming up, the end." All of these different sources of evidence – verbal statements, actions, facial expressions, answers – from different points in the interview seem to point to the interpretation that for Toby, = means "get an answer by adding or subtracting," and that it has nothing to do with equivalence. If I accumulate enough internal evidence of this sort, then I might convince you that my interpretation deriving from the clinical interview is plausible or "valid," because you, as a member of the scientific community, respect evidence. Of course, because I do not traffic in test scores, I cannot provide you with a validity "coefficient" – a correlation of one test score with another. But the evidence I adduce is more valuable: It provides direct information on the operation of Toby's cognitive processes.

Suppose you accept my argument that the validity of clinical interview interpretations must be based largely on examination of the plausibility of inferences employing internal evidence. The next question is: How should such an examination take place? If you are dealing with test scores, then an entire analytic apparatus is at your disposal for examining validity. You can compute correlations of various types; you can conduct factor analyses. But what are the procedures for examining the plausibility of clinical interview interpretations?

The answer is that there really are no well-developed procedures of this type. Nevertheless, there are several possibilities. One is that we might have several judges review the videotape of the interview and ask them to evaluate the soundness of my interpretations. These judges would of course share a common theoretical framework with me and understand the purposes of the investigation. They would not be "blind" to the purposes of the study. They would have to decide: Does a particular interpretation make sense? Does the evidence of the interview support it? Did I make errors of inference? Did I point to evidence which does not support my point?

The judges' job would be made easier if I had written "interpretive summaries in order to make [my] reasoning explicit and to document [my] interpretations as [I] collect and use evidence" (Delandshire & Petrosky, 1994, p. 14). These authors also suggest that the interpretive summaries could be structured along certain lines designed to facilitate the judges' evaluations. For example, I could be asked to specify the critical pieces of evidence that I used and how I derived inferences from them. In evaluating my interpretations, the judges could then rely heavily, but not exclusively, on this information. In effect, this procedure amounts to establishing the validity of the researcher as an interpretive instrument.

3. *Inter-interpreter reliability.* Another method for evaluating the validity of interpretation involves a kind of inter-interpreter reliability. Suppose that I show the videotape of Toby to an independent judge, also well versed in the theoretical framework and purpose of the study. Suppose that this judge arrives at an interpretation remarkably similar to my own. I would be happy. The reliability of interpretation would lead me to conclude that I must have made reasonable inferences from the available data and that both interpretations should therefore be convincing. In this case, reliability may provide evidence concerning validity. Yet the evidence is not conclusive. It is possible, although unlikely, that both the independent judge and I ignore the evidence, make invalid inferences, and yet reach a common bizarre interpretation because we share common delusions, or for some other reasons. And it is possible, although even more unlikely, that this same kind of agreement would occur among five independent judges, all similarly incompetent and deluded.

The bottom line, I think, is this: None of these sources of evidence is conclusive. But if I construct my interpretation through an interactive group process, drawing on the perception and wisdom of other knowledgeable individuals; and if my methods for arriving at the interpretation are carefully examined and found sound; and if other independent judges use the same evidence to arrive at a similar interpretation of the clinical interview – if all these pieces of the jigsaw puzzle have been put into place, then my interpretation must be reasonably valid and you should be persuaded by it.

Replication. Another way to evaluate the clinical interview is to determine whether results and interpretations can be replicated by independent investigators. Thus, Piaget's great collaborator Inhelder (1989) argues: "The validity of the results is essentially a function of their convergence: each theme is studied via a considerable number of different experiments [interviews] which complement one another" (p. 215). In other words, if independent researchers repeatedly discover that children fail to conserve number under certain conditions, then one should be reasonably convinced of the "validity" of the result.

Similarly, when asked how long it is necessary to collect clinical interview data on a particular issue, Piaget (quoted in Bringuier, 1980) replied that "I have only one criterion. I consider an investigation finished when we no longer find out anything new" (p. 24). Repeated replications should contribute to the persuasibility of the evidence and to the desire of the researcher to conclude the enterprise. This is similar to the "historical validity" described earlier in connection with the focused use of the clinical interview.

Yet replication too is an imperfect indicator of the validity of the clinical interview. Replication may establish the basic soundness of the empirical data. Yes, children do fail conservation problems as traditionally presented. Nevertheless, frequent replication of inter-pretations *within* the Piaget school does not guarantee the persuasive-ness of the interpretation. Critics seldom question Piaget's basic em-pirical data, but they do challenge his theory of conservation – his interpretation of the clinical interview results – and offer alternative explanations (e.g., Donaldson, 1978). Usually, the critics maintain that the conditions under which Piaget's findings were obtained bias the results and that modifying the clinical interview in particular ways will result in different outcomes, which in turn suggest alternative interpretations. But whatever the critics' reasoning, it is clear that replication of findings and even interpretations does not ensure persuasiveness.

Effects on the interviewer and the subject. Another consideration in evaluating the clinical interview is whether it produces benefits for interviewer and for subject. Is it a "good experience" for both?

First, consider the interviewer. Experience in teaching the clinical interview suggests that those who learn it well tend to acquire a central theoretical insight, namely that other minds can be different from one's own. Of course, we all know that in a general, abstract way, but we don't *really* know it until we have the experience of discovering in the course of an interview that the child thinks differently about a certain topic than we do. For the teacher, it can come as quite a shock to learn that Toby does not see = as equivalence even though that is what the teacher believes it is and that is what the teacher has been teaching for the past year. For the practitioner, it can be disconcerting to learn that a clever method of solution, even a brilliant one, underlies the child's incorrect response to an IQ test item. For the researcher, it can be a revelation to discover that the child is engaged in a mental activity more complex than what is described in the literature. My students routinely report that experience in conducting interviews is extremely meaningful and in some cases even transforms their entire views of children and their capabilities. Thus, the clinical interview can be beneficial for the interviewer's intellectual development.

What about the subject, usually the child? The clinical interview may produce several benefits for children. First, the clinical interview may stimulate introspection and interest in cognitive processes. We have seen that children often experience difficulty in introspection and its expression, and that schools often do not encourage (and sometimes discourage) these activities. But the kind of discourse required by the clinical interview should help to stimulate introspection. As we saw in the example of Toby, it is possible that children can learn to improve their introspection in the course of an interview.

On a larger scale, "in the course of some 70 experiments we have employed numerous methods for probing mental processes in young people, and a frequent side effect has been that the children themselves became actively interested in what the experimental procedures were allowing them to discover about their mental processes" (Scardamalia & Bereiter, 1983, p. 62). Children "are very interested in analyzing their cognitive processes, and . . . they are interested in them in much the same way as cognitive psychologists are" (p. 69). In general, "children's metacognitive development may be aided by giving them greater access to data arising from their own cognitive processes" (p. 61). Even 5- and 6-year-old children can learn to examine and think about their own learning and thinking (Pramling, 1988).

In brief, both informal observations and some research findings suggest that interviews may promote children's interest in and understanding of their own thinking. Of course, this kind of development is unlikely to occur within a brief, five-minute period. Repeated exposure to interviewing is probably necessary for lasting effects of this type to occur. This is an interesting and important research topic: How can children be helped to learn about their own thinking? What might a "curriculum" in introspection and metacognition comprise?

Second, the clinical interview may stimulate the child to reorganize cognitive processes (Sigel, 1979, p. 166). At the outset, Piaget (1976a) pointed out that interviewing may cause the child to conceptualize an issue never before considered. Indeed, the interview may place the child in a position of disequilibrium, which may lead to new insights and modes of thinking. The clinical interview experience, particularly countersuggestions, may expose the child to different points of view and thereby challenge the child's egocentrism, much in the manner of argument and discussion with peers (Piaget, 1962). From another point of view, the interview provides a kind of indirect adult assistance which can help to advance the child through the Zone of Proximal Development (Vygotsky, 1978). In any event, whatever the explanation for the effect, the clinical interview may benefit the child's intellectual development. This may complicate interpretation of the interview, but that is a problem for the researcher or practitioner, not the child.

Summary

Most traditional psychometric criteria are irrelevant for evaluating the intensive use of the clinical interview in both practice and research. Instead, evaluation requires considering the skill of the interviewer, the engagement of the child, the plausibility of interpretation based on internal evidence, the possibility of replication, and the effects of the interview on both interviewer and child. Can these criteria help shed light on the goodness and objectivity of the intensive clinical interview? We need to find out.

CONCLUSIONS

History has shown that the clinical interview can make valuable contributions to research and practice. Theory suggests that the method can be more sensitive than other procedures for examining children's thought. But we lack a comprehensive body of empirical evidence providing insights into the workings and effectiveness of the clinical interview. The task for the future is to develop rigorous analytic schemes and methods to evaluate and refine this powerful but delicate research instrument.

CHAPTER 6

Toward The Future: The Clinical Interview and the Curriculum

At least a year of daily practice is necessary before passing beyond the inevitable fumbling stage of a beginner. It is so hard not to talk too much when questioning a child . . . ! It is so hard not to be suggestive!

Piaget, *The Child's Conception of the World*

"Please, Dr. Piaget, every other day?"
Eileen Tang, Teachers College, Columbia University

This chapter treats the role of the clinical interview in the curriculum. First, the chapter discusses the need for virtually all students of psychology, other social sciences, and education to learn the clinical interview. Why? It promotes a way of thinking fundamental to psychology and it is a tool for research, formal and informal. The chapter then describes various techniques, including reports and an interactive video method, for helping students to learn interviewing. Second, the chapter argues that practitioners too need to learn the clinical interview. It helps them to think in a genuinely clinical fashion, that is, to develop theories of individual process. The chapter then presents special methods, some of which draw upon standardized testing, designed to help practitioners use the clinical interview to conduct assessments. Third, the chapter offers a proposal concerning the use of the clinical interview to foster a central aspect of schooling at all levels, namely thinking about thinking, which should be one of the primary goals of education.

THE CLINICAL INTERVIEW AS A WAY OF
THINKING AND AS A RESEARCH TOOL

I believe that virtually *all* students in the various branches of psychology and related social sciences should receive training in the use of the clinical interview. They greatly enjoy learning to interview, and it can provide several benefits.

How Students Can Benefit

First, the actual *use* of the clinical interview, not just reading about it, promotes an important perspective on psychology. The interviewer learns that an important goal of psychology is to create theories of mental process – accounts of how the individual subject goes about solving a specific problem, thinking about a particular issue, etc. The clinical interview almost requires a focus on process, on function. To say that the child solved the problem by means of "intelligence" or failed to solve it because of "learning disability" is perhaps a tautology; at the very least it does not provide much explanatory power. The issue is how the hypothetical entity – the "intelligence" or the "learning disability" – actually operated in these cases. Use of the clinical interview helps the student to conceptualize behavior in terms of particular processes that can produce the observed outcomes. My experience suggests that students can fairly easily get the hang of doing this.

Second, the use of the clinical interview makes psychological theory concrete and immediate for the student. For many students, psychology is merely another academic subject. A topic learned from books, it applies mainly to what one reads in books, not to everyday events. Once I served on the doctoral committee of a student who was purported to be an expert on memory. He could cite large chunks of the research literature in the area and was very sophisticated in analyzing experimental studies. But during the thesis defense, he was stymied when I asked him how he could remember in the morning where his cereal was located. The student was not able to use academic concepts he had acquired to analyze this everyday, practical

210

situation. Because the topic was not covered in the literature, the student could not deal with it.

This is not an isolated occurrence. Many students find it difficult to use their knowledge of child development to interpret the behavior of particular children. And unfortunately, many teachers are unable to make use of the theories learned in psychology courses to understand the learning of children in their classrooms. "That's only theory," the teachers say, as if theory must be something useless, abstract, and irrelevant. For them, theory is certainly not considered to be a useful tool, a practical set of ideas for interpreting everyday behavior.

Of course, it is true of school learning generally that students have a hard time in connecting the academic with their personal concerns. For many students, the very term *academic* has come to mean "irrelevant" and "without practical significance." They see what is learned in school as, well, something to be learned in school, but not as something that has meaning for *them*. Indeed, many students struggle before they reach the stage of "connected knowing," in which academic knowledge is connected with personal concerns (Belenky, Clinchy, Goldberger, & Tarule, 1986).

We want to get the student to go beyond "book learning" – to see that psychological concepts are meaningful, to learn that they can be used in interpreting specific instances of behavior. Cognitive notions *can be* among the most immediate and personally relevant of all psychological concepts (Neisser, 1975), and use of the clinical interview can help students realize that possibility. Again, my informal experience suggests that students can develop an interest in cognitive concepts and can learn to apply them to specific situations. And students do not seem to need a great deal of psychological background to perform well as interviewers. Indeed, I have found that mathematics education students are often quite good at interviewing, even though they often don't know much psychology.[1]

Third, students should study the clinical interview because it can be a useful research tool. We often train students very well in what are usually seen as the more "rigorous" aspects of psychological research: experimental design, test theory, statistics. But we often fail to help students learn the various "qualitative" methods. (Caveat: *qualitative* is a misleading term. The clinical interview can result in quantitative data. The qualitative–quantitative distinction is a red her-ring.) Even if you believe that the clinical interview is useful mainly to serve an exploratory function, you should want students to learn it, for exploration is an essential aspect of research. It can help students to acquire an appreciation, a sensitivity, a "feel," however brief, for how other minds function. This experience of thinking deeply about what someone else is thinking (or feeling, etc.) can help students understand what a psychological theory must explain and can make it possible for them to generate meaningful research questions to be investigated through more formal methods of assessment. And if you believe that the clinical interview is one of the most powerful research methods for exploring cognitive process, you certainly should want students to learn it.

Fourth, the clinical interview can be particularly useful in helping students to understand children who are different in some way, cul-turally or educationally. Many students are middle-class and main-stream. They have little experience with poor children, with minor-ities, with those who are culturally different, and with children who perform poorly in school. At the same time, students may hold various stereotypes about these matters, and indeed some of these stereotypes may even be reinforced by the psychological research literature. The clinical interview may help students learn to under-stand different children and overcome stereotypes. It can do this by providing concrete, immediate experience with such children, experi-ence which many students have not had. Students should go out and observe and interview different children. They may be surprised at what they find.

Can everyone learn to interview really well? Probably not.[2] But that does not mean we should not study it. All psychology students learn statistics and experimental design, even though we know that many will not use these procedures well, and that many will not use them at all. Learning these things is seen to be an essential aspect of being literate in psychology. Just so, students should learn the clinical interview. Here are a few ways they can do it.

212

Methods for Learning the Clinical Interview

In several courses (e.g., Cognitive Development, Research Methods, and Development of Mathematical Thinking) I use a three-step procedure for introducing the clinical interview.

LECTURE AND READINGS

First, I give a lecture on the topic, reviewing Piaget's theory, the logic of the method, etc., much as in chapters 1 and 2 of this book. Presumably this lecture and the associated readings provide students with historical and theoretical background and some general appreciation of why the method can be useful for certain purposes. All this is very "academic."

INTERACTIVE VIDEO

The second step introduces an interactive video experience designed to accomplish several goals: to show students an actual interview, unedited, in "real time," with all its virtues and flaws; to engage students in a process of analyzing the video from the point of view of interview method; to help students learn to interpret both the interviewer's and the child's behavior during the course of the interview. In particular, the students need to learn to use evidence as a basis for developing plausible conjectures (miniature theories) concerning the thought processes of both interviewer and child. What was the child thinking about in that situation? Why did the interviewer ask that question? Did the question confuse the child? Did the child understand it?

The interactive video experience operates in this way. The first requirement is producing or obtaining a videotaped clinical interview containing rich material that could provoke discussion concerning a wide array of interview techniques and children's thinking. The video should be not only intellectually stimulating but captivating and enjoyable to watch. There is no point in showing students a dull video or one that is a poor example of the clinical interview. Fortunately, this is not much of a problem. Most good clinical interviews are fascinating, easily attracting students' interest. And finally, the video should show that the interviewer makes some mistakes. This empowers the students to engage in critical thinking concerning the interview process. What did the interviewer do well and not so well? When the video interviewer is the classroom instructor, students are particularly keen on identifying weaknesses in technique. More important, however, a video of this type also conveys the message that if the "expert" can make mistakes, then it won't be so terrible if the students do too. In my class, I show students the unedited, real-time version of the interview with Toby, from the beginning, including all my hesitations, mistakes, and things I wish I had not said.

A key feature of the interactive method is the way in which videos of this type are employed in the classroom. The video is not simply *shown* to students as an "educational" TV program. Instead, the instructor leads the students in an active discussion of the interview. The instructor shows a short excerpt, asks the students what it means, encourages their interpretations of it, promotes discussion of their interpretations, encourages disagreement among students, pushes students to cite the evidence employed to arrive at a particular interpretation, etc. Then the instructor might play the same clip again, in order to clarify what the child actually said, to reexamine the child's hand movements or the interviewer's facial expression and tone of voice, and the like. The instructor asks key questions to challenge the students' interpretations, to push students to examine evidence carefully, and to lead them to reflect on issues that they may have ignored. The students are constantly encouraged to consider the evidence and what it means for their interpretations, which of course can be revised and refined as the process of examining the videotape proceeds. A minute of rich videotape can generate a good 10 minutes of discussion; in a typical class, the instructor may use 10 or 20 minutes of tape.

This interactive method of using video is based on several principles.

a. *Evidence:* Rich videos provide students with evidence to analyze. The videos are a kind of laboratory experiment.[3]
b. *Construction:* The method encourages construction, in the sense that the students are given evidence which can be used to create

miniature theories, in this case about the interviewer's strategy and the child's thinking.

c. *Activity:* Most students get actively involved in the process of interpretation. The memorization of material does not work in the video discussion setting, as it does in all too many university classrooms, which basically require taking notes and committing them to memory.

d. *Connection with informal knowledge:* The concrete experience afforded by videos – that is, seeing an interviewer pose questions to a child solving problems – allows students to connect the academic exercise (learning about clinical interview technique) with their "everyday knowledge" about conversations and social interaction.

e. *Formalization:* The interaction around the videos also helps students to formalize their everyday knowledge as it is applied to the new phenomena presented on video. The instructor helps the students to develop a more organized, "scientific" approach and to develop conceptualizations that can be shared with others and that draw upon the available and conventional concepts of psychology.

f. *Social context:* In the context of discussing the videos, students have to relate their ideas to what others say (and perhaps experience a clash in viewpoints). They need to put their ideas in a form that can be clearly communicated to others. Moreover, they observe others' struggles in engaging in this activity. It must be salutary to see that others have to engage in a difficult process of thinking before they can obtain a reasonable solution. Students learn from each other. One notices an important feature of behavior that the second missed, but the second offers an interpretation that did not occur to the first.

g. *Practice:* Students repeat the processes of interpretation over and over, and this kind of practice makes perfect, or at least better.

h. *Images:* This experience provides useful "images" or "cases" for memory. Students say: "I never forgot the video where the interviewer was asking one question but Toby was solving another." Images like these guide their later thinking about children's mathematical thinking.

Informal experience shows that students seem to learn a good deal from the interactive video method. Students say that the videos enhance their understanding of clinical interview method in a way that lecture does not. Observation in the classroom shows that students tend to wake up when the videos are shown and the discussion of them is conducted. Furthermore, students not only develop some understanding about interview technique, but also learn to construct interpretations based on evidence. They come to realize that different interpretations may be legitimate, and that the process of interpretation takes time, may involve missteps, and is not so scary. Perhaps most important, students learn that it is possible for them to construct sensible cognitive interpretations of interesting "real-life" events.

THE EXERCISE

Next the students are required to conduct at least one clinical interview themselves. They are given an assignment (a copy of which is given in Table 6.1) that requires them to select a topic for the interview, interview a child or adult suitable for the topic, and write it up. Consider the various steps.

The first is for the student to choose a topic for the interview. The topic should be one that has the potential to yield interesting clinical interview results and that is of interest to the student. Some students find the Piaget material fascinating because basically they find the results hard to believe. How could a child possibly say those things? Other students prefer to examine other topics, for example parents' ideas concerning the nature of development (Goodnow & Collins, 1990). The content of the interview is of lesser concern than is the experience of interviewing.

The second step is to develop a protocol giving a preliminary list of questions. Ideally, the questions should be based on relevant research and theory. More advanced students may base them on pilot work, hunches, and intuitions. In general, the questions will center on the solution of specific problems.

Third, the student needs to get a subject. Usually I handle this informally, especially if the class is large and I can't find subjects for all the students. I ask students to interview a friend, acquaintance, or family member. Usually this means that the student ends up inter-

Table 6.1 *A clinical interview exercise*

The goal of this exercise is to give you experience in conducting and writing up a clinical interview. The interview may focus on any topic you are interested in, with one subject at any age level.

1. Choose a topic you are interested in and know something about.

2. Prepare a protocol giving a preliminary list of questions. These should be based on your hunches and intuitions and on relevant research and theory that you may be familiar with. In general, ask your subject to solve specific problems about which you will ask questions.

3. Get a subject – friend, acquaintance, family member. Describe your study and its purpose to the person or parent and get permission to do it.

4. Do the interview, recording it on audiotape. In general, do not try to teach during the interview.

5. If it is successful, write it up; otherwise, do it again with another subject. Success is defined by your having interesting material to write about.

6. The write-up should be typed, no more than eight pages, double-spaced, and should include
   - the goal of your interview;
   - background information about the subject, such as age, sex, and any other information relevant to the questions;
   - a description of the testing conditions and how the subject responded to them;
   - your preliminary protocol;
   - specific findings and interpretations, in sequence, using key iquotations from the interview (it is not necessary to use statistics);
   - discussion of results in general; and
   - self-criticism.

viewing a younger sibling or a neighbor's child. Of course, the student is required to describe the study and its purpose to the person or parent and get permission to do it.

Fourth, the student goes out and does the interview, recording it on audiotape, which is usually sufficient, especially if the student takes notes on relevant behaviors as the interview proceeds. Of course, richer information can be provided by videotaping, although it may not be available to many students, and it is harder to make transcripts from videotape than from audiotape. The interview should be conducted as early as possible in case it does not work in the sense of not yielding interesting behavior to interpret and write about. If for any reason (fear, boredom, whatever) the subject says very little of interest, then the student has nothing to interpret and should find another subject to interview.

Fifth, the student writes up and submits an account of the interview. I place on reserve in the library an exemplary student report which is typed, in 12-point font; is no more than eight pages, double-spaced, 1-inch margins (you might be surprised what students hand in if you don't make this clear); and, more important, includes several features:

a. A description of the goal of the interview, including a brief discussion of relevant literature that led to design of the protocol. Here students are encouraged not to write a lengthy literature review but to give a brief account of the sources they consulted. Typically this is done in a page or so.

b. Background information about the subject, such as age, sex, family characteristics, and anything else that is relevant. A lengthy description is not necessary. After all, the student does not intend to generalize the results; this is an exercise.

c. A description of the testing conditions and how the subject responded to them. Interpretation of the interview may depend at least in part on an account of the subject's motivation, interest, etc.

d. A copy of the preliminary protocol. This establishes where the student is starting from, and hence how much improvisation and originality is displayed in the course of the interview.

e. Specific findings and interpretations, in sequence, using key quotations from the interview. This seems to be the hardest thing for students to learn. The student needs to select key episodes from the interview, illustrating an interaction between interviewer and child, and then discuss how the episodes lead to a particular interpretation. The form should be something like this: "The subject said x, which seemed to suggest interpretation a. But then the interviewer used a particular probe which resulted in the subject's response y, which now suggested b. A follow-up question resulted in response z, which confirmed interpretation b." Students need to learn to use evidence, to cite it accurately, and to show how a pattern of evidence leads to certain interpretations.

f. Discussion of results in general. The student needs to consider what the interview as a whole reveals about the subject and suggests about the topic under study. "This is only one subject, but it's amazing how similar the results are to Piaget's."

g. Self-criticism. This is a key part of the exercise in which the student examines his or her interview technique and tries to describe where it may have gone astray, what other questions could have been asked, where the interview was extremely successful, and the like. The tone should be constructive. Realizing that all interviews are imperfect, the student discusses how to improve his or her technique.

Students seem to enjoy the exercise and indeed many claim that it was one of their most valuable learning experiences in a psychology course. Other writers also report favorable results (Ormrod & Carter, 1985). Try it.

TIME

Informal experience suggests that learning the clinical interview does not have to take a year's daily practice. Some students catch on fairly quickly. But of course, interviewing is a skill that one develops throughout a lifetime. There is always room for improvement.

IMPORTANT DIGRESSION: THE GENERAL USE OF THE METHOD

I have described the three-step process of teaching the clinical interview – lecture and readings, interactive video, and student interview – in considerable detail because it is of general relevance for the teaching of psychology. Many topics in psychology can be taught in a meaningful fashion by first presenting some introductory material, then engaging students in interactive discussion and interpretation of videotape illustrating the phenomenon, and finally having students go out to work with the phenomenon themselves (through the clinical interview, naturalistic observation, or replication of experiments). The key feature of the method is that it allows students to relate the formalizations of psychology to their own concrete experiences (involving viewing behavior on video, conducting their own interviews or observations or replications, etc.). Connecting the student's informal knowledge (common sense) with the formal knowledge of a discipline (psychology or anything else) is one of the key challenges of education.

THE CLINICAL INTERVIEW AS PRACTITIONER'S TOOL

Students intending to engage in practice of various types – school psychology, clinical psychology, counseling psychology, clinical social work, pediatrics, education – can also benefit from the method. The practitioner's main goal is to understand and help the individual. Thus, the school psychologist needs to obtain a comprehensive assessment of the individual child's psychological functioning, especially as it impacts on school learning. In this case, the goal is less to contribute to an understanding of the nature of "learning disability" in general than to understand the specific processes that interfere with this child's learning of particular academic content. Similarly, the clinical psychologist, counseling psychologist, and social worker aim at obtaining insights into the individual child's inner world view. How does the child portray the parents and construct the self? What are the child's defenses and how do they manifest themselves in his or her style of thinking? The pediatrician may wish to understand the individual child's view of his or her illness, the reasons for it, and what can be done about it. And of course the teacher wants to know how the individual child solves problems, thinks about key concepts, and understands important content.

What does it mean to understand the individual child? In all these cases, the practitioner obtains various sorts of empirical data and interprets the information through the lens of relevant theoretical concepts (along with a good dose of hunch and intuition) to arrive at a "miniature theory" of the individual. The information obtained often consists largely of conventional tests (achievement, IQ, projective, and the like), but it should not be limited to them, for all the reasons already discussed. The practitioner can, and in most cases should, also observe the child on the playground or in the classroom, obtain factual information about family functioning, examine the child's schoolwork, administer questionnaires, interview the child, and employ clinical interview techniques. Having obtained all this information, the practitioner then weighs and interprets the various forms of evidence in order to obtain a miniature theory – a psychological portrait – of the individual child's mental functioning.

Use of the clinical interview can often make important contributions to the process of creating this psychological portrait. The clinical interview affects practitioners' general orientation, just as it does researchers'. It can help both to focus on psychological process and to make meaningful connections between general theory and the everyday behavior of the individual child. The clinical interview also provides practitioners with specific capabilities they might otherwise lack. Practitioners can use the clinical interview to explore the patterns of thinking that underlie scores obtained from standardized tests, especially IQ and achievement tests; to probe deeply into responses to questionnaires; to conduct interviews more effectively; to understand children's learning in the classroom; and in general to obtain a more accurate view of the child's construction of the personal and social world. The clinical interview can help practitioners gain access to the child's inner world and to achieve an understanding of children who fall outside the mainstream. It can enrich the process of practitioners' (clinical) judgment, just as it can enrich the process of psychological research.

How can students learn to engage in clinical interviews for the purpose of practice? I suggest several procedures. Some of course are virtually identical to those used for researchers. The practitioner needs to hear and read about the clinical interview, particularly with respect to its origins in clinical practice. The practitioner also needs to understand how cognitive theory generally can have an important role in understanding psychological difficulties. The practitioner does and should not focus only on personality, emotion, and motive but on how the individual conceptualizes the world of family, friends, and self, processes different kinds of information, solves problems, and in general constructs a personal world. From its origins in S. Freud's *Interpretation of Dreams* (1961), through ego psychology (A. Freud, 1946; Shapiro, 1965), and through the psychology of self (Greenberg &

Mitchell, 1983), clinical theory has always been at its core heavily cognitive.

The student practitioner should also engage in interactive video workshops, preferably involving clinical interviews with children with learning and/or emotional problems, children suffering from illnesses, and children engaged in academic learning. And of course the student practitioner should conduct clinical interviews and write up reports on them.

In addition, a special exercise, involving the probing of responses to standardized test questions, may be useful for training practitioners. Suppose that the student has been engaged in administering an IQ test in the standard manner. The result is a pattern of correct and incorrect responses, a profile, and an IQ score. The student can then select a few items – some on which the child was successful and some unsuccessful – for further examination. At first, the student can employ a limited number of more or less standard probes (e.g., "How did you get the answer?" and "How did you figure that out?") to investigate the child's thinking. Once the student feels some confidence, he or she can employ the clinical interview in a more flexible manner to investigate hypotheses concerning the child's thought. Note that this is similar to the procedure Piaget followed at the outset of his research: use of the clinical interview to explore the meaning of children's responses to standardized test items. Eventually of course Piaget extended his research beyond the test items; the practitioner should do the same.

A similar but more structured approach is to train the student in use of the DAB (Newcomer & Ginsburg, 1995) and TEMA (Ginsburg, 1990) probes described in chapter 5. In these cases, the limited extensions of the clinical interview are spelled out in detail for every test item, so that the student need not invent them. The disadvantage, of course, is that the structured probes are available for only two tests.

Whether the student invents probes for test items or uses available probes, this approach can gradually lead to more flexible questioning. The probes are a kind of halfway house; they provide a secure transition to the clinical interview. In my experience, this security is essential. Students may find the clinical interview intimidating and can benefit from a gradual introduction to it. The use of probes has an additional but not insignificant benefit: It teaches students as much about the role and limitations of standardized tests as about the power of the clinical interview.

In brief, a productive sequence is something like this: Students need to read and hear about the nature, logic, and origins of the clinical interview, and particularly about its origins in clinical work and the centrality of cognition in clinical theory. Students can benefit from the interactive video experience, particularly if it involves individuals of the kind the practitioner will later encounter. Then, students can undertake probes of responses to standardized test items as a transitional step toward flexible interviewing.

A special word should be said about the training of prospective teachers. Many students do not understand the difficult intellectual activity that is involved in teaching. Teachers, like the other practitioners described above, are engaged in a process of forming miniature theories of the psychological functioning of students – all 30 or so of them – in a classroom, as they are engaged in one of the most significant and emotionally charged activities of their young lives, namely learning academic content in school. Teachers need to develop an understanding of what Rochelle is learning, how she learns it, what difficulties she experiences, how her feelings interfere with her reading, whether she enjoys it, what she aspires to accomplish, and the like. Teachers need to understand the whole child – and remember that there are likely to be about 30 of them in an American classroom (and about 40 in Japan and 50 in Korea). Teachers' theorizing must cover a broad range, not just academic learning but general cognitive abilities, personality, and social relations. The teacher's intellectual job is at least as complicated as the clinical psychologist's, who after all might see 8 or 10 different *individual* children on a given day and who may focus on a relatively limited range of child behavior.

Teachers are faced with extraordinary intellectual challenges every day. As James (1958) puts it, the teacher's "intermediary inventive mind" must transform abstract theory into a practical form useful for understanding and serving individual children and fulfilling the "ethical" goals of education. I am in awe of the teachers who can develop useful miniature theories of the performance of the 30 or so individual children in the classroom. It makes no sense whatsoever that the prestige (not to speak of the pay) of this profession is far less than that of, say, the clinical psychologist.

In any event, prospective teachers can benefit a great deal from training in the use of the clinical interview. One variation of the probe technique described above is useful for prospective teachers. They can begin to learn interviewing by probing achievement test items, examination questions, and homework problems given in textbooks. They can employ the key clinical interview questions ("How did you do it?" "How did you get the answer?") to learn how children understand and go about solving academic problems as represented in material of this type. Other techniques are available too. For example, one textbook publisher (Silver Burdett Ginn, 1995a) provides for grades K through 8 a series of pamphlets in "authentic assessment," which include some practical guidance in the use of the clinical interview in assessing children's mathematical learning. Eventually, prospective teachers can make several different uses of the clinical interview in the classroom, including interviewing individual children, interviewing children in the group setting, and helping children to interview each other (Ginsburg, Jacobs, & Lopez, in press).

I can imagine, or rather hope for, a future in which practitioners make extensive use of the clinical interview. Practitioners can use the clinical interview to explore the psychological processes underlying test scores; to supplement questionnaires and standardized interviews; to understand learning in the classroom; and in general to obtain a more accurate view of the child's construction of the personal and social world.

THE EXAMINATION OF THINKING AS PART OF THE CURRICULUM

Think of what Toby learned during the course of the interview. With some encouragement to "figure it out," Toby seemed to enter easily into a new form of discourse, namely conversation in which the major topic is her thinking. She learned that the adult's task was not simply to identify right and wrong answers but to ask her about the ways in which she dealt with problems. She became thrilled that the interviewer was fascinated with what she was doing. She learned that her job was to talk about her own thinking, and not just to try to get the right answers. Over time, she became increasingly adept at introspection and at expressing her method of solution. She became proud that she was competent at solving problems. She soon saw that thinking is enjoyable, and indeed a great source of stimulation. Occasionally, Toby managed to correct wrong answers during the course of explaining her method of solution. Perhaps in the process of formulating her thinking, it developed, becoming more careful and accurate. As the session went on, she became increasingly comfortable and open with the interviewer. She trusted him enough to freely reveal her thinking, including her ignorance, failure, or inadequacy. After a period of time, she even gained some understanding of interviewing and occasionally assumed that role herself. And perhaps she learned too that the interview was not the kind of talk she was accustomed to in her classroom.

In brief, she learned

- to expect that an adult could be interested in and respect her thinking,
- to introspect and express her thinking,
- to enjoy her competence in thinking,
- to reorganize her thinking,
- to become open concerning her ignorance, and
- to develop the skills of interviewing.

That's not bad for a 40-minute interview. But how general is this phenomenon? Does the clinical interview produce similar beneficial effects in other children? We don't really know. There has been little research on the effects of interviewing. However, some evidence already reviewed suggests that children can indeed gain a great deal from participation in the clinical interview. In about 70 studies that examined mental processes, children were found to become interested in and apparently relatively adept at examining their own thinking (Scardamalia & Bereiter, 1983).

Now suppose that this phenomenon is real and substantial. Suppose that many, if not most, children – even young children – can indeed get interested in analyzing their mental processes and can benefit to some degree from the experience, much as Toby did. If it is at least approximately true, then the finding suggests an interesting approach to education: teaching and the curriculum should promote thinking, the analysis of thinking (both its successes and its failures), the expression of thinking, the enjoyment of thinking, and the investigation of others' thinking.

For many years, some psychologists and educators have proposed that schooling emphasize thinking as opposed to rote learning. Thus, in the early days of psychology, Dewey proposed: "Knowing the nature and origin of number and numerical properties as psychological facts, the teacher knows how the mind works in the construction of number, and is prepared to help the child to think number" (McLellan & Dewey, 1895, p. 22). According to Brownell, the teacher

> will insist on an interpretation and upon a defense of [the child's] solution. She will make the question, 'Why did you do that?' her commonest one in the arithmetic period. Exposed repeatedly to this searching question, the child will come soon to appreciate arithmetic as a mode of precise thinking (Brownell, 1935, p. 29).

Similarly, more recently, Bruner (1966) set the tone for a good deal of educational research and practice when he proclaimed: "We teach a subject not to produce little living libraries on that subject, but rather to get a student to think . . . for himself . . . to take part in the process of knowledge getting. Knowing is a process, not a product" (p. 72).[4]

The case of Toby and related research suggest that we not only encourage children's thinking but take the additional step of helping them to analyze their thinking, both successful and not so successful, to put their thinking into words, to enjoy the process of thinking, and to investigate the thinking of other people, both children and teachers. The clinical interview can play an important, but of course not exclusive, role in implementing these goals.

Consider how this might work in an area we are all familiar with, the early learning of mathematics. In the first few grades, children are taught the elementary number facts, like 5 + 3. The traditional approach, which is probably still dominant, stresses drill and rote learning. Aided by flash cards or similar activities, now often presented by computer, children learn to memorize the facts until they become so automatic that no thinking or calculation is required to get the answer. By contrast, the thinking approach maintains that it is essential for children to be able to use reason to obtain the facts. Children should understand that $5 + 3$ is 8 because this fact is based on a concept of addition (combining two sets gives a larger set) and because one can obtain the sum by a reliable procedure (like counting on from the larger number: 5 . . . 6, 7, 8) or by a process of reasoning ("I know that $5 + 2$ is 7, so $5 + 3$ must be 1 more"). One advantage of the thinking approach is that if children are helped to reason in these ways, then they can produce the desired number facts if they are not available in memory.

Suppose we go a step further. In addition to encouraging the children to use their heads (and not only their memories) in learning number facts, the teacher should also help the children to think about how they try to find the number facts. She might give them a new number fact they haven't studied before, ask them solve it any way they want, and then engage them in conversation about the different ways they went about solving the problem. Even the textbook should facilitate the process by asking for children's original methods of problem solving. "Find two ways to get the answer to $3 + 6$. Ask how your friend solved the problem." Or "Describe in words how you solved $9 + 7$."

Activities like these accomplish several educational goals. They show children that the focus is on thinking, not only on the correct answer. The activities give children permission to solve the problem in different ways. This is a radical idea in many classrooms, particularly mathematics classrooms, in which it is all too often assumed that there is only one correct way to solve problems. The activities also prompt children to examine their own thinking and to learn how to tell others about it. As time goes on, the children find that the process of figuring out ways to solve problems is stimulating and enjoyable. Discussing methods of solution helps children to learn that other children may approach problems in many different ways, sometimes successful, sometime not. As the teacher uses something like the clinical interview to question everyone about their thinking, the children in the classroom learn to ask probing questions too, and the query "How did you get the answer?" becomes a natural part of everyday discourse. And if the textbook too offers exercises and lessons which require thinking and introspection, then the message is even more strongly reinforced: The curriculum in this classroom is thinking and thinking about thinking.

Is this scenario within the realm of possibility? Sure it is. I have seen classrooms operating in this way. Some textbooks (Silver Burdett Ginn, 1995a, 1995b) offer lessons of the type described.[5] And some national educational organizations propose "standards" which encourage these kinds of activities (National Council of Teachers of Mathematics, 1989).

Although it is possible to take an approach like this, many do not want to. For example, when the California State Department of Education proposed a "framework" suggesting activities of this kind, there was a tremendous backlash among educators and citizens in the state. Thus, a newspaper columnist wrote:

> If the proposed framework is approved, California's third graders could be taught that even math is relative. [The program] would teach children that there are different "strategies" for solving simple equations. Instead of memorizing 5 + 4 = 9, the program would tell children to find creative ways to find the answer, such as: "I think of 5 + 5, because I know that 5 + 5 = 10. And 5 + 4 is 1 less, so it's 9." . . . Maureen DiMarco, Governor Wilson's point person on education and candidate for state schools superintendent, dismisses new-new math as "fuzzy crap." (Saunders, 1994a, p. A20)

In a later article (Saunders, 1994b), the journalist invoked the imagery of religion to describe those advocating the reforms as "math agnostics."

Clearly, the decision to focus on thinking is at least in part a question of values. Some of us think that it should be precisely one of the main aims of education to encourage children "to find creative ways to find the answer, such as: 'I think of 5 + 5, because I know that 5 + 5 = 10. And 5 + 4 is 1 less, so it's 9.'" Others take the opposing view that such activity is "fuzzy crap" and even an expression of agnosticism (and thus by implication a rejection of orthodox religion). The conflict is essentially one between modernity and fundamentalism.

Where does this lead us? The clinical interview, which is based on key values, especially an ethic of respect for the individual's construction of reality, leads to an interesting and distinctive view of education that stresses thinking and children's examination of it. The question is not so much whether this thinking approach is practical but whether educators and citizens value it sufficiently to attempt the implementation.

CONCLUSION

The clinical interview can vitalize the curriculum. It can help psychologists, both researchers and practitioners, to see children in a different way, as independent thinkers. And it can help children to achieve this vision too. Do we value these goals?

Transcript of the Interview with Toby

As the scene opens, there are four people in the room. Toby (T) and Herbert Ginsburg (H) are sitting at a round table, with papers on it. Rochelle Kaplan is sitting on the side, and Takashi Yamamoto is operating the camera. T is looking bewildered. [] indicate actions and { } indicate elapsed time.

H: Let's start here . . . this is a show and it's on now? Let's have a little music, Toby. Da da da da – Welcome to Children's Math. [Pointing at that phrase written on the board.] And Toby wrote her name on the board. [Pointing to that.] Do you have Toby's name? All right. Very good. Now we come over here and I say, "Hi Toby, how old are you?"

T: 6.

H: 6 years old. And what grade are you in?

T: First.

H: How do you like that? I already knew that already, didn't I? OK, and what we're going to do today is to do some fun math things. OK? And we'll start off real easy by asking you to count, as high as you can. Let's hear you count.

T: [Shrugs her shoulder at the very outset as if to indicate that she finds this relatively easy.] 1, . . . [Counts correctly and deliberately, with little expression, until she reaches about 12, when she shows a slight smile.], . . . 44 [She is correct up to here, and then H interrupts her.] {1:00}

H: OK, why don't you start now with 87. Just keep going from 87.

T: 87, 88, eighty-niiiiiine – [Long pause.] a hundred? [Raising her voice.]

H: OK, keep going.

231

T: A hundred and one, a hundred and two, a hundred and three, hundred and four, hundred and five, hundred and six, hundred and seven, hundred and eight, hundred and nine? [Raises voice again.]

H: Yeah, keep going.

T: That's all. [With a shrug and a bit of a nervous laugh and smile.]

H: That's all. Oh, wow, you counted real high. OK? [She seemed to frown and does not look too happy.] What if I tell you some numbers now and you tell me what comes next. OK, like if I said, 1, 2, . . . , you would say . . .

T: 3.

H: OK. 57, 58, . . .

T: [Jumps in quickly.] 59.

H: OK . . . ah . . . 68, 69, . . . {2:00}

T: [Hesitates a little.] 70.

H: Aaaahhh . . . 84, 85, . . .

T: 86. [Nods to confirm what she has said.]

H: . . . 87, 88, . . .

T: 89.

H: 89, . . .

T: Eighty-tennnn . . .

H: Uh-huh [Encouraging.] . . . eighty-ten . . . what's next?

T: [Looks up as she thinks and then shakes her head to indicate that she does not know the answer.]

H: OK . . . 98, 99, . . .

T: [Looks up and thinks for a little bit.] A hundred.

H: Very good. A hundred and eighteen, a hundred and nineteen, . . .

T: [Quietly.] A hundred and twenty.

H: A hundred and eighty-eight, hundred eighty-nine, . . .

T: [She hesitates and then shrugs her shoulders; she smiles a bit. She starts to play with the sleeve of her shirt.]

H: OK . . . those are really big numbers, I mean that's very very high. OK? Can you count by twos? 2, 4 [She nods.], 6, . . . , keep going. {3:00}

T: [As if reciting a song.] 2, 4, 6, 8, 10, 12 [Hesitates at 12, long pause.], . . .

H: What do you think comes after 12? 10, 12, . . . [Pause.]

T: [She shrugs.]

H: 15?

T: [She nods slowly, not sure of herself.]

H: Maybe. How could you figure it out? Suppose you do 10, 12, . . . How could you find out what comes next?

T: [She shrugs.]

H: You know like what comes . . . well after 12 is what? Is . . .

T: 13. [Quietly, but with confidence]

H: 13 . . . after 13 is . . .

T: 14.

H: OK . . . now how, if you're counting by twos, and you're at 12 . . .

T: 15 . . .

H: Yeah . . .

T: . . . 18 . . .

H: Uh-huh . . .

T: . . . 21 [Nods and smiles as she says this.] . . . 24 . . . 26 . . . {4:00}

H: Uh-huh . . .

T: . . . 28 . . . 31 . . . 34 . . . [She nods as she says each number.]

H: OK, now say you're at 31, and you say the next one is 34, how did you know that 34 comes next?

T: 'Cause I was counting by [Holds up two fingers.] . . . um . . . this . . . I was skipping two of them. [Seems excited.]

H: Ohhh . . . on your fingers? [She looks at H as though she does not understand.] . . . You were skipping . . . using your fingers to do that? [She shakes her head.] No? But you just . . . you were doing it in your head, skipping two? [She nods.] Tell me out loud how you do it. So, suppose you had, what was it, 31? [She nods.] How would you do it? Tell me out loud how you would think to yourself.

T: [Jumps in quickly; looks straight ahead into space.] I was like, thinking like . . .

H: Yeah, like how?

T: . . . 31, 32, 33, . . . [Turns to the interviewer.] I was like talking to myself.

H: Ah-hah . . . so what did you say to yourself when you were talking to yourself?

T: I was saying . . . I was like skipping two, and then saying the next one, and then skipping two and saying the next one. [She gestures with her hands as she explains.]

H: Ooooo-K, so if you're at 31 you'd go . . .

T: 34 . . . [Nods.] {5:00}

H: 'Cause you skipped . . . 32 and 33. [She nods slowly.] OK, say you had 34 now. Tell me out loud how you'd do this, OK?

T: Like . . . I talk to myself . . .

H: Uh-huh. What do you say to yourself?

T: Ummm . . . I like say, skip two of them.

H: Uh-huh. . . well do it for me, OK? Say, 34 . . . what do you do next?

T: 36.

H: Uh-huh, then 36 . . . what do you say to yourself?

T: 38 . . .

H: Uh-huh . . .

T: 40 . . .

H: Uh-huh . . .

T: 43 . . .

H: Uh-huh . . .

T: 46 . . .

H: OK, now what did you say? You were at 43 . . . and then what did you say to yourself to get to 46?

T: I said like skip . . .

H: You said . . . did you whisper some numbers to yourself sort of . . . or like which numbers did you say? {6:00}

T: Like if there was one, I would like say 1, 2, 3, and I would skip to 4 [Gesturing with her fingers.].

H: Ohhh . . . OK, OK . . . so you're using two numbers in the middle there, right? [She nods.] OK, very good. Now, we're going to do something a little different, OK? [She nods.] We have two friends here that you looked at before . . . [Interviewer puts on the table two small animal figures that Toby had seen before the interview began.]

T: Ohhh, they're so cute. [She was very excited about working with the animals.]

H: Do you know what else we could use . . . they are very cute . . . I'm going to put a piece of paper here in the middle for aesthetic purposes, OK? So we have two animals here. OK what is this? [Points to one of the animals.]

T: Rabbit.

H: Uh-huh, rabbit and . . .

T: A squirrel.

H: A squirrel. OK. Now rabbit had 5 carrots. We're going to make-believe rabbit has 5 carrots and squirrel has 3 carrots. OK? [She giggles.] What's so funny? A squirrel likes carrots? {7:00}

T: Nuts. [Giggles.]

H: Yeah well, this squirrel likes carrots. OK? All right . . . so rabbit has how many carrots? [Pause.] 5, remember he had 5, and squirrel has . . .

T: 2.

H: 3. OK . . . so rabbit has 5 carrots, squirrel has 3 carrots. How many do they have altogether?

T: 7.

H: 7! How did you know that?

T: I counted before you asked. [Very proud of herself.] I knew you were going to ask me that!

H: You knew that! Ohhh . . . how did you count?

T: I counted like, there were 7 . . .

H: No, 5 and 3; tell me how you do it.

T: 5 and 3. I counted 7, I counted 3. [Uses hands to gesture toward each animal; looks at interviewer.]

H: 5 and 3 . . . can you do that out loud for me, how you get 7?

T: I thought, like, 7, I was thinking, 7 + 3 and I got 10. {8:00}

H: You got 10! 7 + . . . how do you get 10 if you do 7 + 3? I mean do it out loud for me; count out loud for me.

T: I had 7 . . .

H: Uh-huh, and then what do you do?

T: I have 3, so that makes 10. [She gestures that she counts on her fingers.]

H: Oh, you do it on your fingers? [She nods.] OK. Can you do 5 + 3 for me now?

T: 8.

H: OK, do it out loud, how do you, you know when you count these things, how do you . . .

T: I wasn't counting. I was figuring it out.

H: Figuring it! How do you figure it?

T: Like, you're thinking . . .

H: Yeah . . .

T: All different things . . . but . . . um . . . you think, um, that . . . you think it.

H: Uh-huh . . .

T: . . . what's going to come next.

H: OK, how . . . can you think that out loud for me? If somebody didn't know how to do it and you were trying to tell them . . .

T: I was like trying to help them.

H: Uh-huh, how would you help them? {9:00}

T: I would like help them and try to explain it.

H: Could you explain it for me then?

T: What?

H: 5 + 3?

T: There's 5 . . . [She seems to refer to the five fingers of one hand.]

H: Right . . .

T: . . . and 3 . . . [Seems to refer to the other hand.]

H: Right . . .

T: So that altogether makes 8. [Again, she gestures with her hands to the animals on the table.]

H: OK, but how do you figure out that it makes 8? How do you figure out that it makes 8?

T: 'Cause, um, when you think, you're like thinking about it . . .

H: But what do you think?

T: I think what's going to come next.

H: Uh-huh, suppose I don't know . . . all right? Let's do a new one, OK . . . we're going to do a new one? This one's going to be 4 + 3. OK? Now I want to hear how you think about it, OK? What do you start with?

T: I'm starting with 4 . . . [Puts both hands on the table, as if to count on her fingers, but she does divide the fingers clearly into four fingers on one hand and three on the other.]

H: OK, then what do you do?

T: . . . 4 . . . I see it 6 . . . 7 . . . so I count 7.

H: You see what 6? You started with 4, right over there, right? [Points to her hands.] Then what? What do you see? {10:00}

T: I see 3, so I see 5, 6, 7. [Still looking at her fingers and lifting each finger for 5, 6, and 7.]

236

H: Aaahhh . . . like that! That's how you think about it! That's a good way of doing it, right? OK, what if we do, what if I ask you now, 6 + 3? How would you . . . do it out loud, OK, all the thinking out loud.

T: I was thinking 6 . . .

H: Uh-huh . . .

T: 9 . . . 6 and 3 is 9 . . . [Her voice rises a little as she says this.]

H: You see three more on your fingers, is that it? [She nods.] And then you count? OK, very good. What about . . . let's say rabbit has 7 carrots.

T: 7 . . .

H: 7 carrots, and we take away 3 carrots. How many does rabbit have left?

T: Four! [Excited.]

H: Oh! How did you know that so quickly? How did you . . . figure that out?

T: [She giggles.] I counted.

H: You counted. Tell me how you counted OK?

T: OK. The rabbit had 7. 6, 7 . . . [She uses her hands to count, indicating that two fingers of one hand represent the 6 and the 7.] and I said 6, 7, and I took away 3 and I got 4. {11:00}

H: On your fingers you took away 3? OK, very good. Let's do some bigger numbers, OK? [Interviewer talks with other person in room.] Tell you what, we'll do some adding first, OK? First of all, let's do 4 + 3 . . . how much is 4 + 3?

T: [A pause as she thinks about the question.] 7. [She answers in a quiet voice.]

H: 7, and how did you do that?

T: I thinked.

H: You thought about it, huh? With counting, huh? How much is 3 + 4?

T: 6.

H: Uh-huh, how did you know that?

T: I was like thinking and counting . . .

H: Thinking and counting at the same time? Can you do that out loud for me, how you do 3 + 4?

T: I had 3 in my head . . . [Pointing to her head.]

H: Uh-huh . . .

T: . . . and I had 4 in my head . . .

H: Uh-huh . . .

T: . . . so I had 3 + 4 . . . [She again uses her fingers to count.] 3, 4, 5, 6, 7 . . . 7. {12:00}

H: 7. 3 + 4 is 7 . . . OK. When you have them in your head, do you have a
picture of the fingers in your head, or do you have a picture of the carrots, or what do you have in your head?

T: It's like it's blank but I'm thinking about it . . . I'm thinking about it.

H: Uh-huh . . . when you're thinking, are you sort of saying the numbers to yourself . . . is that what you do?

T: Uh-huh . . .

H: . . . by sort of saying the numbers to yourself . . . it's not so much pictures you have there . . .

T: No.

H: . . . but . . . yeah . . . you're saying the numbers . . .

T: But I think a lot of different things . . .

H: Right . . . right . . . OK . . . You see, what I like to do is try to find out how kids think about these things, so if you could tell me as much as you can about how you think, that would be good, OK? Let's do some new ones and you can tell me how you think about those, OK? How much is 4 + 2?

T: [Pause.] 6.

H: OK. How much is 2 + 4? {13:00}

T: 6.

H: How'd you know that?

T: Because I counted them backwards.

H: You counted them . . . a different way . . . what do you mean backwards?

T: Like you gave me 2 + 4 . . .

H: Right . . .

T: . . . so I counted 4, 5, 6. [She gestures with her hands. She counted four fingers in one hand and two in the other.]

H: Ohhhh . . . you counted the four first . . . that's good . . . that makes it easier, doesn't it? [She giggles.] Yeah, OK, well let's . . . let's do another one here . . . let's do 5 + 2.

T: 7.

238

H: OK . . . 2 + 5.

T: 7.

H: How'd you know that?

T: Because I counted the other way.

H: Aaahhh . . .

T: It makes it a little easier. [She gestures with her hands, flipping them back and forth.]

H: You did the 5 and then the 2? [She nods.] Aaaahhh, OK . . . very good. Let's do some take away, OK? What about 7 take away 3?

T: 4.

H: OK, what about 8 take away 2?

T: 6.

H: OK, how do you do take away? {14:00}

T: It's like, let's say you had 5. [She uses her fingers to count.]

H: Uh-huh . . .

T: . . . and I took away 2. There would be 3 left.

H: Um-hm . . .

T: So that's how you do it.

H: So you take it away . . . OK . . .

T: But I don't do it with fingers . . . I like do it with round little things.

H: With round things . . . You mean you do it like that in class, is that what you mean?

T: Yeah . . . I try to do it with anything . . . like blocks or whatever.

H: So like something like this, right? [He pours white circle chips onto the table.]

T: Yeah.

H: OK. Maybe you could show me how you would do a harder one, like um, can you do something like 12 take away 4?

T: [She counts using the chips. She counts 12 chips from the pile of chips and takes away 4 chips.] 8.

H: Very good, very good. So 12 take away 4 is 8. What about . . . let's do 15 take away 6.

T: [She counts out 15 chips and takes away 6.] {15:00} 9.

H: All right! Very good. So you practice doing this in class, huh?

T: No, you see, we have this robot book, and that's how you do it, you see, you have all different math . . . it has a robot and, um, there's math on it.

H: So a robot book you have in class, and it has math on it?

T: Yeah with math . . .

H: Is the robot counting chips?

T: Yeah . . . you could count them or count them with your fingers, but the teacher doesn't want you to count with your fingers.

H: She doesn't want you to count with your fingers?

T: No.

H: How does she want you to count?

T: With these. [She gestures to the chips on the table.]

H: Ah-hah, so instead of using your fingers, you use the chips to solve problems with like with adding and subtracting . . . aahhh, OK. OK, would you like to show us on the paper? I'll give you another piece of paper . . . remember this paper is aesthetic . . . {16:00}

T: I know.

H: This has got to stay here to cover this thing up [Gestures to something on the table.], but then this paper is for writing on. Can you show us what's in your robot book?

T: We like have high numbers up to 10 – that's all we can go up to, like . . .

H: Show me . . .

T: 5 + 4 . . . [She wrote the 4 under the 5.]

H: Um-hm . . .

T: . . . equals 9, but they don't have the line . . . no line. [She is referring to the line that would conventionally be written under the 5 and 4.]

H: No line?

T: No, and they don't write this [meaning the answer]; you have to solve it.

H: You have to solve it, and then you have chips?

T: Yeah, like, ummm, I'll write one . . . that you have to solve! [Excited by her idea.]

H: All right, I'll try. {17:00}

T: This one's easy for you.

H: I don't know . . . I'll try . . . 5 + 5 . . . you want me to do it?

T: OK.

H: 9.

T: 10.

H: 10! How come it's 10?

T: 5 + 5 is 10!

H: Ooohhh, OK . . . how would you use . . . but then you would use the chips to solve it.

T: Yeah, I solve it.

H: Oh, OK . . . so the book has a lot of problems like that.

T: Yeah.

H: What's . . . I don't understand what the robot is.

T: OK, it's like a book . . .

H: Yeah.

T: . . . and it has math in it to help you with it.

H: Uh-huh . . .

T: . . . and if I could take the rule book up here I could, um, show you it.

H: Does the rule . . . I see . . . is it pictures of robots in there, is that it?

T: Yeah, they're pictures, but they're mostly these. [She gestures to the paper with the problems written on it.]

H: Mostly problems?

T: Yeah.

H: It's like a workbook or something, lots of work in it?

T: Yeah, and, um, you see, I'll show you the five balloons. [She drew a line of balloons.] {18:00}

H: Um-hm . . .

T: So and there was . . . hold it, hold it, now I'm going to write 5, no, 2, 2, 5. See you could write . . . cross that one out . . . 6, no, 0, 6 . . . and there would be down there 2, 2 . . . I'm just writing this . . . and if you get a mistake, she writes this [a sad face], and you correct it, she does that [happy face].

H: Ohhh . . . but . . . how . . . what do you do with that problem?

T: So, um, this, there's like 2 and there's 1 . . . 6, 0. {19:00} [She writes "2 6 0 1" below the line of balloons.]

H: OK.

T: How this is: I see the 2, so I draw to the 2; I see the 1, so I draw to the 1; I see the 0, so I draw to the 0; I see the 6, so I draw to the 6. See that's how you do it. [She connects the numbers under the groups of balloons with the appropriate numbers in the second line.]

H: Ooohhhh . . .

T: . . . and if I made a mistake, she would do this, and if I didn't, if I'm all correct, she would do this.

H: Aahhh . . . but why is there a 2 under here and why is there a 1 over there?

T: They do it different ways. They do it any way they want.

H: Hm. Is it supposed to mean that there are two balloons there?

T: It . . . no, they try to make it, um, tricky.

H: Tricky . . . they try to trick you? [She nods.] How do you like that? [She smiles.] Why do they try to trick you?

T: Because they want to make sure you know your math very well.

H: Ah-hah, ah-hah.

T: Probably.

H: Probably . . . so there are different numbers under here and then you have to match them up with . . . OK. {20:00}

T: Yeah . . . yeah . . . there could be plus or take away, whichever one she puts down.

H: Plus or take away . . .

T: But there's mostly take away. Pluses are so easy.

H: OK. Plus or minus problems . . . right?

T: But, um, I'm not sure about these, they have this plus and, um, 5 . . . no hold, that's wrong . . .

H: Right . . . what do they have?

T: They have . . . twenty . . . plus . . . a hundred . . . [She writes "a hundred" as "00" and "plus" as "–."] There's something like that and you have to figure it out . . . a hundred and twenty . . . so a hundred and twenty, so plus [She changes the − into a +.] and you have to write the answers down here . . . [below the line] I don't know . . .

H: You don't know how to do it?

T: I don't know how to do it.

H: Let me give you a couple like that, OK? Suppose that . . .

T: 'Cause I don't know the high numbers all that much.

H: Right . . . maybe you could write a few numbers for me, OK?

T: Any numbers? {21:00}

H: Well, no . . . I'll tell you what to write, OK? Can you write 13?

T: Three-oh?

H: Thirteen. [She writes "31."] OK . . . can you write, ah, 16? [She writes "61."] 21? [She writes "21."] OK . . . 42? [She writes "42."] OK, 19?

T: I'm not sure about that . . .

H: OK . . . 18. [She writes "81."] OK, ah, 56. [She writes "56."] Good, one hundred. [She writes "100" and giggles.] OK . . . a hundred twelve.

T: I'm not sure about that. [Her voice is soft.]

H: You're not sure about that . . . a hundred five. [She writes "005."] {22:00} OK . . . a hundred one. [She writes "001."] OK, very good. Now let's do some adding problems where we write 'em down. OK? 14 + 13.

T: 14 + 13. [She starts to write the problem, drawing a box around the number she has written.]

H: I want to give you a new piece of paper, OK? The box is what? Why did you draw a box around that?

T: 'Cause to, um, know which one I'm doing . . . 'cause I could get mixed up.

H: I see . . . OK . . . let me give you a new piece of paper here. Can you write down 14 + 13?

T: 4, 1, 3, 1. [She writes "41 + 31."]

H: OK, now how would you do that if you had to write it, 14 + 13?

T: Could I do it with these? [She gestures to the chips.]

H: OK, so you don't really do it with writing . . .

T: No. [Shakes her head.]

H: OK, well you're in first grade. I don't think they do that till much later do they? OK, well that's very good. {23:00} [She shakes her head.] OK . . . we're going to do something a little bit . . . oh . . . while we're still writing I have an idea what we could write, OK? Can you write this for me: 3 + 4 = 7. [She writes "3 + 4 = 7."] OK . . . can you write 5 = 2 + 3.

T: [She writes "5 = 2 + 3."] I hope . . . yeah, you could . . .

H: You could?

T: I think . . .

H: Can you write it that way?

T: Yeah . . . I just wrote it.

H: You just . . . [He laughs, then she joins in.] You just wrote it . . . but is it right to do it that way? [She shakes her head.] It's not right . . . what's wrong with it?

T: Because this should be over here and this should be over here. [She rearranges the numbers on the paper so that they are "5 + 2 = 3."]

H: Oh . . . but then it would be 5 + 2 = 3.

T: I know.

H: Is that right? {24:00}

T: No . . .

H: Um-hm, OK . . . But you're saying that the plus sign has to be over here and the equals sign has to be over here?

T: It doesn't have to be.

H: It doesn't have to . . . but . . . well which way is right?

T: Maybe once in a while it could . . .

H: Once in a while . . . Let's try another one then, OK. 3 = . . .

T: Oh . . . equals . . .

H: . . . 2 + 1. [She writes "3 = 2 + 1."] Is that right?

T: No.

H: No. What's wrong with that?

T: Because 3 = 2 + 1 and that doesn't make sense. [She gestures to the paper as she explains and shakes her head.]

H: That doesn't make sense? Why not? [She shrugs.] It's just not right, huh? What would be a better way to do it?

T: I'd do it 3 + 4 = 7. [She writes "3 + 4 = 7."] That would be good . . .

H: That would be good. {25:00} What about 7 . . .

T: Yeah . . .

H: . . . = 3 + 4? [She writes "7 = 3 + 4."]

T: Maybe, I'm not sure about it.

H: Not sure . . . do you think that could be right?

T: Maybe . . .

H: Maybe . . . which way is better?

T: Oh, come on . . . [As she says this she changes the equation "7 = 3 + 4" to "7 + 3 = 4."] Ooohhh . . .

H: Mm-hm, to put the plus first and then the equals . . . that's usually the way you do it, huh?

T: It's better.

H: OK. Can you tell me, like in this one right over here, we have 3 + 4 = 7, what does plus mean?

T: I'm not sure.

H: Huh?

T: I don't know.

244

H: I mean, does plus tell you to do something? What is it all about? [A pause; she shrugs.] Not sure? What about equals? What does equals mean?

T: It tells you, um, I'm not sure about this . . .

H: Uh-huh . . .

T: I think . . . {26:00} it tells you 3 + 4, 3 + 4 [She points to "3 + 4" on paper and covers it with one hand.], so it's telling you, that, um, I think, the, um, the end is coming up. The end.

H: The end is coming up . . . that, what do you mean the end is coming up?

T: Like, if you have equal, and so you have 7, then. [She is gesturing to the problem on the paper.] So if you do 3 + 4 = 7, that would be right. [She retraces the "3 + 4 = 7" she had written previously as she explained.]

H: That would be right, so equal means something is coming up . . . like the answer. [They both laugh.]

T: Yeah.

H: Uh-huh . . . Suppose we have . . . let's do a new one here, cause we need more paper . . . {27:00} [The interviewer discusses paper with the others in the room.] Here's another piece of paper. Let's start afresh, here, OK? What if we do, ah, 4 + 2 = . . .

T: Oh, equals . . . [She corrects herself because she has written "+" instead of "=."]

H: What should it be? [A pause, she writes "6."] 6, OK. Now, what does the plus mean in here?

T: The plus?

H: Yeah, what does plus mean there? [She shrugs.] OK, and the equals means . . .

T: I think coming up.

H: Something's coming up. Can you show me with these chips what this means?

T: 4 . . . [She counts out four chips.]

H: OK . . . {28:00}

T: and 2 . . . [She counts out two chips.]

H: OK . . .

T: I'll count 4, I'll take away 2 and . . . I was kidding [She pulls the chips back.] NO. Lemme have these chips altogether, cause 4: 1, 2, 3, 4, and 2, equals 6. I would count it: 1, 2, 3, 4, 5, 6, and I would get 6 altogether.

H: OK, so that's what that means, huh? OK, very good. You see when you said . . . when you were doing this like counting you said 4, right, and then you said *and* 2 more, right . . . the *and* is like the *plus* . . . right?

T: Oooohhhhh . . . [A great revelation has just been made.]

H: Ooohhh, yeah, it means you kind of put them all together, right? And then the equals, what does the equals mean then?

T: Equal . . . mm . . . I think . . . I'm not sure about that.

H: {29:00} Well, you're right, it says the answer's coming up, so you do 4 and 2 . . . equals . . . the whole thing. [The interviewer is gesturing to the chips again.]

T: 6!

H: Right, OK, very good. OK. Let's do a different kind of thing. Do you write take away at all? Subtraction. Like if I said, 5 take away 2?

T: 5 take away 2 is 3. [She says this as if it is fairly obvious; she seems to be getting a little bit fidgety.]

H: OK, can you write that out for me?

T: 5 take away 2 equals 3. [She writes "4 − 2 = 3."]

H: OK, look at that closely, make sure you're right. 5 take away 2 is 3. Did you write it the right way?

T: Yeah . . . Oh! 5. [She crosses out the 4 and writes a 5.]

H: OK, now, can you show me how you would . . . well let me ask you this, what does this take away mean, this minus sign? [He points to the equation.]

T: Minus, take away . . . What . . . what do you mean? {30:00}

H: What does this sign here that you wrote mean?

T: I think, the same as the other.

H: The same as the other? What do you mean the same?

T: The . . . I think . . .

H: You mean like plus?

T: Yeah.

H: Could you write plus there? I mean like, 5 + 2 = 3?

T: If you want . . .

H: If you wanted to you could write that? OK, why don't you write that down, too. [She writes "5 − 2 = 3."] 5 + 2 you said you could write.

T: Oh. [She changes the equation to "5 + 2 = 3."]

H: OK, now is that right?

T: It should be 7. [She changes the "3" to a "7."]

H: Uh-huh . . . So you can't write it the same . . . is that right? [She nods.] OK, what does this minus sign mean? [She shrugs her shoulders.] OK, show me with the chips now, what you would do to do 5 − 2 = 3.

T: 1, 2, 3, 4, 5 . . . = 3 . . . what do you mean? {31:00} 5: 1, 2, 3, 4, 5 [As she says this she counts out the chips, but actually only counts out 4; this throws her off slightly, so she brings one of the chips back and gives a little nod to indicate that she is satisfied.] . . . take away 2 is 2.

H: Is what?

T: Is 2. OK. 5: 1, 2, 3, 4, 5 . . . [After she has said this, she re-counts, still not sure. There is a sixth chip getting in the way.] 5 take away 2 is 3.

H: Uh-huh. Where is 3? [She puts her hands over three chips.] What about this one? [The interviewer is asking about the sixth chip that was confusing her before.]

T: I'm not doing this one. 1, 2, 3, 4, 5, . . . and take away 2 . . . 1, 2, 3. [She re-counts, using the chips; she seems more convinced as she says it.]

H: Is 3. You're not counting this one?

T: No. [The interviewer puts that chip away.]

H: OK, very good. OK, now, let's see . . . let me write a couple of numbers, and I'd like you to read them for me.

T: I'm so tired. [She stretches.]

H: Are you tired now? [She nods.] Do you want to take a little break? [She shakes her head.] Want to keep going a little bit? OK?

T: OK. {32:00}

H: What number is that? [He writes "14."]

T: 14.

H: What number is that? [He writes "18."]

T: 18. [He writes "16."] 16. [He writes "21."] Twen . . . nineteen, I think . . . twenty-one.

H: Which one . . . what is it now? This one . . . you just said it. [He points to the number "21."]

T: 22.

H: This one is . . .

T: 22.

H: [Interviewer writes the number "22."] What's that?

T: [Pause.] I'm not sure. [She is obviously tired by this point.]

H: Take a guess.

T: [She thinks for a moment, then shakes her head. Interviewer writes "31."] 30 . . . 31 . . . [She looks up at the interviewer, as if she is not quite sure of herself.]

H: 31?

T: I think . . .

H: OK. [He writes "19."]

T: 91 . . . [He writes "24."] 42. {33:00}

H: OK . . . [He writes "21" again.]

T: I'm not sure.

H: OK . . . we have some big numbers. I bet they don't write numbers that big in your class, do they? [She sighs and says no.] OK . . .

[Next come some combinations problems not described here.]

T: {37:00} [Toby stretches.]

H: It was hard work, but you did very well. Did you enjoy it?

T: [Nods briefly and looks the interviewer straight in the eye.] Who are you?

H: Who am I? [Everyone laughs, and so does Toby.] At what level do you mean that, Toby?

T: Why do you want to know about different things that children know?

H: I see. You know why we study children? We try to find out how they learn math so that we can help them learn math if they have trouble.

Notes

PREFACE

1. Whenever I go somewhere to speak about the clinical interview, I conduct a contest to rename the method. Although I appreciate everyone's best efforts, no one has yet won the (unspecified) prize. Some suggestions have been cognitive interview, thinking interview, cognitive clinical interview, adaptive interview, tailored interview, depth interview, personalized interview, person-centered interview, sensitive interview, informal interview, interactive interview, individualized interview, task-based interview, and dialogic interview. I have a long list of discarded possibilities, none of which seems to improve on Piaget's original name.

CHAPTER 1. THE NEED TO MOVE BEYOND
STANDARDIZED METHODS

1. Some might call this a "test item." I usually call it a "task," sometimes a "problem."
2. Referring to tests, the words *standardized* and *standardization* have several meanings. The key meaning I wish to convey refers to standardized administration. But the terms have also been used to refer to "standardizing" a test, that is, administering the test to a representative sample in order to obtain normative data. Thus a test may be standardized in its method of administration or in its standardization sample yielding norms.
3. Similarly, Kamphaus (1993): "Why are standardized procedures important? They are crucial because they ensure that the testing was conducted under similar circumstances for both the child currently being tested and the children tested in order to develop the norm tables. The examiner can then feel confident that comparing the child's scores to the norm (referenced scores of children the same age) is justified" (p. 82).
4. This concern with the negative effects of labeling and with ensuring that all children receive the least restrictive (most normal) educational placement is virtually identical to what motivates educational policy in the United States today.

5. Musical auditions are literally color-blind. Each prospective member of a professional orchestra is required to play some music behind a screen, so as to hide race, gender, and other observable characteristics that are irrelevant to the ability to make music.

6. I give many examples of this phenomenon in my book *Children's Arithmetic* (Ginsburg, 1989a).

7. This danger is more widespread than you might initially think. In *any* comparative research in which the investigator does not create the groups by a process of random assignment, there exists the possibility that groups will differ in interpretations of and reactions to the test situation. But random assignment is not a full solution. Even if the investigator is able to assign subjects randomly to conditions, then all that may be accomplished is to equalize the possibility of misinterpretation between groups, but not to eliminate it. Under conditions of random assignment, the experimenter might be able to demonstrate significant effects of the independent variable, but if both groups misinterpret the instructions or react in strange ways to the task, the investigator will not know what the results mean! So it is always crucial to determine how subjects interpret the task you have given them.

8. Indeed, the National Council of Teachers of Mathematics (National Council of Teachers of Mathematics, 1989) has been a leader in advocating the development, dissemination, and widespread use of alternative, nonstandardized assessment procedures. In this respect, educators seem to be stepping ahead of psychologists.

9. Of course, this is often true of school situations too, which is one of the reasons standardized tests are reasonably successful at predicting school performance.

10. This observation was made by my student Charlene Hendricks.

11. This observation was made by my student Sun Mee Lee.

12. In view of the seriousness of this issue it is remarkable and unfortunate that there has been so little research on children's test-taking styles and motivation and on how they are related to ethnic-group and social-class membership.

13. Anastasi (1988) notes that in cross-cultural research, efforts have been made to "rule out one or more parameters along which cultures vary." Thus, if the cultural groups spoke different languages, then "tests were developed that required no language. . . . When . . . illiteracy was prevalent, *reading* was ruled out" (p. 298).

14. Garcia and Pearson (1994) are more pessimistic than I am about the possibility of achieving any reasonable degree of fairness in assessment: "At every level of analysis, assessment is a political act. Assessments tell people how they should value themselves and others. They open doors for some and close them for others. The very act of giving an assessment is a demonstration of power: One individual tells the other what to read, how to respond, how much time to take" (p. 381). Certainly, test makers have had the power to dictate what is important to measure, and their decisions often drive the academic curriculum. But must this be true of all forms of assessment? Can

assessment reflect a politics which respects and attempts to empower the individual?

15. Similarly, cross-cultural researchers "must engage in local ethnographic work to establish the relation of their testing procedures to the local culture and the kinds of experiences that people undergo" (Cole, 1992, p. 780).

CHAPTER 2. WHAT IS THE CLINICAL INTERVIEW? WHERE DID IT COME FROM? WHY DO IT?

1. Actually, distinctions between reality and fantasy are becoming increasingly hard to maintain on television. "Docudramas" are fictionalized accounts of reality; C-Span presents coverage of the U.S. Congress in which our elected representatives *seem* to be talking to a full house but are actually almost alone, except for the cameraperson and a few other representatives who I imagine are dozing; the film *Jurassic Park* presents computer-generated images which seem to be real; and of course for a long time, the news has presented segments which are to some extent distorted by editing, camera angles, etc.

2. For example, Rappaport, a pioneer in the cognitive interpretation of IQ tests, advocated a technique very much like what is involved in determining the "Zone of Proximal Development" (Vygotsky, 1978), which is reviewed in this chapter. "If and when the examiner is satisfied that the subject cannot solve the problem, he should mark the item failed, but give the subject progressive help in order to discover the nature of the difficulty" (Rappaport, 1946, p. 70).

3. In what follows, I disguise specific IQ items (in case any children should read this) and hence the details of response, but it is easy to see what items are being referred to.

4. Clinical interviewing need not be limited to children. Here is an excerpt of an interview with an adult on the topic of abortion (Smetana, personal communication):

> Interviewer (I): Okay, so as a general rule, when do you think abortion should be permitted?
>
> Subject (S): I guess generally I think anyone who – any woman who wants an abortion in the first three months, it should be permitted.
>
> I: Why?
>
> S: [long pause] Well, it just seems like . . . I guess I just think people should . . . not have children they don't want, almost . . . that generally speaking, abortion is better than any sort of unwanted . . . than any child that's unwanted, for whatever reasons . . . whether the reasons are good or bad, bad reasons might indicate emotional instability or immaturity on the part of the person that has them . . . it's not good for the child to be born unwanted.
>
> I: Do you think it would be wrong for a woman to have an abortion after three months?
>
> S: No.
>
> I: Why did you say then it shouldn't be permitted?

S: Oh – it shouldn't be permitted as a general rule.

I: You're saying – well, what are you saying?

S: [long pause] . . . it seems sort of unjustified to have an abortion that late, unless – again, it's a question of some serious emotional problem on the part of the mother. . . .

I: But if the reasons aren't things like emotional stability or health, and a woman just in general wants an abortion after that, do you think that's justified?

S: [long pause] To a certain extent, yes.

I: Can you explain what you mean when you say "to some extent" it would be unjustified?

Again the clinical interview, this time conducted with an adult and concerning a topic very different from those considered earlier, illustrates some basic features: The interviewer begins with a rather standard, open-ended "problem" that was devised beforehand (" . . . as a general rule, when do you think abortion should be permitted?"), then probes for the subject's reasoning ("Why?"), tests the limits of the subject's response ("Do you think it would be wrong for a woman to have an abortion after three months?"), and in general tries to clarify ambiguous responses ("Why did you say then it shouldn't be permitted?"). I cannot imagine obtaining from a standardized test or questionnaire material as rich as what Smetana was able to get from such interviewing.

5. This section is adapted from a talk I gave, with Kathleen E. Gannon, at the Piaget Society in Philadelphia, June 4, 1983, "Sigmund Freud: Cognitive Psychologist."

6. Other cognitive scientists have come to similar conclusions. As Chomsky (1964) wrote in another context: "if anything far-reaching and real is to be discovered about the actual grammar of the child, then rather devious kinds of observations of his performance, his abilities, and his comprehension in many different kinds of circumstances will have to be obtained" (p. 36).

7. To satisfy these methodological requirements in the context of therapy, Freud developed the free-association method. We are not concerned with this technique here, and the fact that it may suffer from damaging weaknesses does not detract from the power of Freud's views on the need for subtle interpretation of cognitive phenomena.

8. For an account of Piaget's life, see his autobiography (Piaget, 1952a) and also the account given by me and Opper (Ginsburg & Opper, 1988).

9. Indeed, Piaget's first attempts at theorizing about children's thinking, particularly in *Judgment and Reasoning in the Child* (Piaget, 1964) were dominated by psychoanalytic concepts. Freud's description of the dreamwork played a major role in shaping Piaget's first cognitive theory, the notion of egocentrism. Piaget felt that the young child's thought was midway between the primary-process ("autistic") thought of the younger child and the realistic thought of the adult. The processes of egocentric thought were said to resemble those of the dreamwork. For example, egocentric thought combines ideas that should not be combined (the notion of condensation) and is dominated by wish fulfillment. Later, Piaget revised his notions of egocentr-

ism; but it is no exaggeration to say that Freud's account of the dreamwork provided the inspiration and basis for Piaget's initial theory.

10. Even this becomes problematic, however, when the test is given to children from various ethnic groups in a diverse society, such as the contemporary United States. In turn-of-the-century France, however, Binet was not faced with this problem. His population of children was relatively homogeneous, so that inferences of retardation were probably reasonably accurate and certainly superior to the idiosyncratic judgments made by "alienists" on the basis of unstandardized procedures.

11. Piaget's argument seems to combine two points I raised earlier. One is that tests are not suitable instruments for studying complex thinking, and the other is that subjects interpret tests in idiosyncratic ways. In Piaget's view the first is true at least partly because of the second.

12. Later, Piaget often used problems involving concrete objects as a basis for exploration. He came to believe that young children in particular have difficulty in dealing with purely verbal material and that concrete objects can provide the child with some food for thought and thereby stimulate it.

13. As in the case of "pure observation," Piaget's initial experimentation was largely verbal, involving spoken problems of the sort used in the moral-judgment example presented here. Later, however, Piaget introduced concrete problems as the basis for the experiment. Thus, in a conservation of number experiment of the type described above (the case of Jimmy), the child might be asked to make judgments involving various arrays of objects, not about hypothetical situations described in words.

14. Note, by the way, how the question is phrased in such a way as not to suggest an answer. Each of the possible alternatives is given equal weight (although of course the order of questions may bias judgment).

15. Later, an attempt was made to call the method "the critical exploratory method," presumably to reflect both its experimental, hypothesis-testing nature (the "critical" test) and its flexibility. But the name never caught on.

16. It is interesting to note that Piaget's monumental research on infancy (indeed, I think it is his greatest piece of work) is based on essentially the same method, with the crucial exception that for obvious reasons no words are used. As in the case of the clinical interview, Piaget's research method for babies involves on-the-spot experimentation based on naturalistic observation.

17. The clinical interview (along with other forms of qualitative method) is perhaps more like jazz than like classical music in the sense that it involves improvisation, guided by underlying principles but improvisation nevertheless (Oldfather & West, 1994).

18. I must relate a personal anecdote. When I began interviewing, I asked children the "How did you get the answer?" type of question all the time, partly because I believed that is what Piaget did. Although I had read a good deal of Piaget, I falsely believed that he did – as a basic part of his method – what *I* considered to be quite natural. I was disabused of my egocentric error only when it was pointed out to me by my colleague Howard Gruber, who spent many years working with Piaget and has great

insight into his way of thinking. Gruber wrote in a letter to me that "it would not have been his [Piaget's] way to ask the child to tell him how it thought or imaged, etc. Rather, he inferred that from the whole collection of material he had." So our beliefs can easily distort our memories.

19. "His clinical method proves a truly invaluable tool for studying the complex structural wholes of the child's thought in its evolutional transformations. It unifies his diverse investigations and gives us coherent, detailed, real-life pictures of the child's thinking" (Vygotsky, 1986, p. 14).

20. For an important critique describing ambiguities in Vygotsky's account of determining the Zone of Proximal Development, see Paris and Cross (1988).

21. Constructivist theorists even differ in their views of the contribution of "reality." According to Piaget: "An object is a limit, mathematically speaking; we are constantly moving towards objectivity, we never attain the object itself. The object we believe we can attain is always the object as represented and interpreted by the intelligence of the subject. . . . The object exists, but you can discover its properties only by successive approximations" (Bringuier, 1980, p. 63). By contrast, some radical constructivists seem to imply that almost everything is constructed, individually or socially, and there does not seem to be any room left for an "objective reality." Thus, Glasersfeld (1990) claims that "when my actions fail and I am compelled to make a physical or conceptual accommodation, this does not warrant the assumption that my failure reveals something that 'exists' beyond my experience" (p. 24).

22. "As a methodological perspective in the social sciences, constructivism assumes that human beings are knowing subjects, that human behavior is mainly purposive, and that . . . human organisms have a highly developed capacity for organizing knowledge. . . . These assumptions suggest methods – ethnography, clinical interviews, overt thinking . . . – specially designed to study complex semi-autonomous systems" (Noddings, 1990, p. 7).

23. Chapman (in Chandler & Chapman, 1991) presents an interesting discussion of the role of verbal justifications in the evaluation of "competence." He argues basically: "By eliminating children's verbal explanations, one does not succeed merely in measuring children's true competence with less error, but in measuring a competence differently conceived" (p. 226). Several chapters in this book provide thoughtful examinations of meanings of the "competence–performance" distinction.

24. To measure such complexity, they recommend more powerful forms of diagnosis but, strangely, to my mind, do not stress the clinical interview.

25. Others have elaborated upon and extended Feuerstein's dynamic assessment procedures (Lidz, 1987). Campione, Brown, Ferrara, and Bryant (1984) have taken a somewhat different, perhaps more standardized and quantified, approach to Vygotsky's Zone of Proximal Development.

26. Shweder (1991) makes a similar distinction between those who choose to investigate the "Platonic" essence of the general human mind, and thus "enter a transcendent realm where the effects of context, content, and meaning can be eliminated, standardized, or kept under control, and the central

processor observed in the raw" (p. 81), and those who choose to investigate, through the lens of "cultural psychology," a mind which is "content driven, domain specific, and constructively stimulus bound; and [which] cannot be extricated from the historically variable and cross-culturally diverse intentional worlds in which it plays a coconstituting part" (p. 87).

27. As pointed out above, the clinical interviewer who treats children as individuals may not be concerned with them as individuals. Thus, Piaget was interested in learning about children in general (or even in knowledge in general, leaving out the children) and not in learning about particular children. He treated children as individuals, *only* in order to obtain accurate knowledge of their competencies. I thank my colleague Howard Gruber for this insight.

28. These notions of fairness also get played out in the legal and political systems. According to Finnegan (1994), in a trial in which a defendant was being tried on charges of violent assault, the judge imposed "objective" standards of fairness – that is, fairness as impartiality. Specifically, the judge prohibited anyone from revealing the defendant's past criminal record. "The great care taken to exclude certain matters from evidence had but one purpose: to protect the rights of the accused. Everyone, starting with the judge, had been intent on providing Martin Kaplan a fair trial" (p. 58). Using these criteria, the jury convicted the defendant. After the trial, Finnegan, a journalist, investigated the defendant's past and concluded that the effect of excluding evidence concerning Kaplan's criminal past was to "weaken his case." Why? Because particular aspects of his criminal behavior made it unlikely that he could have committed the crime in question. Talking later to Finnegan, one witness reflected, "Maybe I should have just got up there and said, 'Martin's a junkie. . . . His hands were bloody when they stopped him because he'd been shooting up in his wrists. He couldn't have beaten up anybody if he wanted to – he was too high" (pp. 58–59). So evidence that was excluded in the interests of "fairness" – that Kaplan's hands were bloody because of drug taking, not because of violence, and that he was too spaced out to be violent – could have exonerated him.

   Notions of fairness are also central to Hochschild's (1981) discussion of American political beliefs concerning "distributive justice," that is, the distribution of resources in a society. One approach, similar in some ways to the concept of fairness as impartiality, is a *"principle of equality* among persons,"* which assumes that "every person may make equal claims on social resources, despite differences in race, sex, ancestry." A second approach is similar to the notion of fairness as sensitivity to the distinctive needs of the individual: "At other times, people begin with a *principle of differentiation* among persons, that is, they assume that differences in race, sex, ancestry, and so on create legitimately different claims on social resources" (p. 50).

CHAPTER 3. WHAT HAPPENS IN THE CLINICAL
INTERVIEW?

1. For example, while the interviewer may see the goal as getting information, in a small Mexican village the "respondents may see the process as entertainment, pedagogy, obtaining cash income, protecting her or his neighbors from outside scrutiny, and so forth" (Briggs, 1986, p. 49).

2. Siegal (1991) claims that young children have a poor understanding of the rules of conversation and therefore respond inappropriately to the adult's questions in the clinical interview, with the result that it underestimates their competence. I think these claims are misguided. For one thing, Siegal tries to demonstrate them by investigating questioning patterns of a type that are more characteristic of a rather standardized experiment than of a truly flexible and sensitive clinical interview. Siegal's subjects get confused because they are essentially given a standardized test, not a clinical interview. His findings have little relevance for the kind of interview I describe here.

3. What Labov and Fanshel (1977) call "representation."

4. Usually there are two, especially when the subject is a child. But there can be more than two, as when a teacher uses a form of the clinical interview with a small group of children or indeed the whole class (Ginsburg et al., 1993).

5. And even if we could record everything, we cannot adequately comprehend everything that transpires at a given time. In the small slice of the interaction under observation, the interviewer is simultaneously asking a question, "relating" to the child, expressing his own confusion, constructing a reasonably grammatical sentence, and perceiving the commotion next door (just for starters). How can we grasp all of this? Imagine how much sensitivity is required of a teacher who is trying to deal with and understand 30 children at once!

6. "[C]onversation is not a chain of utterances, but rather a matrix of utterances and actions bound together by a web of understandings and reactions" (Labov & Fanshel, 1977, p. 30).

7. "The internal consistency and replication of the principles within this interview provides [sic] considerable justification for this approach" (Labov & Fanshel, 1977, p. 8).

8. It is an interesting question as to why individual case studies are not highly valued in psychological research, even in the clinical area. Perhaps because so many psychologists seem to be seduced by the aura of scientific respectability that they believe is provided by the use of statistics, the usefulness of psychological studies involving small numbers of subjects has not been sufficiently appreciated.

9. "[I]t is obvious that the utility of our work will be judged when the reader turns to other cases that he is more familiar with and encounters fresh data that may be assessed within this framework" (Labov & Fanshel, 1977, pp. 7–8).

10. You should be aware, however, of how difficult it is to make even a simple(!) transcript that accurately captures speech. Labov and Fanshel (1977) point

out that they often find mistakes in their transcripts only after repeated viewing: "after 9 years we find that we are still making corrections that are by no means trivial on repeated listenings" (p. 355). I am not interested in the fine level of detail that is sometimes important for Labov and Fanshel, but still, doing a transcript is difficult.

11. Compliments of Lizbeth Ginsburg.

12. Actually, deciding whether and how much information to obtain about the children is no simple matter. On the one hand, it is desirable to have a good understanding of the child to be interviewed. On the other hand, the information from the school may not provide it. The test scores and the teacher may offer a distorted and inaccurate account of the child's abilities. If so, getting the available information may only restrict or bias the interviewer's view of the child.

13. The tapes were eventually published (Ginsburg, Kaplan, & Baroody, 1992), but the outcomes were not exactly as expected (Ginsburg, 1996a).

14. In school, children learn that "teachers' questions entail assumptions that reverse those of the interview session. Whereas in the interview, the questioner is assumed not to know the answer to the question, in the classroom the teacher does know the answer. . . . In fact, teachers often use questions to assess what is already known so that they can add to it. . . . Pupils generally answer such questions with brief comments and come to think that it is proper to answer all adult questions in this way, whereas they give long and complex answers to questions from peers" (Garbarino et al., 1992, p. 181). In this situation, teachers may then underestimate what children know. Short and evasive answers do not inspire confidence in a student's abilities. But if the student has been taught to respond in this way, the apparent ignorance is school induced.

15. Of course, you could conjecture that had I asked the question properly, she would not have said "eighty-ten." There is no evidence in this case to contradict that hypothesis. But I don't believe it, because the "eighty-ten" error is quite common. Furthermore, even if my mistake flustered her, why would she make that particular error rather than saying, for example, "43?"

16. Some relevant evidence is provided by Stigler and Perry (1990), who report that "Japanese teachers . . . often try to slow their students down, asking them to think about a problem and how to solve it, then discuss their thoughts with the class, rather than rushing on to solve the problem. Interestingly, Japanese fifth grade teachers asked their students not to solve but to think about a problem in 7 percent of all segments, something that occurred in only 2 percent of the Chinese and American segments" (p. 340).

17. Actually, I took this quotation a bit out of context. Binet and Simon were referring, not to the interview, but to what teachers could do in the classroom. But the point is the same: Ordinary classroom practice does not frequently enough permit the opening of children's minds.

18. As I pointed out in chapter 2, Piaget's earliest work proposed that the young child experiences difficulty at introspection (Piaget, 1964) and his later research reinforces this finding (Piaget, 1976b). Contemporary researchers concur (Flavell, Green, & Flavell, 1995).

19. Whenever I omit details, they are always reported in the full transcript, which is given in the appendix.
20. As Mishler (1986) puts it: "One way an interview develops is through mutual reformulation and specification of questions. . . . Rather than serving as a stimulus having a predetermined and presumably shared meaning and intended to elicit a response, a question may more usefully be thought of as part of a circular process through which its meaning and that of its answer are created in the discourse between interviewer and respondent as they try to make continuing sense of what they are saying to each other" (pp. 53–54).
21. I might even speculate that if the child is assuming both these roles, she is also working on reducing egocentrism. In learning different points of view, she is learning to see herself differently. Taking the point of view of the other may be useful for introspection. Accurate self-observation requires objectivity; it implies seeing the self as others do. Does introspection involve a kind of role taking?
22. Of course, a clinician might have another interpretation. The child might be implying that in general, adults are out to deceive her, to trick her. The statement about schooling might be a screen for something deeper. This level of analysis may indeed be useful in some cases but does not seem useful in understanding that trusting soul Toby.
23. "Continuous recalibration of communicative conventions is always to be expected in transactions between human beings . . . communicating and learning to communicate always go hand in hand" (Labov & Fanshel, 1977, p. 7).

CHAPTER 4. GUIDELINES FOR CONDUCTING A CLINICAL INTERVIEW

1. The same is true, of course, in art and religion. The violinist's technique takes years to master, as does the monk's discipline.
2. Thanks to Lynn Liben for highlighting this point.
3. Is it possible for an interviewer who thoroughly devalues children's thinking to be sensitive to their constructions and to gain their trust so that they will reveal their thought? Perhaps it is. Some people are very manipulative.
4. My student Kathleen M. Saint Leger reports that in testing a child, 5 years and 3 months of age, "I told Julian that we were going to play a math game, and I will need to ask him some questions. He smartly replied, 'That's not a game, it's a test.'" So much for simple rapport.
5. The ethics of confidentiality in the case of children's interviews are complex. But at least the interviewer needs to be truthful in asserting that the interview will not affect grades and that the details of the interview will not be reported to teachers or parents.
6. "All you need to do is to appear completely ignorant, and even to make intentional mistakes so that the child may each time clearly point out what the rule is. Naturally, you must take the whole thing very seriously. . . . It is

of paramount importance . . . to play your part in a simple spirit and to let the child feel a certain superiority at the game" (Piaget, 1962, pp. 24–25).

7. Carol Collins has been interviewing children about their views of a standardized test as compared with a clinical interview. She finds: "Although tests may be boring in context, and either anxiety producing or gratifying because of their level of difficulty (or in [one child's] words, make her feel a mixture of 'bored, nervous, and proud'), they are in one sense easy; the child is not asked to *explain* but merely to *answer*." For some children, tests are preferable to interviews: The former are safe; the latter require that one not only think but reveal it.

8. The contrast in atmosphere between testing and the clinical interview is striking and deserves empirical study.

9. Or at least that is my conjecture. Further, I suspect that children's understanding and awareness of their wrong answers may take several forms: (1) I'm not sure whether this answer is right or wrong but I'll try it anyway. (2) I'm wrong and I know I am wrong. (3) I'm sure this answer is right. (4) If what I do is different from what you (the adult, the teacher, the smart one) do, I must be wrong. This aspect of metacognition – do you know when you are wrong and how do you know? – seems worthy of further study.

10. I am indebted to members of my seminar, particularly Carol Collins, for this insight.

11. As a child, the Nobel Prize–winning mathematician John Nash had trouble learning math. Or at least that is what one of his teachers thought. His sister commented, "He could see ways to solve problems that were different from his teacher's" (Nasar, 1994).

12. Interviewed by my student Jacqueline Fliegel.

13. Of course, experimentation also involves many other elements (e.g., assigning subjects randomly to conditions) that I do not consider here.

14. For example, you have only one subject, and you cannot easily counterbalance order of presentation.

15. Certainly it does not make sense merely to ask, "Do you understand?" (Garbarino et al., 1992, p. 190).

16. This question was in fact taken from the reading comprehension scale of the DAB-2, a standard test of achievement (Newcomer, 1990).

17. Interviewed by my student Sun Mee Lee.

18. In this companion to the DAB-2, a standard test of achievement, we present organized ways for following up on students' responses by rephrasing questions, asking about thought processes, and examining learning potential.

19. The interviewer was my student Charlie Hendricks, and I am quoting from her report here.

CHAPTER 5. EVALUATING CLINICAL INTERVIEWS: HOW GOOD ARE THEY?

1. Indeed, the general practice in Genevan research was for Piaget to send out legions of students and assistants to interview children on a particular topic. He himself did not conduct many interviews after he became "Piaget."
2. Similarly, Cairns (1986) points out that "certain developmental outcomes are sufficiently unique as to require analysis at the individual, configural level rather than at the sample, population level. Generalizations may be reached by an analysis of individuals *prior* to aggregating them into 'samples' or 'conditions,' not after the aggregation has occurred. . . . [T]he unit of study becomes the individual, not the sample of individuals" (p. 104).
3. Advice to graduate students: I am nearly driven mad by those students who write in the final chapter of their dissertations that one weakness of their study is that it cannot be generalized beyond the subjects employed. If this were indeed the case, the dissertation is worthless. What they really mean is that they are not sure how widely the results can be generalized. That is another, legitimate matter.
4. This constraint was suggested by Liz Peña in conversation.

CHAPTER 6. TOWARD THE FUTURE: THE CLINICAL INTERVIEW AND THE CURRICULUM

1. Of course this is a very tentative finding, but it does make some sense. Mathematics students are trained to analyze problems in terms of the solution processes necessary to solve them. Is this similar to a cognitive analysis of process?
2. This is an empirical question. I imagine that when computers were invented it seemed unlikely that 5-year-olds would be able to use them. But they can – at least under certain conditions and for limited purposes. It is hard to prove the null hypothesis, to say that something *cannot* be done. At the same time, I think it is safe to say that despite our best efforts at training, some individuals can never be really good at clinical interviewing. This deficiency is as likely to characterize practitioners as researchers.
3. Many years ago, before the advent of video, Arnold Gesell pioneered a similar use of motion pictures. "Scientifically controlled cinematography fortunately is a paradoxical form of embalming. It not only preserves the behavior in chemical balm, but it makes that behavior live again in its original integrity. The cinema registers the behavior events in such coherent, authentic and measurable detail that . . . the reaction patterns of infant and child become almost as tangible as tissue" (Gesell, 1952, p. 132).
4. Of course, not all psychologists have agreed with this approach. Thus, for example, Thorndike (1922) emphasized a kind of "drill and kill" approach, and as Lagemann (1989) has vividly argued, "Edward L. Thorndike won and John Dewey lost" (p. 185) in virtually all aspects of educational theory and practice.
5. I was one of the authors of these materials.

References

Allport, G. (1942). *The use of personal documents in psychological science*. New York: Social Science Research Council.

Anastasi, A. (1988). *Psychological testing* (6th ed.). New York: Macmillan.

Baroody, A. J. (1984). The case of Felicia: A young child's strategy for reducing memory demands during mental addition. *Cognition and Instruction, 1,* 109–116.

Belenky, M. F., Clinchy, B. M., Goldberger, N. R., & Tarule, J. M. (1986). *Women's ways of knowing: The development of self, voice, and mind*. New York: Basic Books.

Bigler, R. S., & Liben, L. S. (1993). A cognitive-developmental approach to racial stereotyping and reconstructive memory in Euro-American children. *Child Development, 64,* 1507–1518.

Binet, A. (1969). The perception of lengths and numbers. In R. H. Pollack & M. W. Brenner (Eds.), *Experimental psychology of Alfred Binet* (pp. 79–92). New York: Springer.

Binet, A., & Simon, T. (1916). *The development of intelligence in children*. Baltimore, MD: Williams & Wilkins.

Bloom, L. (1970). *Language development: Form and function in emerging grammars*. Cambridge, MA: MIT Press.

Bloom, L. (1991). *Language development from two to three*. New York: Cambridge University Press.

Briggs, C. L. (1986). *Learning how to ask: A sociolinguistic appraisal of the role of the interview in social science research*. Cambridge, England: Cambridge University Press.

Bringuier, J.-C. (1980). *Conversations with Jean Piaget* (B. M. Gulati, Trans.). Chicago: University of Chicago Press.

Brown, A. L., Bransford, J. D., Ferrara, R. A., & Campione, J. C. (1983). Learning, remembering, and understanding. In J. H. Flavell & E. M. Markman (Eds.), *Handbook of child psychology: Vol. 3. Cognitive development* (pp. 77–166). New York: Wiley.

Brown, A. L., Campione, J. C., Webber, L. S., & McGilly, K. (1992). Interactive learning environments: A new look at assessment and instruction. In B. R. Gifford & M. C. O'Connor (Eds.), *Changing assessments: Alternative views of aptitude, achievement, and instruction* (pp. 121–211). Boston, MA: Kluwer Academic Publishers.

Brown, J. S., & VanLehn, K. (1982). Towards a generative theory of "bugs." In T. P. Carpenter, J. M. Moser, & T. A. Romberg (Eds.), *Addition and subtraction: A cognitive perspective* (pp. 117–135). Hillsdale, NJ: Lawrence Erlbaum Associates.

Brownell, W. A. (1935). Psychological considerations in the learning and teaching of arithmetic. In W. D. Reeve (Ed.), *The teaching of arithmetic (10th Yearbook of the National Council of Teachers of Mathematics)* (pp. 1–31). New York: Columbia University, Teachers College, Bureau of Publications.

Bruner, J. S. (1966). *Toward a theory of instruction.* Cambridge, MA: Belknap Press of Harvard University Press.

Cairns, R. B. (1986). Phenomena lost: Issues in the study of development. In J. Valsiner (Ed.), *The individual subject and scientific psychology* (pp. 97–111). New York: Plenum Press.

Campione, J. C., Brown, A. L., Ferrara, R. A., & Bryant, N. R. (1984). The Zone of Proximal Development: Implications for individual differences and learning. In B. Rogoff & J. V. Wertsch (Eds.), *Children's learning in the Zone of Proximal Development: New directions for child development* (pp. 77–91). San Francisco: Jossey-Bass.

Carraher, T. N., Carraher, D. W., & Schliemann, A. S. (1985). Mathematics in streets and schools. *British Journal of Developmental Psychology, 3,* 21–29.

Ceci, S. J., & Bruck, M. (1993). Child witnesses: Translating research into policy. *Social Policy Report: Society for Research in Child Development, 7*(3), 1–30.

Chandler, M., & Chapman, M. (Eds.). (1991). *Criteria for competence: Controversies in the conceptualization and assessment of children's abilities.* Hillsdale, NJ: Lawrence Erlbaum Associates.

Chomsky, N. (1964). Discussion of Miller and Ervin's paper. *Monographs of the Society for Research in Child Development, 29,* 35–39.

Clement, J. (1982). Students' preconceptions of introductory mechanics. *American Journal of Physics, 50,* 66–71.

Cochran, B. S., Barson, A., & Davis, R. B. (1970). Child-created mathematics. *Arithmetic Teacher, 17,* 211–215.

Cole, M. (1991). Conclusion. In L. B. Resnick, J. M. Levine, & S. D. Teasly (Eds.), *Perspectives on socially shared cognition* (pp. 398–417). Washington, DC: American Psychological Association.

Cole, M. (1992). Culture in development. In M. H. Bornstein & M. E. Lamb (Eds.), *Developmental psychology: An advanced textbook* (pp. 731–789). Hillsdale, NJ: Lawrence Erlbaum Associates.

Cole, M., & Means, B. (1981). *Comparative studies of how people think: An introduction.* Cambridge, MA: Harvard University Press.

Cole, M., & Scribner, S. (1974). *Culture and thought.* New York: John Wiley.

Cowan, P. A. (1978). *Piaget with feeling: Cognitive, social, and emotional dimensions.* New York: Holt, Rinehart & Winston.

Damon, W., & Hart, D. (1992). Self-understanding and its role in social and moral development. In M. H. Bornstein & M. E. Lamb (Eds.), *Developmental psychology: An advanced textbook* (pp. 421–464). Hillsdale, NJ: Lawrence Erlbaum Associates.

Darwin, C. (1955). *The expression of emotion in man and animals.* New York: Philosophical Library.

Delandshire, G., & Petrosky, A. R. (1994). Capturing teachers' knowledge: Performance assessment. *Educational Researcher, 23*(5), 11–18.

Dewey, J. (1933). *How we think.* Chicago, IL: Henry Regnery.

Donaldson, M. C. (1978). *Children's minds.* New York: Norton.

Eisner, E. W. (1991). *The enlightened eye: Qualitative inquiry and the enhancement of educational practice.* New York: Macmillan.

Ericsson, K. A., & Simon, H. A. (1993). *Protocol analysis: Verbal reports as data.* Cambridge, MA: MIT Press.

Erlwanger, S. H. (1975). Case studies of children's conceptions of mathematics, Part I. *Journal of Children's Mathematical Behavior, 1,* 157–183.

Fetterman, D. (1989). *Ethnography: Step by step.* Newbury Park, CA: Sage Publications.

Feuerstein, R., Rand, Y., Jensen, M. R., Kaniel, S., & Tzuriel, D. (1987). Prerequisites for assessment of learning potential: The LPAD model. In C. S. Lidz (Ed.), *Dynamic assessment: An interactional approach to evaluating learning potential* (pp. 35–51). New York: Guilford Press.

Finnegan, W. (1994, January 31). Doubt. *The New Yorker,* pp. 48–67.

Flavell, J. H., Green, F. L., & Flavell, E. R. (1995). Young children's knowledge about thinking. *Monographs of the Society for Research in Child Development 60*(1, Serial No. 243).

Flavell, J. H., Miller, P. H., & Miller, S. A. (1993). *Cognitive development* (3rd ed.). Englewood Cliffs, NJ: Prentice-Hall.

Fordham, S., & Ogbu, J. U. (1986). Black students' school success: Coping with the burden of "acting White." *Urban Review, 18,* 178–206.

Franck, I. (1986). Psychology as a science: Resolving the idiographic–nomothetic controversy. In J. Valsiner (Ed.), *The individual subject and scientific psychology* (pp. 17–35). New York: Plenum Press.

Freud, A. (1946). *The ego and the mechanisms of defence* (C. Baines, Trans.). New York: International Universities Press.

Freud, S. (1953). *A general introduction to psychoanalysis.* New York: Permabooks.

Freud, S. (1961). *The interpretation of dreams.* New York: Science Editions.

Freud, S. (1963). *Three case histories.* New York: Collier Books.

Friend, J. H., & Guralnick, D. B. (Eds.). (1960). *Webster's new world dictionary of the American language.* Cleveland, OH: World.

Fuson, K. C. (1988). *Children's counting and concepts of number.* New York: Springer-Verlag.

Garbarino, J., Stott, F. M., & Faculty of The Erikson Institute (1992). *What children can tell us.* San Francisco: Jossey-Bass.

Garcia, G. E. (1991). Factors influencing the English reading test performance of Spanish-speaking Hispanic children. *Reading Research Quarterly, 26*(4), 371–392.

Garcia, G. E., & Pearson, P. D. (1994). Assessment and diversity. In L. Darling-

Hammond (Ed.), *Review of research in education* (pp. 337–392). Washington, DC: American Educational Research Association.

Gardner, H. (1985). *The mind's new science: A history of the cognitive revolution.* New York: Basic Books.

Geertz, C. (1973). *The interpretation of cultures.* New York: Basic Books.

Gelman, R. (1980). What young children know about numbers. *Educational Psychologist, 15,* 54–68.

Gesell, A. (1952). Autobiography. In E. G. Boring, H. S. Langfeld, H. Werner, & R. M. Yerkes (Eds.), *A history of psychology in autobiography* (pp. 123–142). Worcester, MA: Clark University Press.

Ginsburg, H. P. (1971). The case of Peter. *Journal of Children's Mathematical Behavior, 1,* 60–71.

Ginsburg, H. P. (1986a). Academic diagnosis: Contributions from developmental psychology. In J. Valsiner (Ed.), *Individual subject and scientific psychology* (pp. 235–260). New York: Plenum Press.

Ginsburg, H. P. (1986b). The myth of the deprived child: New thoughts on poor children. In U. Neisser (Ed.), *The school achievement of minority children: New perspectives* (pp. 169–189). Hillsdale, NJ: Lawrence Erlbaum Associates.

Ginsburg, H. P. (1989a). *Children's arithmetic: How they learn it and how you teach it* (2nd ed.). Austin, TX: Pro Ed.

Ginsburg, H. P. (1989b). The role of the personal in intellectual development. *Newsletter of the Institute for Comparative Human Development, 11,* 8–15.

Ginsburg, H. P. (1990). *Assessment probes and instructional activities: The Test of Early Mathematics Ability* (2nd ed.). Austin, TX: Pro Ed.

Ginsburg, H. P. (1996a). Taming the math monster. In G. Brannigan (Ed.), *The enlightened educator* (pp. 3–25). New York: McGraw Hill.

Ginsburg, H. P. (1996b). Toby's math. In R. J. Sternberg & T. Ben-Zeev (Eds.), *The nature of mathematical thinking* (pp. 175–202). Hillsdale, NJ: Lawrence Erlbaum Associates.

Ginsburg, H. P. (1997). Mathematics learning disabilities: A view from developmental psychology. *Journal of Learning Disabilities, 30,* 20–33.

Ginsburg, H. P., & Baroody, A. J. (1990). *The Test of Early Mathematics Ability* (2nd ed.). Austin, TX: Pro Ed.

Ginsburg, H. P., Jacobs, S. F., & Lopez, L. S. (1993). Assessing mathematical thinking and learning potential. In R. B. Davis & C. S. Maher (Eds.), *Schools, mathematics, and the world of reality* (pp. 237–262). Boston, MA: Allyn & Bacon.

Ginsburg, H. P., Jacobs, S. G., & Lopez, L. S. (in press). *Learning what children know about math: The teacher's guide to flexible interviewing in the classroom.* Boston, MA: Allyn & Bacon.

Ginsburg, H. P., Kaplan, R. G., & Baroody, A. J. (1992). *Children's mathematical thinking: Videotape workshops for educators.* Evanston, IL: Everyday Learning Corp.

Ginsburg, H. P., & Opper, S. (1988). *Piaget's theory of intellectual development* (3rd ed.). Englewood Cliffs, NJ: Prentice-Hall.

Ginsburg, H. P., Posner, J. K., & Russell, R. L. (1981). Mathematics learning difficulties in African children: A clinical interview study. *Quarterly Newsletter of the Laboratory of Comparative Human Cognition, 3*, 8–11.

Glaser, R. (1981). The future of testing: A research agenda for cognitive psychology and psychometrics. *American Psychologist, 36*, 923–936.

Glasersfeld, E. V. (1990). An exposition of constructivism: Why some like it radical. In R. B. Davis, C. A. Maher, & N. Noddings (Eds.), *Constructivist views on the teaching and learning of mathematics* (pp. 19–29). Reston, VA: National Council of Teachers of Mathematics.

Goldin-Meadow, S., Wein, D., & Chang, C. (1992). Assessing knowledge through gesture: Using children's hands to read their minds. *Cognition and Instruction, 9*, 201–219.

Goodnow, J. J., & Collins, W. A. (1990). *Development according to parents: The nature, sources, and consequences of parents' ideas.* London: Lawrence Erlbaum Associates.

Green, B. F. (1983). The promise of tailored tests. In *Principles of modern psychological measurement* (pp. 69–80). Hillsdale, NJ: Lawrence Erlbaum Associates.

Greenberg, J., & Mitchell, S. (1983). *Object relations and psychoanalysis.* Cambridge, MA: Harvard University Press.

Greenspan, S. I., & Thorndike-Greenspan, N. (1991). *The clinical interview of the child* (2nd ed.). Washington, DC: American Psychiatric Press.

Gruber, H. E. (1981). *Darwin on man: A psychological study of scientific creativity.* Chicago: University of Chicago Press.

Hochschild, J. L. (1981). *What's fair? American beliefs about distributive justice.* Cambridge, MA: Harvard University Press.

Holt, J. (1982). *How children fail* (rev. ed.). New York: Delta/Seymour Lawrence.

Hughes, J. N., & Baker, D. B. (1990). *The clinical child interview.* New York: Guilford Press.

Inagaki, K., & Hatano, G. (1993). Young children's understanding of the mind–body distinction. *Child Development, 64*, 1534–1549.

Inhelder, B. (1989). Autobiography. In G. Lindzey (Ed.), *A history of psychology in autobiography* (pp. 208–243). Stanford, CA: Stanford University Press.

Inhelder, B., & Piaget, J. (1958). *The growth of logical thinking from childhood to adolescence.* New York: Basic Books.

Itard, J. M. G. (1962). *The wild boy of Aveyron* (George Humphrey & Muriel Humphrey, Trans.). Englewood Cliffs, NJ: Prentice-Hall.

James, W. (1958). *Talks to teachers on psychology; and to students on some of life's ideals.* New York: W. W. Norton.

Johansson, B., Marton, F., & Svensson, L. (1985). An approach to describing learning as change between qualitatively different conceptions. In L. H. West & L. A. Pines (Eds.), *Cognitive structure and conceptual change* (pp. 128–145). Orlando, FL: Academic Press.

Jones, K. (1986). *Clinical interviewing in educational assessment: Empirical validation of the methodology.* Unpublished doctoral dissertation, University of Rochester.

Kamakura, W. A., & Balasubramanian, S. K. (1989). Tailored interviewing: An application of item response theory for personality measurement. *Journal of Personality Assessment, 53*(3), 502–519.

Kamphaus, R. W. (1993). *Clinical assessment of children's intelligence: A handbook for professional practice.* Boston, MA: Allyn & Bacon.

Kimble, G. A. (1961). *Hilgard and Marquis' "Conditioning and learning."* New York: Appleton-Century-Crofts.

Kirk, J., & Miller, M. L. (1986). *Reliability and validity in qualitative research.* Beverly Hills, CA: Sage.

Kohnken, G., & Brackmann, C. (1988). Das Kognitive Interview: Eine neue Explorationstechnik. *Zeitchrift für Differentielle und Diagnostische Psychologie, 9*(4), 257–265.

Kuhn, D. (1992). Cognitive development. In M. H. Bornstein & M. E. Lamb (Eds.), *Developmental psychology: An advanced textbook* (pp. 211–272). Hillsdale, NJ: Lawrence Erlbaum Associates.

Kuhn, D., Garcia-Mila, M., Zohar, A., & Anderson, C. (1995). Strategies of knowledge acquisition. *Monographs of the Society for Research in Child Development, 60*(4, Serial No. 245).

Kuhn, D., & Phelps, E. (1982). The development of problem-solving strategies. In H. Reese & L. Lipsitt (Eds.), *Advances in child development and behavior* (pp. 1–44). San Diego, CA: Academic Press.

Kuhn, T. (1962). *The structure of scientific revolutions.* Chicago: University of Chicago Press.

Labov, W. (1970). The logic of non-standard English. In F. Williams (Ed.), *Language and poverty* (pp. 153–189). Chicago: Markham.

Labov, W., & Fanshel, D. (1977). *Therapeutic discourse: Psychotherapy as conversation.* Orlando, FL: Academic Press.

Lagemann, E. C. (1989). The plural worlds of educational research. *History of Education Quarterly, 29,* 185–214.

Lemaire, P., & Siegler, R. S. (1995). Four aspects of strategic change: Contributions to children's learning of multiplication. *Journal of Experimental Psychology; General, 124,* 83–97.

Lewin, K. (1935). The conflict between Aristotelian and Galilean modes of thought in contemporary psychology. In K. Lewin (Ed.), *A dynamic theory of personality: Selected papers* (pp. 1–42). New York: McGraw-Hill.

Liben, L. S. (in press). Children's understanding of spatial representations of place: Mapping the methodological landscape. In N. Foreman & R. Gillett (Eds.), *A handbook of spatial paradigms and methodologies.* Hillsdale, NJ: Lawrence Erlbaum Associates.

Liben, L. S., & Downs, R. M. (1991). The role of graphic representations in understanding the world. In R. M. Downs, L. S. Liben, & D. S. Palermo (Eds.), *Visions of aesthetics, the environment,* and development: The legacy of Joachim F. Wohlwill (pp. 139–180). Hillsdale, NJ: Lawrence Erlbaum Associates.

Lidz, C. S. (Ed.). (1987). *Dynamic assessment: An interactional approach to evaluating learning potential.* New York: Guilford Press.

Linn, R. L. (1986). Barriers to new test designs. In *The redesign of testing for the 21st century: Proceedings of the 1985 ETS invitational conference* (pp. 69–79). Princeton, NJ: Educational Testing Service.

Luria, A. R. (1968). *The mind of a mnemonist* (Lynn Solotaroff, Trans.). Cambridge, MA: Harvard University Press.

Luria, A. R. (1979). *The making of mind: A personal account of Soviet psychology.* Cambridge, MA: Harvard University Press.

Madaus, G. F., West, M. M., Harmon, M. C., Lomax, R. G., & Viator, K. A. (1992). *The influence of testing on teaching math and science in grades 4–12* (Report to the National Science Foundation). Boston, MA: Boston College.

McDermott, R. P. (1993). The acquisition of a child by a learning disability. In S. Chaiklin & J. Lave (Eds.), *Understanding practice: Perspectives on activity and context* (pp. 269–305). New York: Cambridge University Press.

McLellan, J. A., & Dewey, J. (1895). *The psychology of number and its applications to methods of teaching arithmetic.* New York: D. Appleton.

Messick, S. (1989). Validity. In R. L. Linn (Ed.), *Educational measurement* (pp. 13–103). New York: Macmillan.

Millar, R., Crute, V., & Hargie, O. (1992). *Professional interviewing.* London: Routledge.

Minick, N. (1987). Implications of Vygotsky's theories for Dynamic Assessment. In C. S. Lidz (Ed.), *Dynamic assessment: An interactional approach to evaluating learning potential* (pp. 116–140). New York: Guilford Press.

Mishler, E. G. (1986). *Research interviewing: Context and narrative.* Cambridge, MA: Harvard University Press.

Mislevy, R. J., Yamamoto, K., & Anacker, S. (1992). Toward a test theory for assessing student understanding. In R. Lesh & S. J. Lamon (Eds.), *Assessment of authentic performance in school mathematics* (pp. 293–318). Washington, DC: American Association for the Advancement of Science Press.

Moss, P. A. (1994). Can there be validity without reliability? *Educational Researcher, 23*(2), 5–12.

Nasar, S. (1994, November 13). The lost years of a Nobel laureate. *The New York Times,* pp. 1, 8.

National Council of Teachers of Mathematics (1989). *Curriculum and evaluation standards for school mathematics.* Reston, VA: Author.

National Council of Teachers of Mathematics (1995). *Assessment standards for school mathematics.* Reston, VA: Author.

Neisser, U. (1975). Self-knowledge and psychological knowledge: Teaching psychology from a cognitive point of view. *Educational Psychologist, 11*, 158–170.

Newcomer, P. L. (1990). *Diagnostic Achievement Battery* (2d ed.). Austin, TX: Pro Ed.

Newcomer, P. L., & Ginsburg, H. P. (1995). *Assessment probes for comprehension, thought processes, and learning potential.* Austin, TX: Pro Ed.

Nichols, P.D. (1994). A framework for developing cognitively diagnostic assessments. *Review of Educational Research, 64*, 575–603.

Noddings, N. (1990). Constructivism in mathematics education. In R. B. Davis,

C. A. Maher, & N. Noddings (Eds.), *Constructivist views on the teaching and learning of mathematics* (pp. 7–18). Reston, VA: National Council of Teachers of Mathematics.

Oldfather, P., & West, J. (1994). Qualitative research as jazz. *Educational Researcher, 23*, 22–26.

Ormrod, J. E., & Carter, K. R. (1985). Systematizing the Piagetian clinical interview for classroom use. *Teaching of Psychology, 12*, 216–219.

Paris, S. G., & Cross, D. R. (1988). The Zone of Proximal Development: Virtues and pitfalls of a metaphorical representation of children's learning. *Genetic Epistemologist, 26*, 27–37.

Paris, S. G., Lawton, T. A., Turner, J. C., & Roth, J. L. (1991). A developmental perspective on standardized achievement testing. *Educational Researcher, 20*(5), 12–20.

Peshkin, A. (1993). The goodness of qualitative research. *Educational Researcher, 22*(2), 23–30.

Piaget, J. (1952a). Autobiography. In E. G. Boring, H. S. Langfeld, H. Werner, & R. M. Yerkes (Eds.), *A history of psychology in autobiography* (pp. 237–256). Worcester, MA: Clark University Press.

Piaget, J. (1952b). *The origins of intelligence in children* (M. Cook, Trans.). New York: International Universities Press.

Piaget, J. (1955). *The language and thought of the child.* Cleveland, OH: World.

Piaget, J. (1962). *The moral judgment of the child* (M. Gabain, Trans.). New York: Collier Books.

Piaget, J. (1964). *Judgment and reasoning in the child* (M. Warden, Trans.). Patterson, NJ: Littlefield, Adams.

Piaget, J. (1971). *Biology and knowledge* (B. Walsh, Trans.). Chicago: University of Chicago Press.

Piaget, J. (1976a). *The child's conception of the world* (J. Tomlinson & A. Tomlinson, Trans.). Totowa, NJ: Littlefield, Adams.

Piaget, J. (1976b). *The grasp of consciousness: Action and concept in the young child* (S. Wedgwood, Trans.). Cambridge, MA: Harvard University Press.

Piaget, J. (1977). Psychoanalysis in its relations with child psychology. In H. E. Gruber & J. J. Voneche (Eds.), *The essential Piaget* (pp. 55–59). New York: Basic Books.

Pillemer, D. B., & White, S. H. (1989). Childhood events recalled by children and adults. In H. W. Reese (Ed.), *Advances in child development and behavior* (Vol. 21, pp. 196–229). New York: Academic Press.

Pittenger, R. E., Hockett, C. F., & Danehy, J. J. (1960). *The first five minutes.* Ithaca, NY: Paul Martineau.

Pramling, I. (1988). Developing children's thinking about their own learning. *British Journal of Educational Psychology, 58*, 266–278.

Rappaport, D. (1946). *Manual of diagnostic psychological testing.* New York: Josiah Macy Foundation.

Resnick, L. B. (1989). Developing mathematical knowledge. *American Psychologist, 44*, 162–169.

Royer, J. M., Cisero, C. A., & Carlo, M. S. (1993). Techniques and procedures for assessing cognitive skills. *Review of Educational Research, 63*(2), 201–243.

Rudman, H. C. (1987). The future of testing is now. *Educational Measurement: Issues and Practice, 6*(3), 5–11.

Sacks, O. W. (1995). *An anthropologist on Mars: Seven paradoxical tales.* New York: Knopf.

Saunders, D. (1994a, September 26). Duck, it's the New-New Math. *San Francisco Chronicle,* p. A20.

Saunders, D. (1994b, October 21). Math agnostics breed math illiterates. *San Francisco Chronicle,* p. A25.

Scardamalia, M., & Bereiter, C. (1983). Child as coinvestigator: Helping children gain insight into their own mental processes. In S. G. Paris, G. M. Olson, & H. W. Stevenson (Eds.), *Learning and motivation in the classroom* (pp. 61–82). Hillsdale, NJ: Lawrence Erlbaum Associates.

Scheffler, I. (1991). *In praise of the cognitive emotions.* New York: Routledge.

Schoenfeld, A. H. (1985). Making sense of "Out Loud" problem-solving protocols. *Journal of Mathematical Behavior, 4,* 171–191.

Schwandt, T. A. (1994). Constructivist, interpretivist approaches to human inquiry. In N. K. Denzin & Y. S. Lincoln (Eds.), *Handbook of qualitative research* (pp. 118–137). Thousand Oaks, CA: Sage.

Shapiro, D. (1965). *Neurotic styles.* New York: Basic Books.

Shweder, R. A. (1991). *Thinking through cultures: Expeditions in cultural psychology.* Cambridge, MA: Harvard University Press.

Siegal, M. (1991). A clash of conversational worlds: Interpreting cognitive development through communication. In L. B. Resnick, J. M. Levine, & S. D. Teasly (Eds.), *Perspectives on socially shared cognition* (pp. 23–40). Washington, DC: American Psychological Association.

Siegler, R. S. (1987). The perils of averaging data over strategies: An example from children's addition. *Journal of Experimental Psychology: General, 116,* 250–264.

Siegler, R. S. (1988). Strategy choice procedures and the development of multiplication skill. *Journal of Experimental Psychology: General, 117,* 258–275.

Siegler, R. S., & Crowley, K. (1991). The microgenetic method: A direct means for studying cognitive development. *American Psychologist, 46*(6), 606–620.

Sigel, I. E. (1979). Cognitive-developmental assessment in children: Application of a cybernetic model. In M. N. Ozer (Ed.), *A cybernetic approach to the assessment of children: Toward a more humane use of human beings* (pp. 151–170). Boulder, CO: Westview Press.

Silver Burdett Ginn (1995a). *Authentic assessment: Grades K through 8.* Morristown, NJ: Author.

Silver Burdett Ginn (1995b). *Mathematics: Exploring your world, Grade 1.* Morristown, NJ: Author.

Smetana, J. G. (1982). *Concepts of self and morality: Women's reasoning about abortion.* New York: Praeger.

Smetana, J. G. (1995). Morality in context: Abstractions, ambiguities, and applications. In R. Vasta (Ed.), *Annals of Child Development* (Vol. 10, pp. 83–130). London: Jessica Kingsley.

Stake, R. E. (1994). Case studies. In N. K. Denzin & Y. S. Lincoln (Eds.), *Handbook of qualitative research* (pp. 236–247). Thousand Oaks, CA: Sage.

Stigler, J. W., & Perry, M. (1990). Mathematics learning in Japanese, Chinese, and American classrooms. In J. W. Stigler, R. A. Shweder, & G. Herdt (Eds.), *Cultural psychology: Essays on comparative human development* (pp. 328–353). New York: Cambridge University Press.

Thorndike, E. L. (1922). *The psychology of arithmetic.* New York: Macmillan.

Toulmin, S. (1982). The construal of reality: Criticism in modern and postmodern science. In W. J. T. Mitchell (Ed.), *The politics of interpretation* (pp. 99–118). Chicago: University of Chicago Press.

Valsiner, J. (Ed.). (1986). *The individual subject and scientific psychology.* New York: Plenum Press.

Vygotsky, L. S. (1978). *Mind in society: The development of higher psychological processes.* Cambridge, MA: Harvard University Press.

Vygotsky, L. S. (1986). *Thought and language* (A. Kozulin, Trans.). Cambridge, MA: MIT Press.

Wainer, H. (1992). *Measurement problems* (Program Statistics Research No. 92–12). Educational Testing Service.

Waller, W. W. (1932). *The sociology of teaching.* New York: Russell & Russell.

Weinstein, R. S. (1993). Children's knowledge of differential treatment in school: Implications for motivation. In T. M. Tomlinson (Ed.), *Motivating students to learn: Overcoming barriers to achievement* (pp. 197–224). Berkeley, CA: McCutchan.

Wixson, K. K., Bosky, A. B., Yochum, M. N., & Alvermann, D. E. (1984). An interview for assessing students' perceptions of classroom reading tasks. *Reading Teacher, 18,* 346–352.

Index